Yun-hua Chen

Mosaic Space and Mosaic Auteurs
On the Cinema of Alejandro González Iñárritu, Atom Egoyan, Hou Hsiao-hsien, Michael Haneke

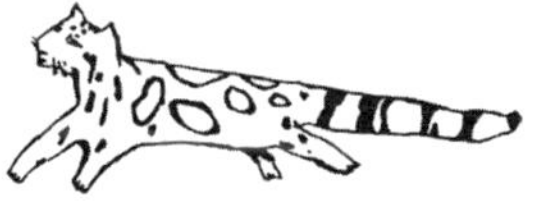

Yun-hua Chen studied Linguistics and Film Studies in Taiwan, France, and Scotland, and obtained her PhD degree in Film Studies at the University of St. Andrews (Scotland) in 2011. She writes both academic articles and film reviews, in English, Chinese and German. Her articles can be found in *Directory of World Cinema: China* and *Journal of Chinese Cinemas*, among others.

Yun-hua Chen

Mosaic Space and Mosaic Auteurs

On the Cinema of Alejandro González Iñárritu, Atom Egoyan, Hou Hsiao-hsien, Michael Haneke

Neofelis Verlag

Gedruckt mit freundlicher Unterstützung der Geschwister Boehringer Ingelheim Stiftung für Geisteswissenschaften in Ingelheim am Rhein.

Bibliografische Information der Deutschen Nationalbibliothek
Die Deutsche Nationalbibliothek verzeichnet diese Publikation in der Deutschen Nationalbibliografie; detaillierte bibliografische Daten sind im Internet über http://dnb.d-nb.de abrufbar.

Umschlaggestaltung: Marija Skara
Lektorat & Satz: Neofelis Verlag (mn/ae)
Druck: PRESSEL Digitaler Produktionsdruck, Remshalden
Gedruckt auf FSC-zertifiziertem Papier.
ISBN (Print): 978-3-95808-044-7
ISBN (PDF): 978-3-95808-107-9

Contents

Chapter 3
Hou Hsiao-hsien: Historical Mosaic of Multilayered Mise-en-Scène

Part III: Three-dimensional Mosaic: Horizontal and Vertical

Chapter 4
Michael Haneke: Fluid Mosaic, Crossing and Recrossing Boundaries

Appendix

Introduction

1. What Is Mosaic? – Mosaic Space and Mosaic Auteurs

A troupe of clowns enters a castle to entertain king and queen who suffer from childlessness. A promiscuous king lies among naked female bodies next to a fountain. A middle-aged king caresses a gigantic flea with love. A runaway princess is chased by her ogre husband along the top of rugged cliffs. A beautiful young woman, transformed from an elderly woman, examines her new flesh in the forest. A pair of look-alike pale-skinned friends dives into the depth of a lake together. In *Tale of Tales* (*Il racconto dei racconti*, IT 2015, D: Matteo Garrone), with a script inspired by 17th century fairy tales, the paths of kings and queens, princes and princesses from three neighbouring castles diverge for the most part of the film and only briefly converge at ceremonies. By intercutting between tales, suspense is well kept throughout the film; each encounter with the characters remains fresh and untainted. This is a 'mosaic', in which narrative threads are interwoven from different characters' perspectives, instead of following one single storyline. In fact, since the late 1980s and arguably until roughly the first decade of the 21st century, this is a trend which can be observed in a great diversity of films across genres, nations and filmmaking contexts. They range from the commercially successful *Pulp Fiction* (USA 1994, D: Quentin Tarantino) and the Oscar-winning *Crash* (USA 2004, D: Paul Haggis), to the Indian horror *Darna Mana Hai* (IN 2003, D: Prawaal Raman) and the relatively low-budget Taiwanese production *Do Over* (*Yi Nian Zhi Chu*, TW 2006, D: Yu-Chieh Cheng). This recurring global phenomenon, in no ways the dominant narrative paradigm in contemporary cinema, catches the zeitgeist of the turn of the century and reflects certain observations, concerns, and understanding beyond the scope of national cinema.

These multi-strand and multi-character films have been widely investigated by scholars such as Thomas Elsaesser, Warren Buckland, and David Bordwell, under the banners of "mind-game films"[1], "puzzle films"[2], "forking path narrative", and "network narrative"[3], and in terms of spectator engagement, narratology, cognitive psychology and socio-politics. Yet the linkage between cinema and film production and distribution context, especially important to the making of these films, has not been established. This book hence provides a different understanding of multi-strand films and argues that the bringing-together of narrative threads infers a larger mosaic of geopolitical spaces, which are interwoven through a variety of cinematic means, including narrative as well as camerawork, framing and mise-en-scène. In addition, a correlation between the construction of filmic mosaic space and the transnational filmmaking contexts can be observed in some auteurs' filmmaking; as the auteurs in question draw talents, resources, and subject matters from a wide range of geopolitical spaces along their border-crossing journeys, their films juxtapose diverse spatial configurations. In this book's model these auteurs are termed 'mosaic auteurs' and the assembled film space 'mosaic space'. To stress its allegiance to the bigger framework of mosaic space, the multi-strand narrative, which functions in conjunction with framing, camerawork, mise-en-scène and other cinematic means, is called 'mosaic narrative'. In fact, the word 'mosaic' is used here as a spatial metaphor, putting emphasis on the visual image of spaces and linking space, narrative and authorship into a multidimensional model of spatial compilation. It is a mosaic which gathers, groups, juxtaposes, and re-arranges spaces. Without the intention of being exhaustive and productive enough to solve all the issues of the phenomena or provide a global explanation, this model offers a reading of mosaic beyond an exclusive focus on narrative.

1 Thomas Elsaesser: The Mind-Game Film. In: Warren Buckland (ed.): *Puzzle Films: Complex Storytelling in Contemporary Cinema.* Chichester: Wiley-Blackwell 2009, pp. 13–41, here pp. 15–16.

2 Warren Buckland: Introduction: Puzzle Plots. In: Id. (ed.): *Puzzle Films: Complex Storytelling in Contemporary Cinema.* Chichester: Wiley-Blackwell 2009, pp. 1–12, here p. 6.

3 David Bordwell: *The Way Hollywood Tells It.* Berkeley / Los Angeles: University of California Press 2006, pp. 72–75.

The spatial aspects of mosaic will be explored in terms of representations of space, understood through theories of space, and spatial aesthetics, in terms of formal cinematic aspects such as editing, framing, and mise-en-scène. At the level of spatial representations, at the same time that narrative threads are interwoven, the mosaic joins together geopolitical spaces of different kinds, including: the developed world, where we can see immigration for different reasons and the phenomenon of diaspora, developing areas visited by tourists from developed countries, global cities with interconnected local networks of information, people, and capital, colonial and postcolonial countries, regions at a time of peace, and regions experiencing an ongoing state of war. In addition, within the mosaic, the actual diegetic image and virtual reframed and remediated images are brought onto the same spatial plane. These spatial configurations complement and interact with each other dynamically. They are analysed with the aid of the theories of space, such as Gilles Deleuze's concept of "any-space-whatever"[4] as the deserted but inhabited wasteland where people do not know how to react, the smooth (nomadic and open space) and the striated (sedentary and demarcated space), and deterritorialisation (distanciation from the territory) and reterritorialisation (reapproximation with the territory)[5]; Marc Augé's places (relational and historical) and (contractual and unrelational, such as airport lobbies and supermarkets) in supermodernity[6]; Saskia Sassen's global city, which is the meeting locale between flows of people, images, finances, technology,

4 Gilles Deleuze: *Cinema 2: The Time-Image*, trans. from French by Robert Galeta / Hugh Tomlinson. London: Continuum 1989, p. xi. Gilles Deleuze has cited Pascal Augé in *Cinema 1* and this has led to many instances of confusion between Marc Augé and Pascal Augé, cf. Gilles Deleuze: *Cinema 1: The Movement-Image*, trans. from French by Barbara Habberjam / Hugh Tomlinson. London: Continuum 1986, p. 109. A detailed explanation can be seen in the communications between Charles J. Stivale and Les Roberts, cf. www.langlab.wayne.edu/CStivale/D-G/DuellingAuge.html (accessed 08.03.2011). Here I am considering Gilles Deleuze's any-space-whatever and Marc Augé's non-places as two independently developed concepts, agreeing with David Martin-Jones' belief that Pascal Augé in fact refers to Deleuze's student Pascal Auger at Université Paris VIII, instead of Marc Augé, as in David Martin-Jones: *Deleuze and World Cinemas*. London: Continuum 2011, p. 249.

5 Gilles Deleuze: *A Thousand Plateaus*. London: Continuum 2004, pp. 10–11, 23, 356–367, 523–551.

6 Marc Augé: Paris and the Ethnography of the Contemporary World. In: Michael Sheringham (ed.): *Parisian Fields*. London: Reaktion 1996, pp. 175–179, here pp. 177–178.

information and goods[7]; Mike Featherstone's "glocalism", the amalgam of increasing interdependencies across nations and daily local activities[8]; and Arjun Appadurai's flows and disjunctures of various aspects which he terms ethnoscapes, mediascapes, technoscapes, financescapes, and ideoscapes[9]. Instead of confining and restraining the scope of films, these spatial theories present new ways of reading films. The spatial concepts are not seen as binary and categorical in the framework of mosaic space, but rather as fluid, dynamic, interactive, and therefore productive. In fact, the global/local theorised by scholars of globalisation, places/non-places of Augé and the smooth/striated of Deleuze overlap in various ways. The global space where different flows of people, finances, and information meet is where non-places proliferate. Because of its facilitation of exchanges, the global space also approximates nomadic smooth space, which has fluid boundaries and is open to redefinition. On the other hand, the local space, demarcated and fragmented by clear borders, tends to be the striated space that is divided and defined by lines. It is also where Augé's anthropological places remain. Yet the interconnectedness of the spatial configurations has to be contextualised in order to be meaningful. The second half of section three in this introduction is dedicated to the discussion of these spatial theories, which interweave into a complex and interactive mosaic.

The mosaic is not only formed by the encounter between spatial configurations of different kinds, but also by the conglomeration between images on screen in terms of spatial aesthetics. It is through mosaic narrative, as well as through framing, mise-en-scène, choices of setting, and cast that the multi-dimensional mosaic manifests itself. Mosaic narrative, assembling different characters' storylines through crosscutting between perspectives and spaces, is the most discernible and most discussed aspect. Yet apart from mosaic narrative, mosaic

7 Saskia Sassen: Spatialities and Temporalities of the Global: Elements for a Theorization. In: Arjun Appadurai (ed.): *Globalization*. Durham: Duke UP 2001, pp. 260–278, here p. 267; ead.: *Territory. Authority. Rights. From Medieval to Global Assemblages*. Princeton: Princeton UP 2006, pp. 402–403.

8 Mike Featherstone: Localism, Globalism, and Cultural Identity. In: Rob Wilson / Wimal Dissanayake (eds): *Global/Local: Cultural Production and the Transnational Imaginary*. Durham: Duke UP 1996, pp. 46–77, here pp. 46–47.

9 Arjun Appadurai: *Modernity at Large: Cultural Dimensions of Globalization*. Minneapolis: University of Minnesota Press 1996, pp. 32–35, 49.

space can also be composed of images of bodies and object parts which are fragmented through framing; it can also piece together layers of the mise-en-scène with great depth of field. Sometimes the mosaic juxtaposes linguistically and culturally diverse spaces through a mismatch between the origin of the cast and the film setting. Whereas the interweaving narrative strategy has been the prevailing route to understand the surge of multi-strand films, this book branches out from narrative concerns to explore a broader variety of mosaic aesthetics, including some elements which are rarely considered in scholarly works. In section two, I will demonstrate how we can understand cinematic formation of mosaic beyond the realm of narrative, as well as how different cinematic techniques work together in specific filmmaking contexts to construct mosaic.

The spatial mosaic, assembling a diverse range of spatial configurations and deploying cinematic aesthetics to construct them, is correlated to the travelling and filmmaking mode of the auteurs in some situations. Alejandro González Iñárritu, Atom Egoyan, Hou Hsiao-hsien and Michael Haneke are four chosen examples of the mosaic auteurs here. As most scholarly works on multi-character narrative tend to predominantly draw examples from films produced and distributed in the West, apart from Patricia Pisters' example of Faouzi Bensaidi's *WWW: What a Wonderful World* (FR 2006)[10] and Bordwell's rather comprehensive scope of network narrative in *Poetics of Cinema*[11], I choose four auteurs from three continents as an attempt to broaden the geopolitical range while considering spatial assemblages. These auteurs are the travelling-auteurs who constantly cross borders and incorporate financial resources, cultural materials, industrial networks and film talents from diverse contexts into a unique mosaic auteur space, thanks to high speed transportation and diverse global flows. As a consequence, the mosaic auteurs' experiences of the shifting spatial configurations in the age of globalisation help them transcend the confinement of nation-based scope and explore transnational filmmaking milieus. Their films also travel

10 Patricia Pisters: The Mosaic Film – An Affaire of Everyone: Becoming-Minoritarian in Transnational Media Culture. In: *Proceedings of the Second Encountro Murcia-Amsterdam on Migratory Aesthetics*, 19–21.09.2007. http://home.medewerker.uva.nl/m.g.bal/bestanden/Pisters%20Patricia%20Encuentro%20Migratory%20Politics%20READER%20OPMAAK.pdf (accessed 21.07.2011).

11 David Bordwell: *Poetics of Cinema*. New York: Routledge 2008.

across boundaries, for they are consumed in circuits of international film festivals and in different local spaces across the globe. As a part of the theoretical framework I build, side by side with the theories of space, in the first half of section three I will review major debates in film authorship and discuss my framework of mosaic authorship, as well as the way it works to compile spaces in filmmaking contexts. Mosaic authorship will then be examined in relation to other important frameworks of transnational authorship, such as Mette Hjort's typology of transnationalism, Hamid Naficy's accented cinema, and Laura Marks' intercultural cinema.

These branches of space, aesthetics and authorship are intertwined into a mosaic. Hence, this book lies in the intersection between the cinematic manifestations of mosaic space, spatial representations, and transnational filmmaking networks facilitated by authorship. By introducing the concept of mosaic, the understanding of multi-character films is not restricted to the consideration of narrative, but rather, enables us to see these films from a spatial perspective. The framework of mosaic also connects the film space on screen and filmmaking contexts in the nuanced analyses of auteur cinema. These key elements will firstly be examined with an analysis of the last eight minutes of Michael Haneke's *71 Fragments of a Chronology of Chance* (*71 Fragmente einer Chronologie des Zufalls*, AT / DE 1994) to build up the multidimensional mosaic. I will then exemplify my framework of mosaic space and distinguish it from other models, before moving on to discuss mosaic authorship and theories of space which facilitate the contextualised understanding of mosaic. A chapter-by-chapter breakdown can be found at the end of the introduction.

2. Mosaic Space: Visual Spatial Assemblage

Mosaic Space and *71 Fragments of a Chronology of Chance*

Haneke's *71 Fragments* is a good example to illustrate my framework of mosaic space and its spatial reading of multi-character films. Space, aesthetics, and authorship are interwoven into a multidimensional model in which diegetic representational spaces are brought together through cinematic means, at the same time that human and material resources are gathered together extradiegetically in the making.

Haneke's third feature film, *71 Fragments*, inspired by a real-life shootout in Vienna, follows the intertwining lives of several people from diverse socioeconomic and geopolitical backgrounds, over the course of ten days before Christmas Eve. It culminates in an unexpected shootout on the 23rd December inside a Viennese bank. As the resulting mosaic is in correspondence to the transnational filmmaking context established by the travelling auteur, it is helpful to put the film in its context before analysing it. *71 Fragments* is an international production which pulls funding resources and cast mainly from three major West European countries: Austria, Germany and France, even if Haneke's transnational filmmaking networks are more limited at this early stage of his career. This indicates Haneke's early border-crossing and transnationality in the European context, which are subsequently expanded and broadened through the progressive milieu-building process. Following *The Seventh Continent* (*Der siebente Kontinent*, AT 1989) and *Benny's Video* (AT / CH 1992), the first two films in his debut trilogy, Michael Haneke's third feature, *71 Fragments*, is an European coproduction of the Austrian Wega Film based in Vienna, German Camera Film based in Berlin, German television channel ZDF (Zweites Deutsches Fernsehen), and the Franco-German television channel Arte. In addition to gathering filmmaking resources from different West European countries, the actors and actresses are also recruited from Germanophone countries across national boundaries in Western Europe: Austria (Lukas Miko, Otto Grünmandl), Switzerland (Anne Bennent), and Germany (Udo Samel, Claudia Martini). In addition, Branko Samarovski, playing the role of the guard Hans, who was born in Yugoslavia and fled to Austria with his parents at the age of five, brings the dimension of political migration within Europe into the picture. Upon its release, the film did not attract much attention and its distribution was first confined to a limited number of distribution networks, such as the Catalonian International Film Festival, Rosebud in Greece, and Sputnik Film in Germany. It is only after the critical and box office success of Haneke's *Caché* (FR / AT / DE / IT 2005) that *71 Fragments* was widely re-released on DVD as part of Haneke's debut trilogy by Tartan in the UK and Alamode Film in Germany. It was even released in theatres in the US by Kino International in 2006. The consumption of this film has thus extended from a rather limited circuit within Western Europe to a global network of art cinema thanks to Haneke's increasing significance as an established auteur. Given its original transnational filmmaking context within Europe, it is not surprising that the film's subject matter evolves around the issues which deeply concern the continent: wealth divides between wealthy and underprivileged countries in Europe, the resultant migration, and discrepancies between bourgeois and working-class Europeans; all of which are present in the daily life of Europeans from different socioeconomic and geopolitical backgrounds. As these experiences have only intensified with the global flows of information, people, finances, and technologies accompanied by new tools of communication and high speed transportation since the 1990s, *71 Fragments* remains relevant to both the European and the global audience two decades after its release.

The film follows the characters' snippets of life before the random shooting of university student Max. Throughout the film they are represented in segments completely segregated by editing, which confine them within individual snapshots and reinforce the feeling of separation. Instead of following one main character's trajectory closely, the spectator gets to know several characters at the same time through fragments of their daily life separated by black-outs. Without knowing the characters' family history or psychological state, we see static shots of Hans walking past his wife who is feeding their baby in the morning, Max talking in a public phone booth in front of his dormitory, a reframed shot of Mrs. Brunner teaching Marian simple German words such as "star" and "people" while driving through the city centre, and a panning shot showing Tomek carefully donning a suit, waistcoat, and tie and putting Christmas presents in a bag. It is through the accumulation of fragmented information like this that the spectator gradually realises how eargerly wealthy Mrs. Brunner, living in the spacious flat she shares with her husband, wants to adopt a child to fill the void she feels. She later hosts the homeless Romanian boy, Marian, who has recently been caught by the police for illegally entering Austria. The lonely middle-class elderly man, Tomek, communicates with his bank clerk daughter face-to-face only in the bank as a customer. The middle-aged working class bank guard, Hans, struggles to make ends meet in a cramped filthy dwelling and to emotionally connect with his wife and their infant daughter. As for Max, who is intensively trained for table tennis, he has won a stolen handgun from his friend in a mind game. Hence the mosaic narrative progressively weaves together snippets of information, which are kept parallel to one another until the moment of encounter. For example,

Marian's nomadism has no direct relation to Tomek's isolation or his daughter's alienation from him. Max's frustration is also unrelated to the unhappiness of Hans' family. They are finally brought together into the same spatial plane when these characters of diverse generations and socioeconomic backgrounds end up in the Viennese bank on the 23rd December 1993, one day before the major cultural occasion for most of the Western world, Christmas Eve. Mrs. Brunner drives Marian around for Christmas shopping and stops by the bank to withdraw money. Tomek wants to give his granddaughter's Christmas presents to his alienated daughter in the bank. Hans transports money from an armoured truck to the bank as his daily routine. And Max, on his drive home for Christmas, realises that he does not have enough cash after refueling his car. He then experiences a series of obstacles in his hasty attempt to withdraw money, including a rude cashier in the gas station, a dysfunctional cash machine, a violent customer at the bank counter and an aggressive passer-by in a car.

At the moment that Max, Tomek, his daughter, Mrs. Brunner, and Hans appear together in the same diegetic time and space on screen for the first and only time, the spectator experiences this encounter from Hans' perspective. Framed from the waist up, the camera follows Hans walking along the corridor in the closest plane. At the pace of Hans' steps, we glance around the crowd in the hall. In the background, the bank customers, separated from the guard by wooden counters, are out of focus but still somehow recognisable as the characters we know amidst the ones we don't know. With Hans' gaze we first see Mrs. Brunner talking within a circle of people, Tomek waiting patiently in the back of a long queue, and his daughter talking to a customer across the counter. By the time that Hans crosses the half-size wooden door to enter the main hall, we see in the background Max entering the frame by pushing through the glass door with a gun on his right hand; he is first seen from Hans' perspective as an anonymous blurry undersized image behind the door. The camera then swiftly zooms in to a medium shot facing Max, as he shoots towards different directions offscreen without any warning or explanation. Max's face is expressionless against the sound of a woman's shouting and no reverse shot of the object of his gaze is given.

Through this example, we can see that *71 Fragments* chooses to represent the events prior to the shootout in fragments from the characters' respective perspectives, and then reassembles the previously parallel lives of the shooter and the victims into the same spatial plane in the tracking with Hans' gaze. In this way, it shows how seemingly insignificant and trivial fragments of everyone's lives can evolve into an unexpected and tragic encounter. Without dwelling on any melodramatic moment or providing psychological explanation, the fragments always end before the spectator gets familiar with a certain setting or involved with a certain character. Accordingly, the way Hans glances through the group of people in the bank in the tracking shot is similar to the way we follow the fragments of each character one by one without really getting to know them in depth. The diegetic world is experienced in snippets, in the same manner that Hans perceives people in the bank hall in fragments. Because of the fragmented perception, the spectator is not omniscient and does not have a privileged access to the characters' inner state. While these characters' pieces of life are edited together, the assemblage is not only of various lines of the story, but also of spatial configurations from diverse socioeconomic and geopolitical backgrounds. All living in the developed and wealthy capital of Austria, the characters carry with them the spaces of the bourgeois, the working-class, the young, the middle-aged, the elderly, the educated, the uneducated, the thriving Western Europe, and the less developed parts of Europe in the small area around the bank. This patchwork of spaces correlates with the filmmaking context, in which funding and cast from different European nations gather in the same production. *71 Fragments* thus constructs a mosaic through editing, which brings together not only narrative threads but also diegetic spaces and extradiegetic spaces.

In addition to bringing actual representations of socioeconomic and geopolitical spaces together, the mosaic of *71 Fragments* also interweaves the actual film diegesis and the virtual images within the diegesis. The diegetic film is in fact bracketed by doubly-mediated images; it opens with an unsolicited zapping of news footage of violence and political conflicts familiar to households of Western Europe: civil wars in Georgia, Somalia and Haiti in 1993, in which the United Nations and/or the Clinton government intervened. Following the usual televisual convention, the segments of news items are separated by the introduction of a news broadcaster emotionlessly talking straight at the camera. The footage provides shaky and abruptly cut images that we are used to seeing on news programmes, oscillating between bird's-eye shots providing an overview and medium shots to close-ups revealing human emotions. Despite the geographical diversity between these locales undergoing civil wars, they are commonly portrayed with medium shots of soldiers on tanks driving by, swarms of distressed civilians and refugees, long shots of surveying helicopters and jet fighters flying overhead, and close-ups of machine guns juxtaposed with the sounds of gunfire in the background. The same kind of news footage is placed in the very end of the film as well. After the last diegetic images created by Haneke which show Max collapsing dead on the steering wheel and the patiently waiting Marian within respective reframed car spaces, the real-life news report on the aftermath of Max's random killing is cut in after a brief black-out. We see medium shots of bodies being carried out of the bank, policemen carefully collecting biological evidence, and a close-up of the gas station cashier in a cursory interview. These images are simultaneously the actual news footage broadcasted on TV in the real extradiegetic world, and the doubly-mediated virtual images reframed by TV sets and also consumed by the diegetic characters within *71 Fragments*. The news report is followed by a repetition of the news zapping, which has already been inserted into the diegesis before the characters start moving towards the bank. It starts with the failed cease-fire agreement in Bosnia before Christmas, portrayed by medium shots of two young children decorating a Christmas tree at home, long shots of civilians in Sarajevo running to escape the bullets from sharpshooters, a close-up of a young woman commenting on the high price of Christmas decoration, and a medium shot of a mother running to the hospital with her infant child whose leg has been scraped by shrapnel. The footage of masked surgeons treating the child cuts to the news report on Michael Jackson's child abuse charge, which ends abruptly in the middle of an archival image of his stage performance with the voice-over of a news commentator in the middle of her sentence. Without any indication of a closure the film returns to complete black with white letters giving credits to production companies. In fact, all the zapped doubly-mediated images represent images of violence readily consumable by Western Europeans from their comfortable sofas on a daily basis: large-scale violence in countries in turmoil, smaller-scale violence right inside the centre of Western Europe in a Viennese bank, and suspected sexual abuse in the luxurious household of a world famous rock star in the USA. By editing together the news footage of the actual gunshot's aftermath circulated on virtual platforms and a selection of unrelated news footage on violence in different corners of the world, and placing them before and after Haneke's virtual representations in the diegesis, *71 Fragments* is interwoven into a mosaic of different virtualities and broader geopolitical contexts, while commenting on the consumption mode of journalistic materials and short attention span of the news spectator.

While the bracketing and mirroring of the doubly-mediated virtual images of news footage provide the outer layer, there is also an inner layer of mirrored images bracketing the diegetic film of *71 Fragments*. After the gunfire, a canted overhead shot shows Max walking across the busy four-lane road between the gas station and the bank, towards his car, where he shoots himself in the head. Accompanied by the sounds of honking and swearing, some cars reluctantly stop while Max fires a couple of bullets randomly towards the drivers. This portrayal of Max's path towards suicide, before the news footage in the very end of the film, is visually similar to Marian's crossing of a river towards Austria in darkness right after the opening news zapping. Although Max and Marian come from very different backgrounds, Max being a future intellectual from a middle-class Austrian family and Marian being a homeless boy from rural Romania, they are filmed 'indiscriminately' while they cross over to a different stage of life (or death). In both instances, Max and Marian cross the screen space diagonally from bottom left to top right, and the camera follows them closely from high above and keeps them in the centre of the frame. In Marian's crossing, he is momentarily obscured by the green leaves of a tree which grows by the shore, whereas Max's crossing is temporarily obstructed by some cars which almost run over him; Marian's traversing of the demarcation of national boundaries in the nature is mirrored with Max's crossing of the artificial urban lines. While the outer brackets of news footage provide a different layer of virtualities, the inner brackets of the canted overhead shots of Max and Marian with analogous composition illustrate the visual mosaic of the interconnected individuals despite their wealth and cultural divides.

Apart from the mirroring between the beginning and the end, mosaic narrative also works in combination with an assemblage of disembodied close-ups, which are isolated from the immediate visual contexts through framing. In *71 Fragments*, the narrative line often progresses by aligning a sequence of close-ups with different durations. These close-ups isolate objects or body parts from their immediate surroundings and hence detach them from the contextual information of the images. Bodies and objects are truncated in the screen space by framing, and are never re-embodied again in the film. For example, Hans' routine trajectory is portrayed by a close-up of Hans' disembodied finger pushing a red button on a dashboard embedded on a wooden door, which is cut to a close-up of his truncated lower body and two silver cases beside it while pushing open that door. This is then followed by close-ups of a microphone and a piece of paper being signed by a pen held by a hand. The sequence leading to the eventual gunshot is also composed of a chain of close-ups: a nozzle coming out of a gas cap, a hand twisting the cap back on, disembodied hands searching for money in the wallet, taking a couple of bills out and putting them back in, a "hole in the wall" ATM, and a credit card being ejected by the machine. In fact, the use of close-ups in *71 Fragments* intentionally differentiates the film's fragmentation from the news footage's conventional representations of violence in pieces. Instead of zooming in to give a closer look, Haneke's close-ups substitute for conventional shots and reverse shots. They fragment, truncate, and dissociate without providing an overview of the situation. Hence, the film leaves all the fragments unexplained and does not pretend to provide a complete picture. When the close-ups appear on screen for an unusually long duration, its effects become even stronger. For example, after Max's suicide in his car, which is represented offscreen with an overhead medium shot of the car roof juxtaposed with the sound of a gunshot, we see a canted static shot of a fragment of a torso for almost 90 seconds. The face down truncated torso and the right arm slant across the screen space and compose an asymmetrical composition. During these 90 seconds, we see red blood flowing very slowly in silence from underneath the body on the white floor towards the bottom of screen space. We can recognise that the torso wears the grey uniform of Hans, and the white marble floor belongs to the hall of the bank. Although the headless torso does not provide facial expression, the combination of the close up and long take creates an especially striking mosaic of colour contrasts between grey, red, and white. By forcing the spectator to stare at the blood flowing out in its duration, this close-up portrays violence in sharp contrast to the quick zapping of news reports in the beginning and the end of the film. No matter how much the spectator wants to zap away from the scene of the violence's consequences, the close-up of the torso rolls on and refuses to cut.

Not only a mosaic assembled by snapshots of the socially diverse characters' day-to-day life which are edited together, *71 Fragments* is also a mosaic of mirroring sequences, and a mosaic of disembodied body and machine parts isolated from their immediate visual contexts by framing. Therefore, its explicit multi-character structure does not stand in isolation from other cinematic means, but instead, all the formal aspects work together in the construction of a mosaic. Furthermore, narrative threads as well as spatial configurations represented in the diegesis and filmmaking resources are joined together in the mosaic. At the same time that the characters' fragments are woven in the bigger picture, their diverse geopolitical socioeconomic spaces are also brought together on the same plane. Correlating with the transnational filmmaking mode through which film professionals, funding, and settings from different national contexts are drawn together, the rich and the poor, the Easterners and the Westerners, the young and the elderly, the fictional representations in the diegesis and the doubly-mediated news footage all meet in the film's mosaic. In the following section I will differentiate my framework of mosaic from other scholarly works.

Literature Review: Multi-Character Narrative

71 Fragments belongs to a group of films with mosaic narratives cutting back and forth between the narrative threads of several protagonists. This group of films has precursors as far back in history as D.W. Griffith's *Intolerance* (USA 1916), and also develops out of Jean-Luc Godard's polemical works in the 1960s, European art films like Alain Resnais' *Last Year at Marienbad* (*L'année dernière à Marienbad*, FR 1961), and US auteur films like Robert Altman's *Nashville* (USA 1975). It starts to become a more popular, and at times mainstream, narrative strategy during the late 1980s. Some recent examples of widely-circulated multi-character films include *Short Cuts* (USA 1993, D: Robert Altman), *Pulp Fiction*, *Magnolia* (USA 1999, D: Paul Thomas Anderson), *Mulholland Drive* (USA 2001, D: David Lynch) and *Crash*. Significantly, this trend traverses boundaries of geopolitics and film genres without being restricted to big budget productions in the US. Its far-reaching scope can be seen in film productions from a wide range of regions including Scotland (*Festival,* UK 2005, D: Annie Griffin), Spain (*La soledad,* ES 2007, D: Jamie Rosales), Taiwan (*Do Over*), and Argentina (*Historias minimas,* AR 2002, D: Carlos Sorin). In addition, the mosaic narrative strategy has been employed in both auteur cinema such as Jorge Fons' *Midaq Alley* (MX 1994) and Maria Notaro's *El jardin del Eden* (MX 1994), and genre films such as the Hindi horror *Darna Mana Hai* and the Hindi romantic comedy *Life in a Metro* (IN 2007, D: Anurag Basu)[12]. Films with mosaic narrative can also be found in American independent productions such as *Fragments* (also called *Winged Creatures,* USA 2008, D: Rowan Woods), *Do the Right Thing* (USA 1989, D: Spike Lee), and *Slacker* (USA 1991, D: Richard Linklater). Sometimes interweaving narrative becomes the trademark of certain filmmakers and film professionals, such as Wong Kar-Wai (*Fallen Angels / Do Lok Tin Si*, HK 1995 and *Chungking Express / Chung Hing Sam Lam*, HK 1994), Alejandro González Iñárritu[13] (*Amores Perros,* MX 2000; *21 Grams*, USA 2003; *Babel*, USA / FR / MX 2005), and the scriptwriter Guillermo Arriaga who wrote scripts for Iñárritu's first three feature films and later directed his own multi-character film with temporal disorder, *The Burning Plain* (USA 2008). The use of interweaving narrative in diverse contexts, which has been comprehensively documented by Bordwell's alphabetical list at the end of *Poetics of Cinema*, demonstrates that it is a phenomenon beyond national cinemas, generic conventions, and cultural backgrounds.

In this book I theorise the films with intertwining narrative such as *71 Fragments* in connection to interweaving spaces and transnational filmmaking contexts; this understanding of multi-character films is significantly different from other scholarly works. As we can see in the example of *71 Fragments*, the narrative threads are interwoven

12 The bringing-together of narrative threads from different characters in these Hindi films is different from typical popular Indian narratives, which are very often multi-strand due to the influence of discursivity in the precursor epic texts, which are characterized by generally autonomous fragments without closure. Cf. Vijay Mishra: *Bollywood Cinema: Temples of Desire*. London: Routledge 2002, p. 4.

13 Subsequent to Iñárritu's falling-out with the scriptwriter Guillermo Arriaga, Iñárritu intentionally diverted from multi-strand narrative, to the extent that his award-winning *Birdman* (USA 2014) appears to be one single take.

towards the end of the film through the gunshot, without forking into a loop of possibilities and alternative courses of events like *Run Lola Run* (*Lola rennt*, DE 1998, D: Tom Tykwer), *Blind Chance* (*Przypadek*, PL 1981, D: Krzysztof Kieślowski), *Sliding Doors* (UK 1998, D: Peter Howitt), and *Too Many Ways to be No.1* (*Jat Go Zi Tau Di Daan Sang*, HK 1997, D: Ka-Fai Wai), which are grouped together as "forking-path narrative" by Bordwell who attributes its development to the filmmakers' immersion in labyrinthine storytelling techniques enabled by the innovations of VCRs, DVDs and computer games[14]. Mosaic narrative films interweave diverse storylines together in one encounter, which can be face-to-face or in a less tangible form, instead of forking from one temporal point towards a range of outcomes as a result of one particular decision or coincidental event. The example of *71 Fragments* also shows that although the spectator has the task of actively assembling the mosaic narrative, it does not engage the spectator in the process of folk-psychological game-playing with trick endings like Thomas Elsaesser's "mind-game films"[15] do, or operate with characters suffering from schizophrenia, memory loss, or other psychology-related diseases, as has been suggested in Warren Buckland's "puzzle films"[16]. It is different from Allan Cameron's "database/modular narrative"[17], and what David Martin-Jones calls "the manipulation of narrative time"[18] in *Deleuze, Cinema and National Identity*. The former signifies "narratives that foreground the relationship between the temporality of the story and the order of its telling"[19] whereas in the latter model, the "multiple narratives" of *Sliding Doors* and the "disrupted, jumbled or backwards narratives" of *Memento* (USA 2000, D: Christopher Nolan) are used to demonstrate the narrative's reterritorialisation of national identity.[20] Unlike these two models, the framework of mosaic narrative does not dwell on chronological disorder but regards it as an

14 Bordwell: *The Way Hollywood Tells It*, pp. 72–75.

15 Elsaesser: The Mind-Game Film, pp. 13–16.

16 Buckland: Introduction: Puzzle Plots, p. 6.

17 Allan Cameron: Contingency, Order, and the Modular Narrative: *21 Grams* and *Irreversible*. In: *The Velvet Light Trap* 58,1 (2006), pp. 65–78, here p. 65.

18 David Martin-Jones: *Deleuze, Cinema and National Identity: Narrative Time in National Contexts*. Edinburgh: Edinburgh UP 2006.

19 Cameron: *Contingency, Order, and the Modular Narrative*, p. 65.

20 Martin-Jones: *Deleuze, Cinema and National Identity*, p. 1.

option within the mosaic. Hence it includes films which deliberately subvert chronological order, such as *21 Grams*, as well as those which follow chronological linearity like *71 Fragments*.

Compared to the aforementioned frameworks, definitions such as Jason Mittel's "narrative complexity"[21], "fractal films"[22] by Wendy Everett, Maria del Mar Azcona Montoliú's "multi-character narrative"[23], "scrambled narrative"[24], and "multi-protagonist film"[25], Bordwell's "network narrative"[26] and "degrees of separation films"[27], and Hsuan L. Hsu's "ensemble film"[28] are more pertinent to the current model for their focus on the complicated and perplexing entanglement of narrative threads brought together by different characters. Yet mosaic narrative diverges from these definitions in terms of its strong focus on the visual bringing-together of spaces, using examples drawn from a wide range of geopolitical contexts, and its understanding of narrative strategy in relation to the bigger framework of mosaic space. The key examples of scholarly works in this respect are Bordwell's "network narrative" and "degrees of separation narrative", and Montoliú's "multi-character narrative", both of which attribute the influence of chaos theory, degrees of separation theory and butterfly effect to the emerging alinear narrative since the late 1980s.[29] Both Bordwell's and Montoliú's frameworks discuss the interweaving narrative of films such as *71 Fragments* and *Amores Perros*, but they hold different opinions when it comes to this narrative's convergence or divergence in relation to mainstream

21 Jason Mittel: Narrative Complexity in Contemporary American Television. In: *The Velvet Light Trap* 58,1 (2006), pp. 29–40, here p. 29.

22 Wendy Everett: Fractal Films and the Architecture of Complexity. In: *Studies in European Cinema* 2 (2005), pp. 159–171, here p. 160.

23 Maria del Mar Azcona Montoliú: A Time to Love and a Time to Die: Desire and Narrative Structure in *21 Grams*. In: *Journal of the Spanish Association of Anglo-American Studies* 31,2 (2009), pp. 111–123, here p. 112.

24 Ibid., p. 114.

25 Maria del Mar Azcona Montoliú: *The Multi-protagonist Film*. West Sussex: Wiley-Blackwell 2010, p. 2.

26 Bordwell: *The Way Hollywood Tells It*, pp. 100–102.

27 Ibid., pp. 71–75.

28 Hsuan L. Hsu: Racial Privacy, The L.A. Ensemble Film, and Paul Haggis's *Crash*. In: *Film Criticism* 31,1–2 (2006), pp. 132–156, here p. 132.

29 Montoliú: A Time to Love and a Time to Die, p. 114; Bordwell: *The Way Hollywood Tells It*, p. 100.

storytelling techniques. For Bordwell, the narrative in these films essentially remains linear, causal, signposted, and hierarchical in order to aid audience comprehension, and does not radically differ from the classical narrative.[30] Montoliú, on the other hand, proposes that causal linearity is in crisis, and that the visible and self-conscious multi-character films form a contemporary genre in response to our increasing experiences of inexplicable forces and events.[31] The current model is distinct from both of these, for mosaic narrative does not work as a subversive genre, or remain fundamentally linear and classical. Instead, it works in correspondence with other cinematic strategies to form the bigger mosaic space and correlates with the transnational filmmaking contexts of certain auteurs. In this alternative way of understanding this trend of filmmaking, not only are narrative threads brought together, but so too are spatial representations and extradiegetic resources in geopolitical contexts.

Among all the works on alinear and multi-character narrative, the term "mosaic" is not unused in existing scholarship. In *Poetics of Cinema*, David Bordwell cites Italo Calvino in the beginning of his chapter "Mutual Friends and Chronologies of Chance":

> What interests me is the whole *mosaic* in which man is set, the interplay of relationships, the design that emerges from the squiggles on the carpet ... These human presences defined only by a system of relationships, by a function, are the very ones that populate the world around us in our everyday lives, good or bad as this situation might appear to us.[32]

What Bordwell calls "network narrative" and "degrees of separation films" in *The Way Hollywood Tells It* and *Poetics of Cinema*, different from his "forking path narrative" in his article "Film Futures", is essentially a "mosaic" of characters' lives and relationships with a focus on human relationships embedded in the narrative. Pisters also uses the word "mosaic" in her article on the becoming-minoritarian of mosaic film. Her article encompasses films with "multiple main characters, multiple interwoven story lines, multiple or fragmented spaces, different time zones or spaces or paces" which seem to reflect "the migratory nature and politics of our times", and discusses *Babel*, *WWW. What*

30 Bordwell: *The Way Hollywood Tells It*, pp. 100–102.
31 Montoliú: A Time to Love and a Time to Die, p. 114.
32 Bordwell: *Poetics of Cinema*, p. 189.

a Wonderful World, and *Kicks* (NL 2007, D: Albert Ter Heerdt).[33] In comparison to Bordwell's and Pisters' usage, the visual metaphor of 'mosaic' in this book, instead of being confined to the narrative structure, is extended to encompass a multidimensional spatial assemblage at the levels of diegetic space, screen space, and auteurist transnational filmmaking contexts at the same time.

In the chapters that follow, I will analyse the mosaic space in the works of Haneke, Hou, Egoyan and Iñárritu, all of whom have used mosaic narrative in combination with other cinematic tools to construct mosaic space in their own ways. We can observe different levels of causal relationships and different spatial concerns within their uses of mosaic narrative, differences that reflect both the possibilities and constraints of their filmmaking contexts, such as the sources of funding, target audience, and spatial concerns specific to their backgrounds. The characters' chance encounter is often portrayed in a precise and self-reflexive manner in Haneke's films, in a historically laden event in Hou's films, in a complex contemplation of territory in Egoyan's films, and in a melodramatic and tragic manner in Iñárritu's films. In terms of the chain of cause and effect in mosaic narrative, Haneke and Hou employ causal relationships as a narrative device to a far lesser extent than Egoyan and Iñárritu. Limiting the causal relationship between events to its minimum, Haneke and Hou's multi-character narrative is established on a looser, subtler, and less determined relationship between characters. They are more concerned with fluidity of space and narrative, and consciously leave fragments unexplained, unconnected, or irrelevant to the narrative. In their films, some fragments exist only for their own sake and do not serve any narrative purpose. In Egoyan and Iñárritu's films, on the other hand, it is made clear to the spectator that one character's deeds lead to another character's delight or suffering, and that all threads will be tied up in the narrative at the end. This will be illustrated in detail in the following chapters.

In section two, I have demonstrated that films like *71 Fragments* employ mosaic narrative in combination with framing, bracketing, and spatial composition to interweave narrative threads from different characters, and bring together spaces from different virtualities and geopolitical contexts in the process. I thus argue that the

33 Pisters: The Mosaic Film, p. 1.

framework of mosaic differs from other frameworks of interweaving narrative because it takes into account not only the interweaving narrative but also the assembled filmmaking resources and spatial configurations. This is when the theories of film authorship and of space become very helpful to the framework. Whereas film authorship situates the mosaic space in relation to the auteurist transnational filmmaking context, theories of space help us understand the dynamism of the geopolitical spaces represented on screen.

3. Theoretical Frameworks: Mosaic Authorship and Mosaic Space

Mosaic Authorship

I will start with a literature review on the debate of authorship and discuss the framework of mosaic authorship in relation to it. Taking on board the shifting focus in the debate of authorship from personality and vision to a more contextualised notion, mosaic authorship considers aesthetics as well as filmmaking's collaborative and commercial aspects. Instead of a fixed and coherent personality, mosaic authorship is rather a collective trajectory, facilitated by the privilege of travelling and affected by globalisation. Thanks to the unique transnational filmmaking mode established through border-crossing, mosaic auteurs assemble the combination of the cheapest film set, best film professionals and cast, best opportunities for fundraising, and biggest audience appeal, and their films are widely circulated within film festival circuits and international distribution networks.

As the mosaic auteurs' works are created along with their border-crossing, they cannot be fully explored by the framework of national cinema and should be contextualised in relation to the transnational filmmaking mode. This is where Hjort's typology of transnationalism, and especially cosmopolitan transnationalism, becomes pertinent to the forming of the current model. In the following section I will first briefly review the long-standing debate surrounding authorship, and then demonstrate how mosaic authorship develops out of Hjort's original definition and differs from it. Subsequently I will differentiate mosaic authorship from Naficy's "accented cinema" and Marks' "intercultural cinema", for the former has the privilege of border-crossing and hence ready access to multiculturalism and multilingualism. The four auteurs Haneke, Hou, Egoyan and Iñárritu, who have all built unique transnational filmmaking milieus through travelling, are chosen as examples for methodological reasons to demonstrate the model and the nuances within it. Their respective milieu-building and mosaic-forming in terms of travelling, production and distribution modes will be explored in the chapters to follow.

Film Authorship

Film authorship is complicated given the inherently collaborative nature of filmmaking, material demands, and, hence, strong commercial orientation. It stems from the insecure status of cinema, which swings between being a popular commodity and an art form in its own right, and plays a key role moving film theories beyond literary models and establishing film's status as an art form with its specificity of aesthetics and full range of expression. Many academic edited volumes such as *Theories of Film Authorship: A Reader*[34], *Auteurs and Authorship: A Film Reader*[35], and *Authorship and Film*[36] have tackled the debate surrounding authorship extensively, so here I will be content with a brief summary of some important issues and put the main focus on transnational authorship, which is the key to understanding mosaic space and mosaic auteurs.

This debate was first instigated in the 1950s by the *Cahiers du Cinéma* critics, who attributed the unique vision, world-view, and personal stamp of film, conveyed through visual aspects of cinema, to the distinctive personality of the director. The scholars who hold a similar romantic auteurist view include Andrew Sarris and British film critics in *Movie* such as Ian Cameron and Robin Wood. They practice a version of authorship-as-personality analysis and emphasise the coherence between the auteurs and their film works.[37] Sarris' value judgments when conducting a mystical and mystifying analysis

34 John Caughie (ed.): *Theories of Authorship: A Reader*. London: Routledge & Kegan Paul 1981.

35 Barry Keith Grant (ed.): *Auteurs and Authorship: A Film Reader*. Oxford: Blackwell 2008.

36 David A. Gerstner / Janet Staiger (eds): *Authorship and Film*. London: Routledge 2003.

37 Andrew Sarris: Notes on the 'Auteur' Theory in 1963. In: *Film Quarterly* 59 (2007), pp. 6–17; Robin Wood: Ideology, Genre, Auteur. In: Grant (ed.): *Auteurs and Authorship*, pp. 84–92; Ian Cameron: Films, Directors and Critics. In: Ibid., pp. 65–78; Helen Stoddart: Auteurism and Film Authorship Theory. In: Joanne Hollows / Mark Jancovich (eds): *Approaches to Popular Film*. Manchester: Manchester UP 1995, pp. 37–57; Janet Staiger: Authorship Approaches. In: Gerstner / Staiger (eds): *Authorship and Film*, pp. 27–57.

of the interior meaning of the films have often incited debates and criticism from critics such as Pauline Kael.[38] During the 1970s and 1980s, the ciné-structuralists such as Peter Wollen, who are inspired by Claude Lévi-Strauss' structural anthropology, shift the attention from the romantic view of "personal vision" to a more rigorous and systematic study of the film text, focusing more on the narrative than visual aspects.[39] The structuralist approach to authorship was later challenged by the poststructuralist emphasis on the role of reception and a plural, multiple and multiplying text, crystallised in the famous claim of "The Death of the Author" by Roland Barthes.[40] Although many scholars take issue with the poststructuralists' elimination of minor voices,[41] it marks a significant shift from *Cahiers*'s "author-vision" in the immediate aftermath of the Second World War to the notion of "author-brand name"[42] (within a broader discussion of art cinema as institution) of Steve Neale, "author-function"[43] of Michel Foucault, and authors as a critical construct of spectatorship of John Caughie[44]. The demystified notion of authorship continues to develop with a more attentive focus on the commercial and transnational aspects within the film industry. As a result, auteurs are viewed as a constructed marketing brand for various distribution routes, including international film festival circuits, and the spectators as consumers.[45] For example, Timothy Corrigan argues for the

38 Pauline Kael: Circles and Squares. In: Grant (ed.): *Auteurs and Authorship*, pp. 46–54.

39 Virginia Wright Wexman: Introduction. In: Ead. (ed.): *Film and Authorship*. New Brunswick: Rutgers UP 2003, pp. 1–18; Peter Wollen: The Auteur Theory: Michael Curtiz, and *Casablanca*. In: Gerstner / Staiger (eds): *Authorship and Film*, pp. 61–76, here p. 65.

40 Stoddart: Auteurism and Film Authorship Theory, pp. 48–49; Roland Barthes: The Death of the Author. In: Id.: *Image / Music / Text*, ed. and trans. from French by Stephen Heath. New York: Hill & Wang 1977, pp. 142–148.

41 Staiger: Authorship Approaches, pp. 49–51.

42 Steve Neale: Art Cinema as Institution. In: *Screen* 22,1 (1981), pp. 11–39, here p. 33.

43 Michel Foucault: What is an Author? In: Vassilis Lambropoulos / David Neal Miller (eds): *Twentieth-Century Literary Theory: An Introductory Anthology*. Albany: State UP of New York 1987, pp. 124–142, here pp. 124–127.

44 John Caughie: Introduction. In: Id. (ed.): *Theories of Authorship*, pp. 9–16, here p. 14.

45 Timothy Corrigan: *A Cinema Without Walls: Movies and Culture After Vietnam*. New Brunswick, NJ: Rutgers UP 1991, p. 103; Catherine Grant: www.auteur.com? In: *Screen* 41,1 (2000), pp. 101–108, here p. 105; Thomas Elsaesser: *European Cinema: Face to Face with Hollywood*. Amsterdam: Amsterdam UP 2005, p. 51.

commerce of an auteurism framework with the examples of Francis Ford Coppola, Alexander Kluge, and Raoul Ruiz.[46] Yet this stance is not without criticism. Helen Stoddart, for example, criticises this position as overemphasising commercial strategies and reducing the audience to an undifferentiated mass.[47]

Taking into account the current trend of scholarly works on authorship, mosaic authorship in this book does not focus solely on film texts or commercial strategies. Rather, it integrates the consideration of filmmaking contexts within particular film industries into film aesthetics. Mosaic authorship thus nuances different networking contexts and disparate spatial aesthetics according to each auteur's network-building and visual style. As the filmmaking contexts of mosaic auteurs are transnational and variegated, built along their travels, theories of transnational cinema become pertinent to the current framework.

Mosaic Authorship and Transnational Cinema

In Hjort's nuanced differentiation of transnational cinema, she criticises the way in which the term "transnational" has been used with certain assumptions about contemporary "networked and globalized realities" without providing enough semantic content.[48] She thus proposes a nuanced typology which connects transnationalism to a range of different ways of film production, which would facilitate a more polemical and productive discourse. This typology includes epiphanic, affinitive, milieu-building, opportunistic, cosmopolitan, globalising, auteurist, modernising, and experimental transnationalisms, which are not mutually exclusive, and considers the concept of "transnational" as scalar (with different degrees of intensity), instead of binary (assigning the presence or absence of transnationalism).[49]

What Hjort calls "cosmopolitan transnationalism"[50] is especially germane to the mosaic authorship here, because it focuses on transnationalism facilitated by the auteurs' border-crossing. In the

46 Corrigan: *A Cinema Without Walls*, pp. 101–136.

47 Stoddart: Auteurism and Film Authorship Theory, pp. 53–54.

48 Mette Hjort: On the Plurality of Cinematic Transnationalism. In: Nataša Ďurovičová / Kathleen Newman (eds): *World Cinemas, Transnational Perspectives*. London: Routledge 2010, pp. 12–33, here p. 13.

49 Ibid., pp. 15–30.

50 Ibid., p. 20.

cosmopolitan transnationalism of Hjort, the established auteurs who "exercise executive control over the filmmaking process" have "a lived experience of the limits of national belonging and citizenship", and consciously decide "to embrace a particular kind of collaboration beyond national borders".[51] Hjort's understanding of cosmopolitan peripatetic directors is thus focused on "a set of purely personal experiences" and "the particular mix of national, transnational, and post-colonial commitments and opportunities to which these trajectories give rise".[52] As Hjort notes:

> Multiple belonging linked to ethnicity and various trajectories of migration here becomes the basis for a form of transnationalism that is oriented toward the ideal of film as a medium capable of strengthening certain social imaginaries. The emphasis is on the exploration of issues relevant to particular communities situated in a number of different national or subnational locations to which the cosmopolitan auteur has a certain privileged access.[53]

The mode of mosaic authorship I am discussing here is pertinent to Hjort's category of cosmopolitan transnationalism, but pushes the argument forward by further nuancing it, contextualising it, and extending the exploration of cosmopolitan transnationalism to the relationship between this transnational mode of filmmaking in specific contexts and their mosaic spatial aesthetics, manifested in different ways. This mosaic authorship is a part of the much larger phenomenon of the transnational filmmaking mode. By also taking production and distribution aspects of the film industry into account, it does not claim to be a coherent whole but rather a constantly evolving milieu-building process, which develops with time and travelling. Through moving physically, the mosaic auteurs incorporate filmmaking resources such as funding and film professionals from diverse milieus and create an important transnational network. This transnational filmmaking mode is also reflected on the global circulation and consumption of their films within the circuits of international film festivals and arthouse cinema. As Marijke De Valck emphasises, international film festival networks join together the forces of state support, local initiatives, global film circulation, and Hollywood interference, and form an important nodal point at the reception end

51 Hjort: On the Plurality of Cinematic Transformation, pp. 20, 23.

52 Ibid., p. 21.

53 Ibid., p. 20.

of the film products.[54] To a great extent, the mosaic auteurs rely on the global networks of international film festivals, which address the transnational interconnections between technologies, institutions, and markets within the globalised media culture,[55] to ensure visibility and broad circulation of their films, although Iñárritu's films are also circulated through more commercial networks, especially after *Biutiful* (MX / ES 2010). The multiple cultural heritages become their advantage in attracting funding, film professionals, and distribution opportunities, as well as developing a unique perception of transnational space. This transnational authorship is not necessarily a self-conscious decision, as these auteurs, through their travelling, gradually discover the possibility of transnational networks to enable their practices of filmmaking.

Different from Hjort's cosmopolitan transnationalism, my understanding of these mosaic directors is not solely focused on their 'personal' experiences or vision, but rather on their experiences as a collective filmmaking unit, with a nuanced understanding of their milieu-building (the less self-conscious and rule-governed kind of milieu compared to Hjort's milieu-building transnationalism) within the national and the transnational. They are a brand recognised by the public and used as a marketing strategy while they represent the whole group of people with whom they collaborate regularly and the milieus that these collaborators bring together. These auteurs also perform mosaic distribution, as their works widely circulate within international film festival circuits, even Iñárritu who is more popular and commercial compared to Haneke, Hou and Egoyan. This trend is sometimes a reaction to the increasing challenges of globalisation in the film industry. For example, as Ann Marie Stock points out, cinema has become increasingly transnational in Latin America because of the influences of interculturalism and multinational coproduction. In this context, films made with collaborative financing and a transnational production team travel in international film festival circuits in Chicago, Los Angeles, New York, the Twin Cities, and Sundance, as well as in San Sebastian, Rotterdam, Cannes, Venice, and Berlin. Distributors such as Miramax, and cultural centres such as Video del

54 Marijke De Valck: *Film Festivals: From European Geopolitics to Global Cinephilia*. Amsterdam: Amsterdam UP 2007, p. 18.

55 Ibid., p. 30.

Sur, the International Media Resource Exchange, and Cine-Accion facilitate a global reception of the films.[56] A similar reaction to the impact of globalisation on local film industries can also be seen in the case of Taiwanese auteurs such as Hou and Tsai Ming-liang, who seek transnational financing, production, and distribution within the circuits of international art cinema and film festivals to overcome the financial limitations of national cinema; hence, their transnational filmmaking mode and mosaic authorship.

While mosaic authorship approximates Hjort's cosmopolitan transnationalism in some aspects, it is significantly different from her other typological categories. According to Hjort's definitions, epiphanic transnationalism emphasises "the cinematic articulation of those elements of deep national belonging that overlap with aspects of other national identities to produce something resembling deep transnational belonging"[57]. Modernising transnationalism emerges when a certain society employs transnational cinematic practices as a source of modernisation and recognition, whereas experimental transnationalism emerges simply as the "artistically cogent" thing to do, such as the playful experiments of making films under imposed constraints in Lars von Trier and Jørgen Leth's project of *The Five Obstructions*.[58] Milieu-building transnationalism, such as Dogma 95 (an avant-garde filmmaking movement initiated in 1995 headed by the Danish directors Lars von Trier and Thomas Vinterberg which refuses the use of special effects and post-production) and Advance Party (the concept backed by Sigma Films and Zentropa to produce three films by different first-time directors and producers with the same cast), is a rule-governed and collaborative initiative that is often a small-nation's response to the domination of Hollywood.[59] In affinitive transnationalism, filmmaking teams cooperate in film productions because of their close ethnic, cultural and linguistic links.[60] Opportunistic transnationalism is primarily concerned with

56 Ann Marie Stock: Authentically Mexican? *Mi Querido Tom Mix* and *Chronos* Reframe Critical Questions. In: Joanne Hershfield / David R. Maciel (eds): *Mexico's Cinema: A Century of Film and Filmmakers*. Lanham: SR 1999, pp. 269–283, here pp. 269, 272–273.

57 Hjort: On the Plurality of Cinematic Transnationalism, p. 16.

58 Ibid., pp. 24–25, 28.

59 Ibid., p. 18.

60 Ibid., p. 17.

economic issues without having the intention of creating a sustainable network.[61] Auteurist transnationalism is enabled through an intentional and ad-hoc collaboration between auteurs across national boundaries, as can be seen in compilation films.[62] As for globalising transnationalism, one seeks global appeal in international co-production in order to recuperate the astronomical amount of film budget.[63] In contrast to these definitions, mosaic authorship is less systematic and exists on a relatively smaller scale than modernising and milieu-building transnationalisms; mosaic authorship does not function at the level of government policy like modernising transnationalism, and it is far less self-conscious and rule-governed than milieu-building transnationalism. Moreover, more sustainable networks are usually established through mosaic authorship, compared to the mostly one-off collaboration in epiphanic, auteurist, and opportunistic transnationalisms. We can observe this in Haneke's continual integration of European filmmaking resources throughout his career. Mosaic auteurs also cooperate with both culturally affinitive and unaffinitive networks, unlike Hjort's affinitive transnationalism. Hou, for example, works with both culturally affinitive networks in the Japan-based *Café Lumière* (JP / TW 2003) and culturally unaffinitive networks in the France-based *Flight of the Red Balloon* (*Le Voyage du Ballon Rouge*, FR / TW 2007).

Admittedly, mosaic auteurs are sometimes involved in projects which belong to Hjort's globalising and auteurist transnationalism, but these one-off networks are temporary and not their main network-building strategies. For example, some mosaic auteurs such as Hou and Iñárritu, who come from countries which devote relatively limited financial and material resources on film art, can be seen to be using the strategy of "globalizing transnationalism" to overcome the scarcity of funding resources within the nation by resorting to transnational resources and distribution routes.[64] The economic concerns, however, are not the only reason for their transnational cooperation. In addition, sometimes mosaic auteurs practice temporary auteurist transnationalism by joining compilation film projects

61 Ibid., pp. 19–20.

62 Ibid., p. 23.

63 Ibid., p. 21.

64 Ibid.

such as *To Each His Own Cinema* (*Chacun son cinéma*, FR 2007, D: Hou Hsiao-hsien et al.) and *Lumière and Company* (*Lumière et compagnie*, FR / DK / ES / SE 1995, D: Hou Hsiao-hsien et al.). Yet each of these projects compile short films made in respective auteurist contexts into a particular feature film, instead of helping the auteurs build transnational milieus during the process. As the mosaic auteurs' transnationalism is primarily built upon multiplying film milieus through long-term relationships which come with travelling, the framework of mosaic authorship focuses primarily on the long-standing network-building transnational practices instead of temporary associations.

Although mosaic auteurs and their works are hard to define within the framework of national cinema, their careers do start off from a certain national cinema milieu, from which they branch out to multicultural and multilingual environments. Instead of having to choose one particular cultural affiliation and one filmmaking context, their experience as peripatetic directors living in two or more cultural regimes of knowledge enables them to combine multiple identities and resources. Rather than being a fixed and stable personality, the mosaic auteurs mark their trajectories of shifting filmmaking contexts and spatial perception in their works. For example, we can see the shifting mosaic authorship and transnational networks in Haneke's travelling from the Germanophone world to France and to the USA in chapter 4, and in Egoyan's implicit to explicit multiple cultural identities discussed in chapter 2. Through travelling, they operate transnationality on several levels and find the best combination of funding, crew, mise-en-scène, setting, narrative materials, audience, and networks from a diverse range of networks in their unique milieu of filmmaking. Their personal travelling, and their travelling with the filmmaking crew, has an impact on their spatial aesthetics, which reflect the experiences of mobility of our time. This resonates with Caren Kaplan's argument that travelling individuals who dwell in multilingual and multicultural situations and "the various configurations of power and meaning in complex colonial situations" possess the particular ability to see, understand, read, and write culture on multiple levels.[65] Here it is worth noting that all these auteurs'

65 Caren Kaplan: Deterritorializations: The Rewriting of Home and Exile in Western Feminist Discourse. In: *Cultural Critique* 6 (1987), pp. 187–198, here p. 187.

professional travelling and border-crossing is a privilege and an advantage given by their internationally acclaimed authorship and their success in gaining visibility in world cinema. They are relatively free to move across the borders physically, thanks to their auteur status, which enables them to acquire visa and work permits more easily and to generate financial resources for film production without too much struggle. Naturally not every auteur could enjoy this mobility; many independently working exilic and diasporic filmmakers constantly struggle to deal with immigration laws and search for filmmaking funds and distribution routes. Therefore, I am not trying to imply that national boundaries or geopolitical walls are tumbling down in the age of globalisation. Mosaic auteurs are by no means showing the disappearance of borders. In fact, despite their privileged status, frequent border-crossing experiences render them very conscious of the political implications of borders and the imbalanced power relations at border control; to a great extent, their construction of mosaic space is created from this awareness of borders.

At this point, the historical specificity of this type of auteurism is worth briefly mentioning. Although the focus here is on the films of contemporary mosaic auteurs whose films are produced in the contemporary period since the 1980s, and whose major works appear in the 1990s and 2000s, when we see a more rapidly formed interconnectivity across the globe and a growing popularity of mosaic aesthetics, it would be inaccurate to presume that mosaic authorship is solely concerned with contemporary practices of border-crossing after the late 1980s. In fact, Elsaesser traces the genealogy of his framework of mind-game films back to masters of suspense such as Fritz Lang, Luis Buñuel, Alfred Hitchcock, Orson Welles, Akira Kurosawa, Alain Resnais, and Ingmar Bergman,[66] and some of these auteurs can in fact be understood as mosaic auteurs for their practices of transnational filmmaking through travelling. For example, Fritz Lang can be seen as a mosaic auteur whose filmmaking networks are extended from Germanophone Austria and Germany to France and the US through migration before the Second World War.[67] Indeed, the historical

66 Elsaesser: The Mind-Game Film, p. 16.

67 Paul M. Jensen: *The Cinema of Fritz Lang*. New York: Barnes 1969, pp. 112–128; Lotte H. Eisner: *Fritz Lang*. London: Secker & Warburg 1976, pp. 149–176; Robert A. Armour: *Fritz Lang*. Boston: Twayne 1977, pp. 22–24.

context creates a unique transnational network specific to the particular era that the mosaic auteurs live in and the border-crossing condition of that period. Yet due to the complexity and width of the full historical range of mosaic auteurs and mosaic space, it is not possible to include all these auteurs throughout the span of film history in the current project.

In addition, the examples of Haneke, Hou, Egoyan, and Iñárritu in this book are not intended to imply that these four auteurs are the only primary examples of contemporary mosaic auteurs. Krzysztof Kieślowski and Fatih Akin are two good examples of the mosaic auteurs that are not discussed here. The former has incorporated the filmmaking resources and networks of Poland, France, and Switzerland and co-produced with Sidéral Productions (Paris), Tor Production (Warsaw), MK2 Productions (Paris), CAB Productions (Switzerland), Télévision Swiss-Romande (Switzerland), France 3 (Paris), and Studio Canal+ (Paris) for the films *Three Colours: Blue, White, Red* (*Trois couleurs: Bleu, Blanc, Rouge*, FR 1993/94) and *The Double Life of Veronique* (*La double vie de Véronique*, FR 1991), which demonstrate unique and striking mosaic aesthetics.[68] The latter, on the other hand, embraces his Turkish-German dual identities and transculturalism, and has incorporated a wide range of filmmaking resources in Germany and Turkey, including Corazon International (Germany), Dorje Film (Italy), Pyramide Production (France), and Panfilm (Turkey) in the making of *Soul Kitchen* (DE 2009), *The Edge of Heaven* (*Auf der anderen Seite*, DE 2005), *Head-on* (*Gegen die Wand*, DE 2004), and *Short Sharp Shock* (*Kurz und schmerzlos*, DE 1998).[69] Kieślowski's and Akin's film works and transnational authorship also demonstrate a multidimensional mosaic which brings together transnational filmmaking resources, screen spaces and spatial configurations, but as the Germanophone world of Akin

68 Joseph G. Kickasola: *The Films of Krzysztof Kieslowski: The Liminal Image*. New York: Continuum 2004, p. 14; Steven Woodward: Introduction. In: Id. (ed.): *After Kieslowski: The Legacy of Krzysztof Kieslowski*. Detroit: Wayne State UP 2009, pp. 1–16, here pp. 1–3; Emma Wilson: *Memory and Survival: The French Cinema of Krzysztof Kieslowski*. London: Modern Humanities Research Association / Maney 2000, p. 1.

69 Roger Hillman: Transnationalism in the Films of Fatih Akin. In: *Europe and Its Others: Essays on Interperception and Identity*. Bern: Lang 2010, pp. 263–276, here p. 265.

and the Francophone world of Kieślowski overlap with Haneke's European context, they are not included in the book in order to avoid a purely Eurocentric discussion of transnationalism. However, the correspondence between mosaic authorship and mosaic space in the case of female filmmakers does not seem to be as distinct as in the case of male filmmakers, and this would demand further research. For example, the Indonesian-American Fatimah Tobing Rony has made short films in the US and Indonesia, including her recent participation in the Indonesian compilation project *Chants of Lotus* (*Perempuan Punya Cerita*, ID 2007, D: Fatimah Tobing Rony et al.). The Hong-Kong based auteur Ann Hui has multiple identities as she was born in China, has a Japanese mother, grew up in Hong Kong and was educated in the UK, though she has produced films exclusively from Chinese funding, such as Class Limited in the mainland and Golden Harvest Company and Mega-Vision Pictures in Hong Kong. Yet their films do not manifest mosaic aesthetics. Haneke, Hou, Egoyan and Iñárritu, the selected auteurs to be discussed here, offer key examples of mosaic filmmaking by coveing a broad range of geopolitical filmmaking contexts, including Europe, Asia, North America, Latin America, and the intercontinental context between Armenia and Canada in the case of Egoyan, and manifest diverse yet corresponding aesthetics.

It is worth noting that I observe an absence of female filmmakers in the mosaic model. Whereas male travelling filmmakers demonstrate the emergence of such a trend of mosaic aesthetics within mainstream and arthouse cinemas, it is not happening with female auteurs. Within this particular market very much dominated by male filmmakers, the closest female auteur to the mosaic model that I can locate is Claire Denis. She established transnational filmmaking networks through her experience as assistant director, having worked for the Yugoslavian auteur Dušan Makavejev, the Italian production designer and director Beni Montresor, the Greek-French auteur Costa-Gavras, the British director Clive Donner, the German auteur Wim Wenders, and the US auteur Jim Jarmusch. Although Denis' films are mostly funded by French companies, such as Ognon Pictures for *The Intruder* (*L'intrus*, FR 2004), Soudaine Compagnie for *35 Shots of Rhums* (*35 Rhums*, FR 2008), and Arena Films for *Friday Night* (*Vendredi soir*, FR 2002), they are widely distributed in the arthouse cinema circuits through the networks including

Artificial Eye in the UK, Slovenska Kinoteka in Slovenia, IFC Films and Wellspring Media in the US, Imovision in Brazil, and Teleview International in Lebanon. They are also circulated in international film festivals such as Cannes (where *Chocolat*, FR 1988, was nominated for the Palme d'Or), Venice (where *White Material*, FR 2009, and *The Intruder* were nominated for the Golden Lion), and Locarno (where *Nenette and Boni / Nénette et Boni*, FR 1996, won the Golden Leopard). As Martine Beugnet justly points out, Denis uses flashbacks, parallel editing, dissolves, and superimpositions to "create a narrative space where a multitude of lives, of realities, and several time zones seem to collide or to overlap"[70]. Beugnet also relates the interweaving of different characters' trajectories in *I Can't Sleep* (*J'ai pas sommeil*, ES 1994, D: Claire Denis) to Altman's *Short Cuts*, although the characters are always on the verge of meeting without physically encountering one another.[71] Indeed, through the mosaic narrative, *J'ai pas sommeil* juxtaposes the space of the colonial and the postcolonial, the developed and the developing regions of Europe, homosexual and heterosexual, black and white, young and elderly, and the underprivileged and the privileged. *Beau Travail* (FR 1999, D: Claire Denis) also demonstrates mosaic aesthetics by jumping back and forth between the legionnaire and post-legionnaire life, past and present, the actual and the virtual, and recollection-images and dream-images, while at the same time assembling colonial and postcolonial spaces of the vertical dimension. As Denis' European arthouse filmmaking context overlaps with Haneke's network, which would make the book lose the balance of three continents and lean towards a Eurocentric approach, I had to make the difficult decision of leaving Denis outwith the book's scope.

To sum up, we can see that the current framework of mosaic authorship provides new depth to our existing understanding of the issues of authorship, transnationalism, and globalisation, and takes on board the mode of cultural production influenced by the flows and disjunctures of global ethnoscapes. This corresponds to what Arjun Appadurai says:

70 Martine Beugnet: *Claire Denis*. Manchester / New York: Manchester UP 2004, p. 23.

71 Ibid., p. 23.

> It seems impossible to study these new cosmopolitanisms fruitfully without analyzing the transnational cultural flows within which they thrive, compete, and feed off one another in ways that defeat and confound many verities of the human sciences today. One such truth concerns the link between space, stability, and cultural reproduction. There is an urgent need to focus on the cultural dynamics of what is now called deterritorialization. [...] The loosening of the holds between people, wealth, and territories fundamentally alters the basis of cultural reproduction.[72]

Seen in this light, the framework of mosaic authorship tackles exactly the transformed and transforming mode of film production through the auteurs' travelling, where their works are caught in the intersection between global flows of goods, technologies, people, finances and information. The multidirectional movement of transnational cultural flows and such a link between space, motion, and cultural reproduction are manifest in their filmmaking contexts and spatial aesthetics. Being entangled in the transnational network, the mosaic auteurs integrate forces from diverse resources and produce cultural products which are consumed by global audiences. This kind of transnationalism is formed thanks to the privileged access to border-crossing and multiculturalism of mosaic auteurs, which marks its distinction from Naficy's "accented cinema" and Marks' "intercultural cinema".

Mosaic Authorship, Accented Cinema and Intercultural Cinema

Naficy's accented cinema and Marks' intercultural cinema also explore travelling auteurs and their film works, but the multidirectional movement of mosaic auteurs is distinctively different from them. Naficy defines authors in accented cinema:

> [Accented] authors are literally and figuratively everyday journeymen and journeywomen who are driven off or set free from their places of origin, by force or by choice, on agonizing quests that require displacements and emplacements so profound, personal, and transformative as to shape not only the authors themselves and their films but also the question of authorship. Any discussion of authorship in exile needs to take into consideration not only the individuality, originality, and personality of unique individuals as expressive film authors but also, and more important, their (dis)location as interstitial subjects within social formations and cinematic practices.[73]

72 Appadurai: *Modernity at Large*, p. 49.

73 Hamid Naficy: *An Accented Cinema: Exilic and Diasporic Filmmaking*. Princeton: Princeton UP 2001, p. 34.

Like Naficy's accented cinema, mosaic authorship is also interested in the everyday journeymen and journeywomen, but it discusses a different kind of journeying, which is not necessarily a journey of exile. Both mosaic auteurs and accented auteurs travel, but the latter's travelling is concerned with *one* location and *one* accent, whereas the former's border-crossing, thanks to their privilege of travelling, is back and forth, multidimensional and multiplying. I consider mosaic auteurs as interstitial subjects with constant displacement, but, being relatively free to move around, their quest is not necessarily agonising over the loss of a certain location. Nor are their films necessarily accented. In fact, accent is something mosaic auteurs can choose to leave on their film works or not, and they can have more than one single accent. Unlike exilic and diasporic auteurs, mosaic auteurs have the choice of foregrounding the accent of their true origin, or disguising their particular accent and foregrounding other aspects of their cultural belongings according to filmmaking purposes. Hence, a fixed and static cultural root becomes a notion that is difficult to pinpoint for them. Caught in a complicated relationship with different cultures and different cultural affiliations, one can be in exile from different roots with different accents in different contexts. The framework of mosaic auteurs thus provides an alternative category to journeymen and journeywomen filmmakers, as in this case it becomes an impossible question to ask which accent one has and in which direction one moves. Instead of moving to the host country and longing for the home culture, mosaic auteurs' movement between host and home cultures, as well as their belongings and longing, are multidirectional; all the cultural elements are integrated and keep growing in them. My argument here is resonant with Hjort, who, in her analysis of Evan Chan, finds "cosmopolitan" more appropriate than "exilic" and "accented", as long as "this director has the freedom to move back and forth between different sites, where a certain highly enabling insider status is available to him".[74]

Egoyan would be a good example to demonstrate the difference between accented and mosaic auteurs because he is discussed in both frameworks. From the point of view of accented cinema, he is a diasporic Armenian director residing in Canada with agonising quests for his dislocation and identity, making films with relatively small

74 Hjort: On the Plurality of Cinematic Transformation, p. 21.

budgets in an artisanal production mode. However, the framework of mosaic auteurs does not view Egoyan as being tormented by the choice of either the host culture or the ancestors' roots, but rather emphasises Egoyan's integration of filmmaking resources and cultural elements in both contexts. In this mosaic, the consideration of space is not only about displacement and emplacement as such, for displacement and emplacement, and dislocation and relocation are constantly in exchange in these auteurs' privileged stance, which weave into a complex and multidimensional assemblage. Egoyan's movement is thus understood as back and forth, multidirectional and multifaceted, instead of simply being accented. As a matter of fact, in most of Egoyan's films, Canadian and Armenian subject matters intermingle and coexist, though more explicit in some films than in others. His reflections on Canada are rendered more in depth and meaningful through his explorations of Armenia. Meanwhile his Canadian experiences provide him with a refreshing perspective on Armenia.

For a similar reason this book also differs from Marks' intercultural cinema in *The Skin of the Film: Intercultural Cinema, Embodiment, and the Senses*[75]. The focus of intercultural cinema for Marks is a body of works produced in the USA, Canada and the UK by artists who are often cultural minorities, from locations which are economically and politically underprivileged compared to the Western metropolitan centres. She posits, "this movement is an international phenomenon, produced wherever people of different cultural backgrounds live together in the power-inflected spaces of diaspora, (post-or neo-)colonialism, and cultural apartheid"[76]. In contrast to Marks' arguments in intercultural cinema, the mosaic auteurs, belonging to a minority group or not, are the privileged auteurs who are relatively free to establish filmmaking milieus across boundaries, and to explore juxtapositions of spatial configurations. They are residing in power-inflected spaces but do not necessarily consider the geopolitical and cultural space from the point of view of a cultural minority. Their experience as peripatetic directors living in two or more cultural regimes of knowledge is fluid, intangible, less well defined, and thus

75 Laura U. Marks: *The Skin of the Film: Intercultural Cinema, Embodiment, and the Senses*. Durham: Duke UP 2000.

76 Ibid., p. 1.

multiple and multiplying. Therefore, the mosaic directors here do not necessarily "share the political issues of displacement and hybridity"[77] as Marks observes. They do not have a fixed sense of "displacement" because they are always on the move and their networks are always on the move. Whereas Marks argues that the violent disjunctions in space and time experienced by filmmakers under exile and displacement have an impact on their doubt in cinema's representational ability and in notions of truth,[78] my argument here is that the physical effects of travelling, enjoyed by resourceful auteurs, are having an impact on their perception of space, their decision-making, funding resources, and reception of their films, which are manifested in their screen space. While Marks puts special focus on haptic images, which invite experiences of nonaudiovisual senses, this book focuses on spatial aesthetics which reflects upon mosaic space and refuses a unified and coherent perception of space.

Therefore, mosaic authorship is pertinent to but different from Hjort's cosmopolitan transnationalism, Naficy's accented cinema, and Marks' intercultural cinema. It groups together travelling filmmakers who assemble multilingual and multicultural resources and whose film works piece together spatial representations, which will be informed by the theories of space in the following section.

Theories of Space and Mosaic Space

In the framework of mosaic, at the same time that screen spaces are assembled at the formal level and film resources gather thanks to mosaic authorship at the contextual level, a wide range of geopolitical spatial configurations are also put together. As we see in the example of *71 Fragments*, in the diegetic mosaic space the bourgeois and the working-class, and the West Europeans and the East Europeans coexist, clash with, and interconnect with each other. This is where theories of space come into the model, as they help us understand the interweaving of spatial configurations into a myriad and multiplying mosaic at the level of spatial representations on screen. Works by Gilles Deleuze and Félix Guattari, Augé, Marks, Featherstone, Appadurai, Sassen, Antonio Negri and Michael Hardt have all informed the current model. In fact, these theorists of space from various disciplines have all observed the emergence of a new kind of

77 Marks: *The Skin of the Film*, p. 2.

78 Ibid., p. 57.

space, although their focus and terminologies diverge. Deleuze calls the new space "any-space-whatever", Augé "non-places", Featherstone and Sassen "the global", and Negri / Hardt "Empire". In the following section I will discuss these fluid, dynamic, interactive, and, hence, productive concepts, the differences between any-space-whatevers and non-places, as well as their crossovers.

Global/Local

Contemporary scholars such as Featherstone, Sassen, Appadurai, and Negri / Hardt have noted the recently developed space in the age of increasing global interdependencies, which Featherstone, Sassen, and Appadurai call "the global", and Negri / Hardt call "Empire". In their theories, Featherstone and Sassen discuss the increasing exchanges across nation-states on a global scale as well as their impact on the industrial production, circulation, and marketing modes. The globalised world city, taking over the role of nation-states to a certain extent, is an important linking site where the various flows of people, images, finances, technology, information, and goods from the centre and the periphery, and the local and the global intermingle.[79] However, both Featherstone and Sassen caution that the proliferation of global spaces, instead of acting in place of the local, exists in juxtaposition with local spaces.[80] For Featherstone, the era of globalisation develops in the intertwining of globalism, manifested in increasing interdependencies between nations and proliferation of anonymous "no place spaces", and localism, founded on day-to-day interactions in a "place".[81] For Sassen, since the 1980s, globalisation is signaled by a proliferation of specialised global assemblages and a new complex interdependence of global economic dynamic, which exists side-by-side with older historical formations and structures.[82] Hardt / Negri, on the other hand, view this interconnectedness between the local and the global as being under the globalised form of sovereignty, "Empire", which is a new economic-industrial-communicative

79 Featherstone: Localism, Globalism, and Cultural Identity, p. 65; Sassen: Spatialities and Temporalities of the Global, p. 267.

80 Sassen: *Territory. Authority. Rights*, pp. 402–403; Sassen: Spatialities and Temporalities of the Global, p. 265; Featherstone: Localism, Globalism, and Cultural Identity, p. 65.

81 Featherstone: Localism, Globalism, and Cultural Identity, pp. 46–47.

82 Sassen: *Territory. Authority. Rights*, pp. 402–403; Sassen: Spatialities and Temporalities of the Global, p. 267.

machine with a discontinuous structure constantly shifting between centre and margins.[83] As for Appadurai, he portrays a new cultural configuration that takes shape at the conjuncture of mass mediation and migration, and theorises the complex and disjunctive intersection between various flows in the new global cultural economy in terms of ethnoscapes, mediascapes, technoscapes, financescapes, and ideoscapes, which move away from the centre-periphery model. They form a mosaic of imagined worlds with constant negotiation between the global and the local.[84]

Though interweaving different flows of forces, globalisation is not equal, balanced, and universalising. It is a partial and strategic geography of globalisation with a diverse range of rates of acceleration, in which global circulation is often strategically located and constituted in national spaces, themselves never unitary or completely integrated.[85] We can see the manifestations of these interfaces in the example of *71 Fragments*, in which multiplying interchanges between the local and the global are foregrounded in the interdependencies between characters and the visual bringing-together of diverse geopolitical spaces. In the developed metropolis of Vienna, people from urban, rural, bourgeois, working-class, and nomad spaces brush through one another's shoulders at various occasions, from an underground ride to a bank transaction. The city space becomes a linking site which assembles flows of individuals, mediatised images, and products between the centre and the periphery. Yet we see the disparities between people's access to the global resources through the eyes of the homeless Romanian boy Marian, who smuggles himself into Austria by sneaking into a cargo loaded with refrigerators; he follows the same trajectory as the refrigerators, the products made in the underprivileged part of Europe and transported to be consumed in wealthy countries. During his wandering, he encounters a bourgeois mother with two sons, a working-class diasporic newspaper boy, and another homeless boy. From the bourgeois mother playing in a park with her kids, Marian steals a wind jacket to keep himself warm. Though being mutually incomprehensible, he enquires about food

83 Michael Hardt / Antonio Negri: *Empire*. Cambridge, MA: Harvard UP 2000, p. 39.

84 Appadurai: *Modernity at Large*, pp. 32–35.

85 Featherstone: Localism, Globalism, and Cultural Identity, p. 57; Sassen: Spatialities and Temporalities of the Global, pp. 265, 267.

and shelter from the newspaper boy in front of a kiosk. As a game with the homeless boy on the opposite underground platform, they imitate each other, without any verbal communication, by balancing themselves on the very edge of the platform with open arms. These encounters bring together local spaces of people with different languages, socioeconomic status, and imbalanced relationships to global flows of goods, information, technologies, and images. The bourgeois family in the park, as well as Marian's host mother Mrs. Brunner, can easily afford many more wind jackets, refrigerators and TV sets, which are produced in countries which offer cheap labor such as Marian's homeland, to keep themselves warm, comfortable, and connected. Contrarily, Marian, before Mrs. Brunner hosts him, is cut off from all global networks and survives on spare food in the trash bin and remains largely unseen in the middle of the wealthy Western European city.

Marc Augé's Non-places and Gilles Deleuze's Any-space-whatevers
Globalisation, theorised by Sassen, Featherstone, and Appadurai, approximates what Augé calls "supermodernity", which marks a shift into the frequent and expansive exchange of information, people, images, and goods. These are the circumstances under which "non-places" proliferate. From his anthropological perspective, Augé contrasts non-places of contractual relationships, which should be treated by anthropologists with new methods, to anthropological places which are relational, historical, and concerned with identity.[86] Non-places thus refer to transit points where people simply pass through and do not reside, such as airports, hospitals, convenience stores, gas stations, hotel chains, and conference centres. We see non-places in the underground stations, kiosk, and autoroute that Marian passes by momentarily in *71 Fragments*. They are fleeting, temporary, ephemeral, and unaffectionate spaces where people place themselves as spectators without paying much attention to the spectacle. In Augé's framework, places and non-places intertwine in the world of supermodernity; the notion of places presupposes the existence of non-places.[87] The differentiation between non-places and places hangs on the quality of living agents' relation to the space.

86 Augé: Paris and the Ethnography of the Contemporary World, pp. 177–178.
87 Marc Augé: *Non-Places. Introduction to an Anthropology of Supermodernity*, trans. from French by John Howe. London: Verso 1995, pp. 86, 107–108.

This is taken one step forward by James Tweedie who maps "places" with the local, in contrast to the non-places of "global images flows". He writes:

> In the ubiquitous and at times nearly deafening rhetoric of globalization, images and places habitually occupy opposite poles, with "global image flows" as the emblematic border-crossing phenomenon, and the neighborhood, the village, and other place-bound communities standing enduringly for the local.[88]

We can understand this as the pairing between places and non-places, and the local and the global. In a space where non-places prevail, the space loses its local characteristics and becomes more global. Conversely, the more a certain space is filled with relational and sustainable places, the more the space is attached to the local. This resonates with Featherstone's theorisation of globalism and localism, in which he relates the intertwining of globalism to the proliferation of what he calls "no place spaces" and localism to the grounded interactions in "places".[89] Wollen also extends the notion of non-places along the line of globalisation. He proposes that non-places proliferate in cinema as spectacles for touristic consumption of visual pleasure, in opposition to places which are created for dramatic consumption. In his argument, with globalisation and its tendency of immediacy, simultaneity, and juxtaposition, we seem to move away from tactile apprehension of the world to visual and optical apprehension, which implies seeing a spectacle at a distance instead of residing in a certain space.[90] Yet this does not imply that the non-places are always global, and places are on all occasions local. The pairings between them should always be contextualised, for the working of the correlation is complicated.

Although Augé's places and non-places are very productive concepts in understanding space, they are not without pitfalls and criticism. In fact, as Augé attempts to modify in the second English-language edition by emphasising on the "circulation, consumption

88 James Tweedie: Morning in the New Metropolis: Taipei and the Globalization of the City Film. In: Darrell William Davis / Ru-Shou Robert Chen (eds): *Cinema Taiwan: Politics, Popularity and State of the Arts*. London: Routledge 2007, pp. 116–145, here p. 116.

89 Featherstone: Localism, Globalism, and Cultural Identity, pp. 46–47.

90 Peter Wollen: *Paris Hollywood: Writings on Film*. London: Verso 2002, pp. 213–214.

and communication" of what he now calls "empirical non-places"[91], places and non-places should not be taken as a categorical shift from one fixed concept to another fixed concept. In fact, non-places do not replace places in the age of 'supermodernity' but rather increase spatial exchanges and fluidity. Instead of foregrounding the binarism, places and non-places transform and swap their roles constantly. In the example of *71 Fragments*, the supposed home 'places' become unaffectionate for Tomek, whose falling-out with his daughter is apparent in their cold, matter-of-fact interaction at a bank counter and over the phone. The orphanage 'places' are where children like Marian pass by between adoptive families. The supposed transit and functional non-places such as a bank, on the other hand, are where people are forced to stay and establish some kind of a relation because of the gunshot. Moreover, Augé's supermodernity and non-places are the concepts essentially from the perspective of the bourgeois class in a Western society. As a matter of fact, only the leisured class would have the means to experience the so-called 'supermodernity', for only they would have time and money to travel and to experience the transitional non-places such as airport lobbies, border control, and chain hotels. As the underprivileged people, such as Hans' core family in *71 Fragments*, are struggling to maintain even the most basic needs within an anthropological 'place', they do not have the luxury of supermodernity and do not have the resources to 'pass by' anywhere for holidays. Even for the illegal immigrants who eventually 'travel' to somewhere else, their travelling does not involve the same kind of experiences of non-places. As we can see from the cinematic representations of the Romanian boy Marian's journey to the host country, it is devoid of transitional non-places such as airport waiting rooms, hotel receptions, and convenience stores. He literally 'boxes' himself into a cargo, with the camera reframing the image into double squares, and has to travel without food and water like a refrigerator for a long time.

Deleuze's any-space-whatever in *Cinema 2* theorises a different kind of space from Augé's non-places. Although any-space-whatever in *Cinema 1* refers to the background place in the depth of field which loses its spatio-temporal co-ordinates behind the affect images

91 Marc Augé: *Non-Places. Introduction to an Anthropology of Supermodernity*, trans. from French by John Howe. Second Edition. London: Verso 2009, p. viii.

created by close-ups,[92] the use of any-space-whatever here is taken from Deleuze's work in *Cinema 2*. According to Deleuze, the Second World War marks the moment when movement-images give way to time-images, as postwar Europe sees the proliferation of spaces which Europeans find difficult to relate to. These spaces are called any-space-whatevers and are "deserted but inhabited, disused warehouses, waste ground, cities in the course of demolition or reconstruction"[93]. The logical connection between these spaces becomes unknown or vacuous. In the emptied and disconnected any-space-whatevers, purely optical or sound situations, instead of sensory-motor situations prompting a reaction, proliferate.[94] In these spaces, the individuals who no longer know how to react to the new spaces are thus deprived of action and become seers.[95] They are "objectively emptied", absent from their own existence, becoming seers and no longer *actants*.[96]
Although scholars such as Ian Buchanan and David Martin-Jones have argued for the similarities between Augé's non-places and Deleuze's any-space-whatevers,[97] here, I would argue that although both point out a new spatial perception, non-places and any-space-whatevers are essentially two different notions with very different significations and implications. Any-space-whatever, according to Deleuze's definition in *Cinema 2*, is deserted but inhabited, a shantytown, and yet a dwelling nonetheless.[98] Augé's non-places also include shantytowns, refugee camps and slums, but in his framework these are transitory sites where refugees and deprived individuals don't stay for a long time.[99] Hence, individuals inhabit any-space-whatevers without a sense of attachment and the ability to react, whereas non-places are the immediate and transitory spaces with well-defined codes for interaction, where people pass by without residing. Both

92 Deleuze: *Cinema 1*, p. 99.

93 Deleuze: *Cinema 2*, p. xi.

94 Ibid., p. 5.

95 Ibid., p. xi.

96 Ibid., p. 9.

97 Ian Buchanan: Space in the Age of Non-Place. In: Id. / Gregg Lambert (eds): *Deleuze and Space*. Edinburgh: Edinburgh UP 2005, pp. 16–35, here p. 28; Martin-Jones: *Deleuze and World Cinemas*, p. 143.

98 Deleuze: *Cinema 2*, p. xi.

99 Augé: *Non-Places*, pp. 34, 78.

are uninhabitable, but people will still reside in any-space-whatever out of need as opposed to simply passing by non-places.

The Smooth and the Striated, Deterritorialisation and Reterritorialisation
Within any-space-whatevers, we see the smooth and the striated, and deterritorialisation and reterritorialisation, which are theorised in Deleuze and Guattari's collaborative work *A Thousand Plateaus: Capitalism and Schizophrenia*[100], flowing into each other and intermingling dynamically. There are many different ways of understanding the smooth and the striated, including Gary Genosko and Adam Bryx's reading of the smooth and the striated through informatic striation and bureaucratic segmentarities,[101] but the focus here is on the spatial implications of the smooth and the striated and their cinematic manifestation. According to Deleuze / Guattari, the smooth is nomadic space and the striated sedentary space, which crisscross, transform, correlate and juxtapose on each other. They form a circuit in which "smooth space is constantly being translated, transversed into a striated space; striated space is constantly being reversed, returned to a smooth space"[102]. Having well-defined and well-anchored vertical and horizontal lines, the striated is fixed, delimited, and solid with closed intervals. It provides an order and an organism, where one counts, measures and demarcates in order to occupy. Like the outline of fortifications in the Roman Empire, this is an extensive space of measures, with geometrical and linear segmentation which draws lines to mark boundaries. It is "a laying-out of territories" and "a substitution of space for places and territorialities".[103] The smooth space, on the other hand, is open, fluid, mobile, unlimited, continuous, infinite, and amorphous, with no marks of top and bottom, centre and margins. The lines in the smooth space are directional with open intervals, rather than dimensional or metric. Possessing a greater power of deterritorialisation, it is a nomadic space of

100 Gilles Deleuze / Félix Guattari: *A Thousand Plateaus: Capitalism and Schizophrenia*, trans. from French by Brian Massumi. London: Continuum 2004.

101 Gary Genosko / Adam Bryx: After Informatic Striation: The Resignification of Disc Numbers in Contemporary Inuit Popular Culture. In: Buchanan / Lambert (eds): *Deleuze and Space*, pp. 109–125, here p. 110.

102 Deleuze / Guattari: *A Thousand Plateaus*, p. 524.

103 Ibid., p. 233.

intensities where one occupies without measuring.[104] In the case of *71 Fragments*, the countryside landscape with a river and meadow of an indeterminate size, which Marian crosses on foot in the beginning of his journey, is the smooth. From the point he sneaks into the cargo, he enters the world of striation where the living space is constantly demarcated and reframed in front of the camera. In the striation of city space, people are almost always indoors and move between box-shaped rooms and car space.

Deterritorialisation and reterritorialistion, going hand in hand without being reciprocal or binary,[105] imply another kind of spatial relationship. In general, during the process of deterritorialisation one is distanced from the territory, whereas during reterritorialisation one reapproximates and re-engages with the territory. As reterritorialisation brings forth a new territoriality, it does not bring one back to the state of pre-deterritorialisation.[106] Returning to the example of *71 Fragments*, Marian is physically deterritorialised from his homeland Romania after he successfully crosses the frontiers. Some initial reterritorialisation happens in the end of the film when Marian repeats after Mrs. Brunner German words for bank and money and listens to the German radio in Mrs. Brunner's car while waiting patiently for her return.

These theories of space, the global and the local, non-places and places, any-space-whatevers, deterritorialisation and reterritorialisation, and the smooth and the striated will unlock and underpin the different aspects of the mosaics created in each auteur's works examined in the book. The interactive and dynamic assemblage between these spatial configurations compose a myriad and multiplying mosaic on screen, and each auteur constructs different kinds of mosaic through interweaving and different cinematic representations of the spatial configurations.

In conclusion, the model of mosaic exists at the crossroad between spatial aesthetics (through the use of mosaic narrative, framing, reframing, spatial composition, and other cinematic means), transnational authorship (which links transnational filmmaking contexts with the film content), and theories of space (which demonstrate the

104 Deleuze / Guattari: *A Thousand Plateaus*, pp. 525–539.

105 Buchanan: Space in the Age of Non-Place.

106 Deleuze / Guattari: *A Thousand Plateaus*, p. 174.

dynamic flow and juxtaposition between different spatial configurations). At the same time that the mosaic auteur physically crosses national borders and assembles transnational filmmaking resources in his context, spatial representations, and screen spaces are interwoven into a mosaic. Through the meeting, diegetic characters' spaces cease being completely separate entities and are transformed into each other. East and West, privileged and underprivileged class, sedentary and nomadic, places and non-places, smooth and striated, and local and global from different fragments are brought together into the same plane, whereas truncated images, mirroring sequences, and broken screen spaces are spliced. The framework of mosaic space thus provides a different understanding of this trend of filmmaking by encompassing the narrative issue within a bigger framework of space, and relating it to the transnational filmmaking contexts of the auteurs. This correlation between mosaic space and mosaic authorship will be examined in terms of the four case studies in the following chapters on Iñárritu, Egoyan, Hou and Haneke.

4. Chapter-by-chapter Breakdown

I group the four chapters of the book, each dedicated to a mosaic auteur and their particular mosaic, into three parts. In each chapter, the mosaic auteur's transnational filmmaking mode and the characteristics of his respective mosaic will be analysed first, followed by detailed analyses of two films. Part I is "Horizontal Mosaic", which emphasises the mosaic space which compiles contemporary spaces from a wide socioeconomic and geopolitical range. Chapter 1 will use Iñárritu's films as examples of such a mosaic. Iñárritu is a mosaic auteur who extends from a regional Latin American filmmaking network to incorporate filmmaking resources in the USA, Morocco, Japan, and Spain, among others, and establishes his status as both a local Mexican filmmaker and a global filmmaker strongly affiliated with the global networks of art and popular cinema. Corresponding to this transnational authorship, his films weave together narrative threads from protagonists who carry with them diverse spatial planes of class division, ethnical backgrounds, and cultural configurations. As these characters meet and have an impact on one another's lives, physical, emotional, or cultural clashing between them is foregrounded in the globalised space. Hence, the smooth and the striated, places and non-places, and distinctive local elements and interconnected global space are interwoven into a horizontal mosaic. This kind of mosaic space visually portrays the bringing-together of the uneven and imbalanced flows of people, images, goods, and information from disparate contexts connected through global assemblages, posited by theories of global space. In *Amores Perros,* a car crash results in the clashing between three perspectives and three milieus, and therefore a mosaic of an unbalanced metropolitan society interwoven between the local and the global, and the smooth and the striated, while integrating both the specifically Mexican music and concerns and the global issues of social divide and urban violence. The blend of the local and the global in terms of subject matter and visual style becomes a marketable space which helps to reach out to both local and global audiences. *Babel* extends the global scope of the horizontal mosaic by incorporating mosaic pieces from the USA, Mexico, Japan, and Morocco. A shooting in the Moroccan hills results in the clashing and transformation between the striated and the smooth, the local and the global, and nation-states and global forces, with uneven power relations. As spatial configurations are interconnected and juxtaposed in global space, it is not always easy for the protagonists to adapt to the changing degrees of striation once they cross the boundaries between mosaic pieces.

In part II, I examine the "Vertical Mosaic", which investigates the juxtaposition between spaces in relation to historical depth in Egoyan's and Hou's different mosaics in chapters 2 and 3 respectively. Egoyan is a mosaic auteur with multiple identities, being both Canadian and Armenian, and with an established transnational filmmaking network which integrates film production resources and distribution routes across national boundaries. His mosaic of deterritorialisation and reterritorialisation, coupled with actualisation and virtualisation, is foregrounded both in terms of the relationship between diegetic characters and their territories, and the relationship between the spectator and the screen space. In the diegesis, Egoyan's characters, deterritorialised from their actual territories, are the seers residing in the media-saturated post-displacement and/or post-trauma any-space-whatevers who attempt to reterritorialise themselves through virtual means. On the other hand, the spectator, in the process of viewing deterritorialised images which are subsequently reterritorialised, experiences deterritorialisation and reterritorialisation of the screen space which replicate the experience of migration and diaspora. In *Next of Kin* (CA 1984, D: Atom Egoyan) the mosaic space is formed in Peter's deterritorialisation from his actual original WASP family and his intentional reterritorialisation into an ethnic family through virtualisation. *Calendar* (CA / AM / DE 1993, D: Atom Egoyan) uses two settings (Armenia and Canada) and two time frames (before and after the divorce between the photographer and Arsinée) to weave the circular terrain between past and present, actual and virtual, deterritorialisation and reterritorialisation. The photographer and Arsinée, in their separate striated space and smooth spaces, are splitting images of the actual and the virtual, deterritorialisation and reterritorialisation, which project their personal relationship onto mosaic space.

Chapter 3 continues with Part II's exploration of history and traumatic past, and considers the Taiwan-based Hou as a mosaic auteur with multiple identities of both mainlander by birth and nativist by demeanor, who incorporates filmmaking resources from Taiwan, Hong Kong, mainland China, Japan, and France at different stages of his career. He makes use of the East Asian architectural style to compile a vertical mosaic across different temporal points through the construction of multilayered mise-en-scène, which couples with historical depth of the subject matter. With historical depth in the narrative, the layering of screen space is explored through the 'half-outsider half-insider' seer position of the camera, which is often situated right outside the architectural threshold. In this way the camera's vision is partially obstructed by pieces of the furniture or human bodies in the foreground; the screen space is layered with different partial obstructions to vision. The seer position of the camera is also where the Taiwan-born characters are situated in relation to the postwar postcolonial any-space-whatevers in Taiwan. *Good Men, Good Women* (*Hao Nan Hao Nu*, TW / JP 1995, D: Hou Hsiao-hsien), spanning from the Sino-Japanese Resistance, through the White Terror in the 1950s–60s, to 2005, composes a historically informed mosaic which blends uses of several language varieties, actual and virtual images, and present and past. The multilayered mise-en-scène, corresponding to the historical depth of the subject matter, is explored by the camera's wandering gaze along the vertical and longitudinal lines. In *Three Times* (*Zui Hao De Shi Guang*, TW / FR 2005, D: Hou Hsiao-hsien), three segments of historical periods in Taiwanese history enacted by the same pair of actor and actress are interwoven into a mosaic of multilayered mise-en-scène in correspondence to the folding and unfolding of history. The further down into the history, the deeper and more layered the mise-en-scène and the more obstructed the vision of the camera. Going back and forth in history, the spatial juxtaposition in *Three Times* between the pre-industrial and post-industrial life, monarchy and democracy, imprisonment and mobility, innocent and decadent youth, traditional values and modern thoughts is explored through the camera's lingering gaze.

Part III offers a synthesis of the horizontal and vertical mosaics of Part I and II, using the works of perhaps the most exemplary auteur of the mosaic, Haneke, in chapter 4. I will illustrate how horizontal and vertical mosaics are combined and intertwined in film works, which at the same time consider the socioeconomic geopolitical spaces within a certain time frame and the spaces from different periods of time. Haneke is a mosaic auteur who brings together filmmaking resources from the developed Western countries: Austria, France, the USA, and Germany. Corresponding to his transnational filmmaking mode, his films assemble diverse spaces into a fluid mosaic space with the crossing and recrossing of boundaries. At the same time that the horizontal dimension manifests through the fluid exchanges between the smooth and the striated, actual and virtual, places and non-places, underprivileged and privileged, underdeveloped and developed, the vertical aspect brings together colonial and postcolonial worlds. The characters become seers in the image-saturated postcolonial any-space-whatever of the developed West, who no longer know how to react to the surrounding space with constantly changing boundaries. The mosaic of *Code Unknown* (*Code inconnu*, FR / DE / RO 2000, D: Michael Haneke) is woven from incomplete fragments of several characters' respective perspectives, which bring in a range of spaces, from Romania and Kosovo to the very centre of postcolonial Paris, as well as the historical cause and effect. There is a dynamic interplay between Augé's places and non-places, sedentariness and rootedness, and centre and periphery. At the same time that the boundaries between the actual and the virtual become fluid, the developing underprivileged world and the striated developed world are juxtaposed and the characters struggle to reach a balanced state of striation within the mosaic. In *Caché*, the horizontal mosaic of socioeconomic and geopolitical spaces is juxtaposed with the vertical mosaic embedded in the postcolonial Western European bourgeois society. The positions of seer and *actant*, and the smooth and the striated interchange and interact while the haunting past is brought in to the actual space of the present through the virtual doubly-mediated images.

Together these chapters demonstrate different mosaic auteurs operating in different dimensions. Corresponding to their respective transnational filmmaking networks in the contexts of America, Asia, and Europe, their mosaic weaves together narrative threads of different characters, and at the same time the spatial configurations which the characters carry, as well as the screen spaces which are truncated, fragmented, and assembled by the use of editing, framing, mise-en-scène, and the choice of cast and setting. In fact, these mosaic spaces share the characteristic of spatial assemblage but also demonstrate the specific features which emerge out of the geopolitical, cultural, and financial circumstances in which the mosaic auteurs find themselves. Therefore, the concept of mosaic encompasses at the same time the similarities across the body of works and their different manifestations.

Part I

Horizontal Mosaic

Chapter 1
Alejandro González Iñárritu: Contemporary Mosaic of Socioeconomic and Geopolitical Spaces

1. Introduction

Alejandro González Inárritu is a mosaic auteur who assembles filmmaking resources from the regional network in Latin America and the global milieus which incorporate funding, cast, crew, setting, and distribution routes in the USA, Japan, Morocco, and Spain, among others. Correspondingly, his films compose a horizontal mosaic that maps the contemporary wealth gaps of global space and weaves together narrative threads connecting characters from diverse socioeconomic and geopolitical backgrounds through a mosaic narrative, sometimes with chronological linearity and sometimes with temporal disorder, without delving directly into historical issues. At the same time, the characters' spaces are interwoven and interconnected into a mosaic with a dynamic relationship between spatial configurations. In Iñárritu's films we can see a mapping between wealth divides and degrees of striation: the poor geopolitical locations are open smooth space with unhindered vision whereas the wealthy regions of the world are demarcated, regulated, and striated. As chance encounter breaks the originally guarded spatial relationship, places and nonplaces encounter and transform each other, whereas the global space enters local spheres. There is also a struggle over smooth and striated spaces that reflects upon mutually interconnected global wealthy inequalities. While crossing mosaic pieces with different degrees of striation, the characters have the task of adapting to the divergent degrees of striation in respective local spaces. Some characters manage to accommodate to the complete smoothness whereas others underestimate or overestimate the levels of smoothness. As a result

Iñárritu's mosaic demonstrates the increasingly inevitable contact between spaces and their subsequent conflicts and reconciliation in the global space, in correlation with his integration of transnational filmmaking networks. This can be understood through theories of global space, which posit that, although in an uneven and imbalanced process, flows of people, images, goods, and information from disparate contexts are immediately connected through global assemblages, forming a mosaic.

In this chapter, I will first trace his building of transnational filmmaking networks as a mosaic auteur, and then illustrate how his contemporary mosaic of socioeconomic and geopolitical spaces works in the example of *21 Grams*, as the first film with which Iñárritu extends from his original Latin American milieu, in relation to the theories of global space proposed by various theorists, such as Saskia Sassen, Marc Augé, Gilles Deleuze, and Félix Guattari. Detailed analyses of *Amores Perros* and *Babel* will follow and conclude the chapter.

2. Iñárritu's Border-crossing as a Mosaic Auteur

Iñárritu's building of mosaic space correlates with his assembled global filmmaking networks. When he physically moves from one geopolitical context to another, Iñárritu integrates global circulation of money, information, and human resources, and extends his transnational filmmaking networks with the making of each of his films. At the distribution stage, his film products also travel with him in international film festivals and global cities. Born in Narvarte neighbourhood in Mexico City, a neighbourhood very similar to the one of Octavio (Gael Garcia Bernal) and Susana (Vanessa Bauche) in *Amores Perros*,[1] Iñárritu starts his career in the local Latin American filmmaking context, and crosses the Mexico-US border to connect with the Hollywood studio Focus Features and an international group of performers in *21 Grams*. In his third feature film, *Babel,* he extends his networks to the continents of Africa and Asia, by collaborating with local film professionals and amateur actors, whereas by making *Biutiful* in Spain, he reinforces the Hispanic link. With the Oscar-winning *Birdman or (The Unexpected Virtue of Ignorance)* (USA 2014) and the highly anticipated *The Revenant* (USA 2015) Iñárritu becomes well

1 Jason Wood: *The Faber Book of Mexican Cinema*. London: Faber & Faber 2006, p. 64.

established in the mainstream US film industry. As Iñárritu's transnational filmmaking mode is an essential part in understanding his horizontal mosaic space across wealth and geopolitical divides, it is worthwhile to look first at the filmmaking mode, before we turn to the analysis of mosaic space in his film works.

At the same time that Iñárritu's four feature films have extended his networks to the Spanish and English speaking worlds of the North and Latin Americas and elsewhere, his transnational production mode paradoxically comes both from his root in, and his reaction against, national cinema. Since Iñárritu's feature film *Amores Perros*, he refuses the doctrine of the contemporary state-funded Mexican cinema, characterised by cineastes such as Arturo Ripstein, Felipe Cazals and Jorge Fons, all funded by the governmental IMCINE (Instituto Mexicano de Cinematografía)[2]. His reaction against the contemporary state-funded Mexican cinema and cultural policy prompts him to cooperate with the larger network of Latin American cinema. In fact, AltaVista, *Amores Perros*' production company which also owns the distribution company NuVisión, is a Mexican private production outlet, which was "originally set up as a joint venture between Corporación Interamericana de Entretenimiento (CIE), Latin America's leading live-entertainment provider, and investment capitalist Sinca Inbursa"[3]. The film professionals who participate in this production outlet are also not restricted to the Mexican context, as their team is composed of Latin American talent and expatriates in Latin America. Scriptwriter Guillermo Arriaga, cinematographer Rodrigo Prieto, and Martin Hernandez, the sound designer, are from Mexico; Brigitte Broch is a German production designer based in Mexico City; and music composer Gustavo Santaolalla is Argentinean.[4] This transnational model, which promotes a private and unofficial sense of *la mexicanidad* with the Latin American

2 IMCINE was established under the administration of Miguel de la Madrid (1982–1988). For further discussion of the interlinking relationship between state funding organisations and Mexican cinema, see David R. Maciel: Cinema and the State in Contemporary Mexico, 1970–1999. In: Hershfield / Maciel (eds): *Mexico's Cinema*, pp. 197–232, here p. 211; Tomás Pérez Turrent: Crises and Renovations (1965–91). In: Paulo Antonio Paranaguá (ed.): *Mexican Cinema*. London: British Film Institute 1995, pp. 94–115, here pp. 104–115.

3 Wood: *The Faber Book of Mexican Cinema*, pp. 59–63.

4 Ibid., p. 77; Maria Eladia Hagerman (ed.): *Babel: A Film by Alejandro Gonzalez Inarritu*. Photographs by Mary Ellen Mark / Patrick Bard / Graciela Iturbide / Miguel Rio Branco. Hong Kong: Taschen 2006, p. 262.

production networks, proved to be successful. *Amores Perros,* released at a low point of Mexican film industry, when film production had dropped from a hundred films a year in the mid-1980s to four to five a year in 1998, achieved exceptional success, grossing approximately US$ 8.8 million in Mexico alone and ranking the fourth in the country's top grossing films of all time.[5]

From his initial reflection upon the old version of Mexican cinema and the integration of Latin American filmmaking resources, Iñárritu ventures into the filmmaking milieus in North America, Japan, Morocco, and Spain in his following feature films *21 Grams*, *Babel*, and *Biutiful*. Through this broader transnational network, he combines established financial resources, film talents, and distribution routes with the newly formed milieus. Hence, the local elements from different locales are interwoven into the global. To date, he has worked with American studios such as Universal Pictures' Focus Features, Paramount Pictures' Paramount Vantage, Summit entertainment, the French film company Central Films, the Japanese Gaga Communications, and the Latin American branch of United International Pictures, Spanish Mod Producciones, Ikiru Films, Televisió de Catalunya, Televisión Española, in combination with his own Mexican production company Zeta Films, founded in 1991.[6] His choice of cast is also a nexus of the local and the global, mixing the long-time collaborators such as Gael García Bernal and Adriana Barraza from Mexico, professional actors renowned in the global film world, such as Brad Pitt, Sean Penn, and Melissa Leo from the USA, Cate Blanchett from Australia, Naomi Watts who was born in England and grew up in Australia, Charlotte Gainsbourg with an English mother and a French father, Javier Bardem from Spain, Japanese stars Kōji Yakusho and Rinko Kikuchi, and local amateur actors recruited from the filming locations, such as the shepherd's family in Morocco, the veterinarian in *Babel* who is a real town veterinarian, and the deaf-mute school girls in Japan.[7] In terms of the film crew, incorporated into his core team, which has accompanied

5 Wood: *The Faber Book of Mexican Cinema*, pp. 63, 85.

6 Hagerman (ed.): *Babel: A Film by Alejandro Gonzalez Inarritu*, pp. 257, 263; Paul Kerr: *Babel*'s Network Narrative: Packaging a Globalized Art Cinema. In: *Transnational Cinemas* 1,1 (2010), pp. 37–51, here pp. 44–45; Alan Hunter: Alan Hunter in Cannes. In: *Screen International*, 28.05.2006; Mike Goodridge: Mike Goodridge in Cannes. In: *Screen International*, 11.05.2005.

7 Hagerman (ed.): *Babel: A Film by Alejandro Gonzalez Inarritu*, p. 260.

him since the early days of *Amores Perros*, are local professionals such as the Japanese music composer Ryūichi Sakamoto, and the English music writer and singer David Sylvian. The final film products are also distributed through transnational routes, such as international film festivals ranging from the prestigious Cannes Film Festival, to smaller film festivals such as Edinburgh International Film Festival and Bogota Film Festival, and a wide range of film distribution companies such as Gaga Communications in Japan, Mars Distribution in France, Shaw Organisation in Singapore, and Sponge in South Korea. As Iñárritu's films are distributed through both popular and arthouse networks, they are eventually consumed by the global audience of both art cinema and mainstream cinema, including the local audiences in places where the films are shot.

Despite Iñárritu's broadening transnational filmmaking mode across the globe, he remains supportive of the regional Latin American networks by executive producing the US production of Columbian filmmaker Rodrigo García's *Nine Lives* (USA 2005), the Mexican documentary *Toro Negro* (USA 2005, D: Carlos Armella / Pedro González-Rubio), Carlos Cuarón's *Rudo and Cursi* (*Rudo y Cursi*, MX 2008), and Rodrigo García's *Mother and Child* (USA 2009). As Ann Marie Stock and Jeff Menne put it, his transnational movement is a part of the bigger range of mutual flows of influence and interdependence across porous national and cultural boundaries, which reconstitute regional identities into a globally imagined community and hybridise cultural phenomena.[8] Keeping his roots in the Latin American context, he incorporates the regional network with the larger global cultural industry through his accumulated contacts. In this way, he is both local and global, cultivating regional identities and building a global community of film culture at the same time. This differentiates him as a mosaic auteur, rather than an accented auteur, for he has never been unrooted and he represents the world with many different voices without emphasising one particular 'accent' in terms of both film form and use of language. As a mosaic auteur, accent is not a given, but rather, chosen. Maintaining the choice to foreground or downplay his cultural roots, Iñárritu is not agonizing over the identities of either/or but is empowered to be both/and.

8 Stock: Authentically Mexican?, pp. 269, 272–273; Jeff Menne: A Mexican Nouvelle Vague: The Logic of New Waves under Globalization. In: *Cinema Journal* 47,1 (2007), pp. 70–92, here p. 80.

This mode of transnational filmmaking is parallel to the global/local relationship in his aesthetics. While Iñárritu employs a global production mode in his filmmaking, his subject matter is also consciously global, foregrounding interdependence between people of diverse backgrounds. As Montoliú points out, this thematic concern, which captures the zeitgeist of our time, in combination with striking visual effects and strong soundtracks, attracts a wide spectrum of audience and leads to his dual status as both a popular filmmaker and an arthouse auteur.[9] In contrast to Haneke, Hou, and Egoyan, Iñárritu has a wider appeal to a broader range of the audience stemming from his five-year's experience as a radio DJ at WFM, the most important radio station nationwide at the time of his departure, and his five years as a commercial director, producing about eighty commercials a year.[10] His mosaic space, distant from Haneke's unraveling of deliberately hidden or forgotten global events with postcolonial implications, is interwoven through an assemblage of issues at the forefront of global attention, such as the September 11th attacks and subsequent fear of terrorism, global circulation of weapons, the illegal migration between the USA and Mexico, and the extreme wealth divides between wealthy and poor countries as a consequence of globalisation. These issues, which concern a wide range of people regardless of their geopolitical backgrounds, are all extensively broadcasted and discussed in the public sphere. In section 3, I will demonstrate how Iñárritu constructs the mosaic of socioeconomic milieus through mosaic narrative and representations of space, under the transnational filmmaking mode.

3. Mosaic Space of Contemporary Wealth Divides

The mosaic space in Iñárritu's works interweaves different narrative threads carried by characters from different socioeconomic classes in the globalised space. Divided by their wealth, social status, and living milieus, these characters are brought together into the same spatial plane because of a chance encounter which often provokes tragic consequences. As Iñárritu's mosaic assembles fragments from the same time frame and across different socioeconomic spaces, it is a horizontal mosaic, with or without temporal disorder, which concerns our

9 Montoliú: A Time to Love and a Time to Die, p. 116.

10 Wood: *The Faber Book of Mexican Cinema*, p. 65.

contemporary time without delving into an investigation of historical causes. I will first use some key scenes in *21 Grams* to demonstrate this mosaic, because the making of *21 Grams* is the start of Iñárritu's transnational filmmaking journey from the original Latin American filmmaking network to a wider global milieu. It is also the most visually striking mosaic with the most chaotic temporality. This example demonstrates his mosaic of socioeconomic spaces through the bringing-together of characters, narrative threads, and spaces where the characters reside respectively, encompassing the dynamism between the global and the local, places and non-places, and smooth and striated. The chance encounter in non-places between characters disintegrates relational places, smooths the striated, and lets the local spaces meet in the global. Hence, new sets of spatial configurations enter the mosaic.

In *21 Grams*, Iñárritu moves from his familiar environment in Mexico, and integrates his original filmmaking milieu with his newly formed network in North America. He produced this film with a budget of around US$ 20 million, thanks to Ted Hope, the former partner in Good Machine which was later merged with USA Films to form Focus Features ("Focus"). Distribution took place through the major studio Universal Pictures' Focus Features, run by David Linde and James Schamus. It is the critical and commercial success of Iñárritu's debut feature, *Amores Perros,* that enables him to negotiate with Hollywood studios for creative independence in terms of the cast, crew, script, shooting location, and final cut.[11]

As Iñárritu negotiates with transnational filmmaking resources, his films also demonstrate an assemblage of diverse socioeconomic spaces delivered into a mosaic at the cinematic level through mosaic narrative, when the narrative threads of the protagonists from diverse socioeconomic backgrounds are woven together. Admittedly, the interweaving of perspectives is also the trademark of the scriptwriter Guillermo Arriaga, whose style of fragmented narrative structure, influenced by William Faulkner's *Sound and The Fury*[12], *Absalom Absalom!*[13], and *Light in August*[14], tends to mingle threads of various

11 Ibid., p. 145.

12 William Faulkner: *The Sound and the Fury*. London: Cape & Smith 1929.

13 William Faulkner: *Absalom, Absalom!* New York: Random House 1936.

14 William Faulkner: *Light in August*. New York: Smith & Haas 1932.

characters and disturb conventional chronology.[15] But nevertheless the formal quality of the mosaic narrative is still pertinent to the consideration of Iñárritu's works because of his cinematic transformation of the script. In the very beginning of *21 Grams* we see a close-up of Cristina's naked upper body, partially wrapped in a white blanket, on a big double bed in the closest plane. Sitting right next to her in the further plane, Paul smokes and contemplates Cristina's sleeping body which undulates rhythmically with her regular breathing sounds, while blindingly bright sunlight shines from the background across glass windowpanes. This fragment of an intimate moment at a slow pace is then cut to a fast-cutting series of close-ups capturing the joyful faces of Michael and two girls at a local dining place. Before their action of getting ready to leave comes to an end, we see a medium shot of Cristina sitting on a metal chair facing the camera and sharing her experiences as a former drug addict in a therapy group. This shot leads to a sequence of shaky close-ups of the ex-convict Jack preaching to a young delinquent about God in a community church. Then we see a long shot capturing dark profiles of birds flying in flocks around a roof in the dim blue light of sunset. This is when the first non-diegetic sounds, solo guitar tunes of Santaollala and Paul's voice-over, come into the picture, narrating Peter's mood and perspective while being juxtaposed with the point-of-view shots of Paul lying in the hospital sustained by tubes. Medium shots of a ceiling's fluorescent light and of Paul's immobile body seen from the top of his head interchange with the reverse shots of Paul's close-ups. These fragments, jumping from one character's snapshot of life to another, are edited together without any clear linkage, signposting, or transition shots. They are assembled into a visual mosaic of snippets of perspectives and representations of space. At this point, flowing from one diegetic moment to another, the spectator is left puzzled, unsure of either these characters' relationship or these fragments' temporal relationship with one another, or if any sort of relationship between these characters exists at all. It is not until much later in the film that the spectator starts to decipher the intertwining temporalities and relationships, and to see the full picture of the narrative: Jack, the ex-convict and religion fanatic, runs over Cristina's husband, Michael and their two daughters while they are crossing the intersection's zebra crossing. The car accident results in the loss of Cristina's entire

15 Wood: *The Faber Book of Mexican Cinema*, p. 69.

family, her stronghold against drug addiction. Jack is jailed and separated from his wife Marianne and two kids, whereas Michael's heart saves Paul, who refuses to continue with his loveless marriage in his new life. Later on, Paul and Cristina fall in love and embark on a revenge trip to a nameless place of the New Mexican desert, where Jack works in a mine.

The example of *21 Grams* shows us that instead of following one single narrative line throughout the film, Iñárritu jumps between snippets from different characters' perspectives. As they are edited together, the fragments gradually reveal the mosaic picture. Through the interweaving narrative, the characters' paths, which used to be completely parallel and independent, are interrupted and intercepted because of a tragic chance encounter. From the chance encounter onwards, Cristina, Michael, and Jack cease leading separate and unrelated lives and are forced to intersect and deal with the impact they have on one another and the consequences of their behaviour. Mosaic narrative emphasises the meeting of their formerly parallel lives by providing multiple points of view. In this way, the spectator encounters the characters' snapshots one by one and has the task of assembling the mosaic picture in their mind with the progression of the film. As Iñárritu does not employ cinematic means such as the fragmentation of bodies and objects, as seen in *71 Fragments*, his mosaic is mainly built on mosaic narrative with interweaving narrative threads. This is thus the primary route to understand his mosaic space in the first three feature films *Amores Perros, 21 Grams*, and *Babel*.[16] In some of Iñárritu's mosaic narratives, such as *Babel*, the characters impact one another's storylines without appearing together on screen at any given moment; in other cases, such as *Amores Perros* and *21 Grams*, the meeting between the characters is violent, visceral, and salient. Here, in the example of *21 Grams*, the three characters Jack, Paul, and Cristina physically clash with one another during the climactic confrontation scene in the featureless grungy motel of the New Mexican desert near the end of the film, which Michael Stewart calls "the Lynchian, liminal motel fight"[17]. In a series of fast-cutting shaky

16 His subsequent films *Biutiful, Birdman or (The Unexpected Virtue of Ignorance)*, and *The Revenant* interweave narrative threads in a different manner, though arguably also into a mosaic. Yet this is outwith the bounds of the current study.

17 Michael Stewart: Irresistible Death: *21 Grams* as Melodrama. In: *Cinema Journal* 47,1 (2007), pp. 49–69, here p. 53.

close-ups between the gasping Paul against a wall, Cristina striking the offscreen Jack repetitively with a desk lamp, and Jack's face revealing submissive agony under physical pain, the characters encounter one another face to face on screen.

The encounter between these characters not only brings together different characters' perspectives and perceptions, but also their respective socioeconomic spaces. In the example here, the three families, of about the same generation, bring their socioeconomically diverse spaces into the same spatial plane because of Jack's hit-and-run. Michael, an architect, and Cristina, the housewife, are a bourgeois couple living with two daughters in a spacious household situated in a quiet suburban neighbourhood. The walls are impeccably clean, bed sheets shiningly white, and books arranged in an orderly manner on shelves. Paul and Marie, the intellectual couple in their loveless and childless marriage, reside in a bright and clean house elegantly decorated with wooden furniture of good quality, reminiscent of Cristina and Michael's household. On the other hand, the working class couple, Jack and Marianne, lives in an outskirt wasteland of Memphis with their daughter and son. Their household is distinctively different: the yellow wallpaper has darkened with time; carpets and sofa are a faded and dirty grey tone; white paint on the doors has turned black; random tools and boxes are cramped in the corners. Through the chance encounter, the three characters across the socioeconomic spectrum, unwillingly impacting upon one another's lives, bring together into the same spatial plane three distinct spaces with apparent wealth divides. Dramatised on screen, the intersection between their respective spaces creates their misery and suffering, as well as salvation and conciliation.

Furthermore, this joining together of disparate spaces and characters into a mosaic of horizontal socioeconomic spaces is reinforced by the achronological manner in which the fragments are assembled, because the atemporal order disrupts and delays the realisation of the impact that the characters have on one another. As a consequence, the spectator draws the connection between these different spaces more slowly and is rendered more aware of editing's important role in assembling snapshots of life. As described earlier, the film starts *in medias res*, and jumps back to Cristina, Jack, and Paul's separate lives before the car accident. It then goes forward to the painful post-trauma distress of Cristina, and Paul's wife's examination at a gynecologist for childbearing. We then see a brief fragment of Jack's entry into a prison. This jumping back and forth between different time frames, before and after the car accident, continues throughout the film. Within minutes, the spectators are shown a different time and space jarring against the previous time and space. Todd McGowan and Allan Cameron have remarked that Iñárritu's use of editing "reveal[s] contingency operating in the structural point of impossibility" and "display[s], as a central stylistic and thematic concern, a fraught relationship between contingency and narrative order".[18] Within this contingency, any explicit temporal anchoring point is left free-floating within the narrative. It would take the spectator a while to be able to distinguish between fragments before, after and during the car accident. Even after the spectator grasps enough information to locate the temporal point of each fragment during the viewing, the temporal disorder still makes the film appear as if the past, present, and future intermingle and coexist on screen. As a matter of fact, the car accident, which connects the three families, its beforehand, and its consequences are visited and revisited from the three perspectives of Cristina, Jack, and Paul. As the spectator digests all these fragments simultaneously during the viewing, the characters' previous happy moments do not seem to be further away in time, and their subsequent sorrow and pain also do not seem to be forthcoming. In fact, the terms "flashback" and "flash-forward" lose their meanings in this chaos of time, as there is no "here and now" to go back or forward to along a chronological line. This alinearity of time works like Deleuze's crystal of time, in which a before and an after are inseparable and coexist from the perspective of the viewing moment. As Deleuze cites Federico Fellini's Bergsonian sentence, "We are constructed in memory. We are simultaneously childhood, adolescence, old age and maturity"[19]. By editing these fragments of different temporalities together into a mosaic, past, present, and future in *21 Grams* are interwoven, no longer in succession but in simultaneity. Deleuze writes:

18 Todd McGowan: The Contingency of Connection: The Path to Politicization in *Babel*. In: *Discourse* 30,3 (2008), pp. 401–418, here p. 405; Cameron: Contingency, Order, and the Modular Narrative, p. 65.

19 Deleuze: *Cinema 2*, p. 96.

> What constitutes the crystal-image is the most fundamental operation of time: since the past is constituted not after the present that it was but at the same time, time has to split itself in two at each moment as present and past, which differ from each other in nature, or, what amounts to the same thing, it has to split the present in two heterogeneous directions, one of which is launched towards the future while the other falls into the past.[20]

Viewed in this light, the narrative threads are interwoven in the labyrinth of multiple circuits, which keeps on forking into different time frames.[21] As different time frames are juxtaposed, these three characters' different moments are contained in narrative of the same moment. At the same time the tragic car accident has not happened, it is happening, and it just happened. At the same time Paul is inserted with tubes, dying in the hospital, he is transplanted with a healthy heart, and he is lying on his deathbed in the hospital again. The narrative time, instead of being linear, is subjective and circular; it visits and revisits the before, during, and after. This reinforces the impression of a mosaic, which interweaves snippets of different spatialities and temporalities into the same plane.

The horizontal mosaic of wealth divides in Iñárritu's films, with or without temporal disorder, is the terrain where the local spaces are assembled into the global. It is in the globalised space where characters of different socioeconomic, ethnic, and cultural backgrounds bring their respective local spaces along and have what Mike Featherstone calls "a clashing of different interpretations of the meaning of the world formulated from the perspective of different national and civilizational traditions"[22]. Featherstone suggests that instead of assuming the monological accounts of globalisation which "miss the cultural variability of non-Western nation-states and civilizations", "the globalization process should be regarded as opening up the sense that now the world is a single place with increased, even unavoidable, contact".[23] Instead of being segregated in their particular social and regional milieu, much as it seems to be on the surface and as city-dwellers would believe, the encounter between people of different socioeconomic status has a perpetual impact on their existence and assembles their local spaces in the globalised space. However, these

20 Deleuze: *Cinema 2*, pp. 78–79.

21 Ibid., p. 127.

22 Featherstone: Localism, Globalism, and Cultural Identity, p. 58.

23 Ibid., pp. 46–47.

unavoidable contacts and dialogues between nation-states, blocs, dialogical spaces, all embedded with the inherent power relationships, are not always benign and cooperative and also result in conflicts, disagreement and clashing of perspectives.[24] The contacts, dialogues and clashes between the local spaces in Iñárritu's films are portrayed through physical travelling (for example, Maria's illegal migration to the USA, Cheiko's father's hunting trip to Morocco in *Babel*, Jack's drive between the community church and home in *21 Grams*), car accidents (in *Amores Perros* and *21 Grams*), guns (the rifle which leads the Japanese police officer Mamiya to Cheiko's flat in *Babel*), organs (heart transplantation in *21 Grams*), and media broadcasts (Valeria's virtual appearance on the TV screen in Octavio's room in *Amores Perros*). Through different means of interconnectedness, diverse geopolitical and socioeconomic local spaces encounter and interweave into the global. This is the picture of mosaic space where people, caught within the global flows of contrasting wealth and unequal information, are connected in a complex manner through links which are at times intangible. Within the intersecting global networks where flows of people, goods, and information interact and connect, individual identities are no longer defined as separate entities, but rather in relation to and against one another. Similarly, the identities of spaces become less categorical and are constantly redefined against other spatial configurations. This nexus of the local and the global might be more salient in *Babel*, but in the current example of *21 Grams*, we can nonetheless observe the global interconnectedness in the juxtaposition between flows of Latin American auteur and crew and the North American setting and the cast. Furthermore, the script, originally written by Guillermo Arriaga in Spanish and set in Mexico, has been transferred to Memphis with a different set of cultural parameters and urban look with relative ease.[25] Hence, the film product is itself the global, in which the Mexico-based script meets with the filmic setting of Memphis. With the adaptability of the film materials, the local anonymous brick-made downtown towers in Memphis and uncharacteristic New Mexican desert in *21 Grams* portray common emotions of irretrievable loss shared by people across national, linguistic, and cultural boundaries in the global.

24 Ibid., p. 47.
25 Wood: *The Faber Book of Mexican Cinema*, p. 144.

In Iñárritu's horizontal mosaic where the local and the global meet, the unexpected encounter between individuals from different local spaces and socioeconomic backgrounds takes place in non-places. Continuing with the example of *21 Grams*, what Augé calls non-places proliferate in the setting of Memphis: a hospital, uncharacteristic dining places, unrecognisable motorways, group therapy rooms, a desolate motel, a community gym, and featureless crossroads, which the residents pass by with a well-defined purpose without residing in them. In these nameless locations, people usually brush against one another and do not stop to pay attention to other individuals or establish relations of any sort. It is only when the tragic chance encounter between Jack's van, Michael, and the two girls happens in the non-place of an intersection that the façade of separate and independent identities breaks. The chance encounter in the non-place disconnects Cristina's middle-class household from relations. As it breaks through the fortress and invades in the comfort zone of separate, protected, and guarded "places", it strips Cristina's identity as a wife and mother. With a destroyed and disconnected place, Cristina returns to non-places, such as a club that she used to frequent as a drug addict, to seek consolation in anonymity and relationships which are merely functional. We can see another intersecting encounter in a non-place when Paul's wife Mary and Cristina, the two women so closely interconnected through Michael's physical heart and Paul's emotional heart, meet without understanding their link. While Cristina, accompanied by her father and sister, emerges from a hospital corridor in grievance right after the death of her husband and daughters, Paul's wife turns her head to follow them with her gaze from a chair in the waiting lounge. Without their realisation, Paul's new heart is that of Cristina's dead husband; the death of Michael enables Paul to live. What is also unknown to them is that Paul is going to abandon Mary after having a new heart and falling in love with his donor's wife. When the home of Paul and Mary breaks apart, the relational place of Paul and Cristina is established. The contrasting, yet tightly interrelated, happy and sad moments of two families, and the moments of life and death, gain and loss, and falling in and out of love, encounter each other in the non-place of a hospital's waiting lounge.

The tragic chance encounter not only results in the meeting between non-places and places, but also the smoothing of the striated spaces, which forces the characters to open up to more possibilities within the mosaic. Originally Cristina and Michael, Jack and Marianne, and Paul and Mary live in separate corners, in a striated world where everything is in its place and everyone has a designated role to play in their private and professional life. Their previous life is structured around all kinds of institutions such as the hospital (where Paul's life is sustained by tubes before the heart transplant), gym (where Cristina goes swimming regularly), and the community church (which is frequented by the fanatic Jack), whose functions are well defined. This harmonious striation, demarcated by functional and socioeconomic boundaries, breaks down after the car accident and is smoothed out. As a consequence, the characters are forced to leave their safely striated spaces and open up to the smooth and new mosaic pieces. It is through this inevitable smoothing of the striated that the characters acquire a dynamic relationship with the mosaic space, and are pushed to let new sets of spatial configurations come in and to establish new connections. For example, Cristina's striated world no longer holds together as there are no more children to cater for and no timetable to go by. Paul's striated life around the treatment schedule in the hospital also no longer sustains in his new life. Their love affair, which would not initiate in their original striation, is made possible by the smoothing and their loss of anchorage. As for Jack, he goes from his original striation as a loving father to the extremely striated life in prison, where thick metal bars strictly mark both personal and collective spaces. He then exiles himself in the desert of New Mexico, living a smooth life in a run-down motel with no name and no identity. Their former striated spaces and the later smoothing can be seen as mapping the global and local. Their striated spaces are their separate local spaces, demarcated by wealth divides, where they used to reside. The smooth New Mexican desert, where Cristina, Paul, and Jack eventually meet physically, and where lines and boundaries are no longer striated in the same way that they are used to, is the global where people meet. In a similar way that global flows of information and wealth enter the local spaces of the individuals, the bringing-together of socioeconomic spaces forces the characters' striated space to be smoothed. Hence, this complex intertwining between striation/smooth and global/local implies the proximity of striation to the local, the fortress of each household, and the smooth to the global, the meeting between these households and opening up of their fortresses. The striated/local is barred by various lines of demarcation; the smooth/global is an open space where the boundaries are unmarked and undemarcated.

With the example of *21 Grams*, Iñárritu's mosaic space interweaves snippets of perspectives from diverse socioeconomic backgrounds, and at the same time the spaces that they carry with them. This mosaic is the intersection where non-places proliferate and threaten the established places, where the characters' striated spaces are smoothed, and where the global enters local spaces. In the following sections, I will return to Iñárritu's debut feature *Amores Perros* to look at his mosaic before moving to the US and then forward to his third feature *Babel*, the result of a full-fledged transnational film production network, in order to build up Iñárritu's multifaceted mosaic assembled by diverse contemporary socioeconomic and geopolitical contexts.

4. *Amores Perros*

Amores Perros demonstrates how contemporary socioeconomically diverse spaces are assembled into a mosaic through interweaving narrative threads from three characters' (Octavio, Valeria, and El Chivo (Emilio Echevarria)) perspectives, and how these spaces, illustrative of wealth divides, are interconnected through imbalanced access to global networks in Mexico City. This is a mosaic terrain where local and global coexist, intertwine, and interact with each other, in which El Chivo is the only character who can open up new sets of spatial configurations and engage in a more active relationship with mosaic space through his smoothing of the striated.

Not only being Iñárritu's debut feature, *Amores Perros* is also the debut production of the private company AltaVista, composed of Francisco González Compeán, from advertising, and Martha Sosa, a former television journalist, who were as inexperienced in the field of filmmaking industry as Iñárritu.[26] It was released in Mexico just two weeks before the election, which brought an end to the more than seventy years' Institutional Revolutionary Party (PRI) government.[27] As Mexicans were enthusiastic about the new prospects, symbolised in the new National Action Party (PAN) government led by the new

26 Wood: *The Faber Book of Mexican Cinema*, pp. 62–65, 88–89.

27 Paul Julian Smith: *Amores Perros*. London: British Film Institute 2003, p. 16; Wood: *The Faber Book of Mexican Cinema*, pp. 84–86.

president Vicente Fox, the campaign of *Amores Perros* as a "change" from previous Mexican films appealed to local audiences who anticipated positive changes in social, economic and cultural aspects.[28] With a publicity and advertising budget of US$ 1.1 million, the advertising campaign was seen and heard all over Mexico City: promotion on billboards, radio, and television made the film extremely visible to citizens.[29] The film was successful in Mexico as well as in the global film market, both critically and commercially. *Amores Perros* is one of the most awarded Mexican films: winning Cannes Critics' Week prize, a BAFTA (British Academy of Film and Television Arts) Award for Best Film not in the English Language, and a New Directors Award at the Edinburgh International Film Festival.[30] It was also nominated for both Golden Globes and Academy Awards as the best foreign film.[31] The recognition in Cannes drew the Mexican audience's attention to this film, and it grossed approximately US$ 8.8 million in Mexico alone, ranking the fourth in Mexican box office of all time.[32] Distributed internationally by Lion's Gate, *Amores Perros* was quickly sold to France (through the French film company Central Films), Italy, Spain, and Israel following the success at Cannes, and grossed $ 5.2 million in the US and $ 20 million worldwide.[33]

The film starts *in media res*, in the climactic moment of the car crash between Octavio and Valeria which joins the three main characters Octavio, Valeria, and El Chivo together. Without any background set-up or establishing shots, the film starts with indistinguishable aural elements against a completely black screen. The sound of whooshing cars is only rendered meaningful when the first image, rapid tracking of asphalt road and its white dividing lines, is introduced. The tense feeling of the car chase is created by both rapid editing and shaky handheld camera, which also changes frames swiftly. The camera tracks the view from car windows and captures some

28 Paul Julian Smith: Heaven's Mouth. In: *Sight and Sound* 12,4 (April 2002), pp. 16–19, here pp. 16–17.

29 Wood: *The Faber Book of Mexican Cinema*, p. 87.

30 Ibid., p. 90.

31 Smith: *Amores Perros*, p. 10.

32 Wood: *The Faber Book of Mexican Cinema*, pp. 85–86.

33 Kerr: *Babel*'s Network Narrative, pp. 43–45; Estudio Mexico Plans US Distribution Operation. Staff Reporters in Berlin. In: *Screen International*, 11.03.2002.

indiscernible grey tall buildings and trees fleetingly. The tracking is followed by close-ups of Octavio (Fig. 1), his friend Jorge and the dog Cofi, and their rear view and side mirrors, which show the bright red and yellow van following them, which belongs to the gangsters. When the car crash happens, we see some quick overhead shots and profile shots from outside the cars. (Fig. 2) From a distance, El Chivo, passing by the crossroad on his mission to assassinate the businessman Luis, looks at the crash from the pavement. The film then cuts to Valeria, covered in blood, knocking her car window. Although the spectator is left in suspense as these characters appear on screen without any introduction, this prelude, with its speedy camera movement and fast cutting, brings the three spatial planes together in intensity. It also foretells the order of these characters' appearance in the film and sums up their characterisation, beginning with the working class Octavio, whose close-ups occupy most of the prelude, and carries on with the milieu of Valeria, whose trapped existence both in the prelude and in her own segment appears second. El Chivo, wandering in the background of the car crash, is a marginal figure in the globalised Mexico City whose story is revealed last.

Following the prelude, *Amores Perros* branches out into three segments from the three perspectives of socioeconomically distinct and segregated milieus, divided by black screen with intertitles: "Octavio and Susana", "Valeria and Daniel", and "El Chivo and Maru". These segments, each following its inherent chronological temporal order, are gradually assembled into a mosaic picture. The narrative of *Amores Perros* interweaves the threads of three characters of different generations and from different socioeconomic backgrounds, ranging from adolescent to sexagenarian, and from tramp to upper class. Octavio, in baggy hoodies, is a young man under twenty from a working class family in which the supermarket clerk and part-time bank robber brother Ramiro is the sole breadwinner. Sexually obsessed with Romario's wife Susana, Octavio collects runaway funds from dogfights. Elegantly dressed Valeria is a wealthy and prosperous model and TV celebrity of the leisure class in her late twenties, involved in an affair with a married man, Daniel. The bearded El Chivo, in large filthy sport jacket, is a revolutionary-turned-assassin homeless man in his sixties, living in a shantytown, in the urban margins invisible to the bourgeois class. (Fig. 3) He stalks his daughter Maru, who is unaware of his existence, as a daily routine. By intersecting three storylines from the very beginning of the film, mosaic narrative brings together different spaces divided by wealth and status, and foregrounds a variety of social issues, such as social inequality, previous revolutionary leftism, political assassination, business feuds, and police corruption. We can see the divided milieus in the mise-en-scène of their dwellings. The bourgeois Valeria's space is polished with shiningly white walls and wooden floors, decorated with art photos of herself and abstract paintings. The space of Octavio's working class family is messy and cramped with objects in loud colours. El Chivo's space is even more cramped from his hoarding of broken furniture, filthy blankets, metal fragments, and old magazines. His wallpaper is tattered, electric wires exposed, and a lamp without a lampshade dangles from the ceiling. Within this mise-en-scène, El Chivo, who is literally fighting for living space with all the trash-like objects, is constantly reframed behind window frames or metal tubes.

In this mosaic, the bringing-together of spaces also brings them closer to their dogs. Cofi's first owner, Octavio, exploits Cofi's talent of killing out of his desire to run away with his brother's wife Susana. While Octavio transforms Cofi from a domesticated dog to a professional killer, he is transformed from a naïve young boy to a killer himself. The *rapprochement* between Valeria and her poodle Richi is portrayed in a more visual way: right after Valeria's car accident, while chasing a ball, Richi disappears under the assembled wooden floorboards of the part-finished new flat, down the hole which Valeria's high heels made on the move-in day. The hole leads to the completely dark underground space, inhabited by mice, where Richi is trapped. Following a point-of-view shot of Valeria looking down, the reverse shot from Richi's perspective places the camera a step away underneath the wooden floor, looking towards the hole where dim light from the outside world shines in. Whereas the stable camera imitates the trapped position of Richi, Valeria is also physically confined by the metal support which holds her leg straight and immobile, after having been badly injured in the car accident caused by Octavio. The view from the window towards her glamorous image, highlighting her long legs on a huge billboard, is a view back to her previous modelling career. Whereas from Richi's perspective, the outside light is a possible but unreachable exit; for Valeria, her bigger-than-life poster is a beautiful sight but painfully unreachable image.

The meeting point between the three perspectives in this mosaic space is the crossroad in Mexico City, a site of circulation and intrusion, a

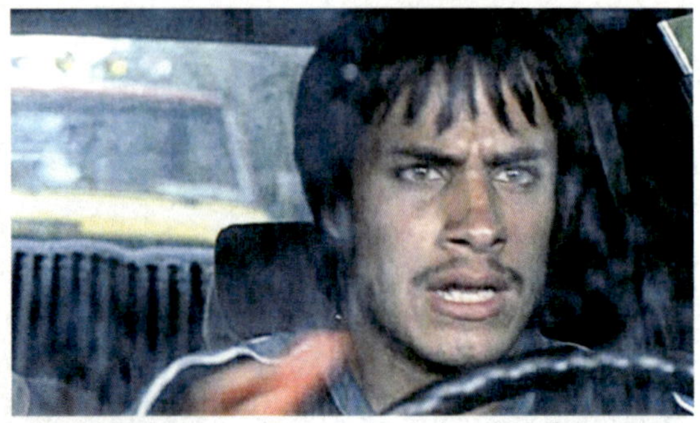

Fig. 1
Close-up of Octavio across the window pane during the opening car chase (*Amores Perros*).

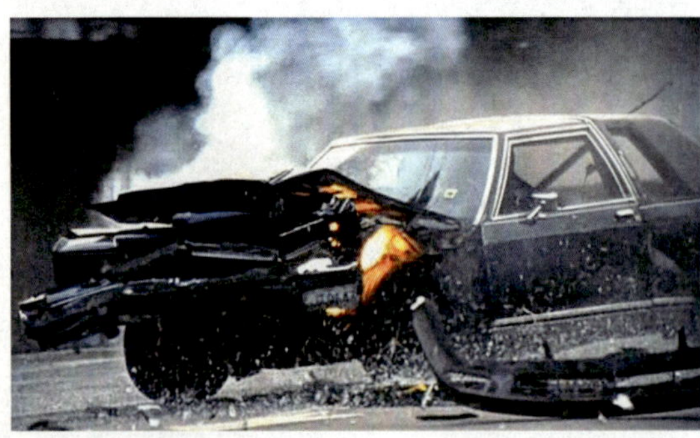

Fig. 2
Chance encounter through a car crash (*Amores Perros*).

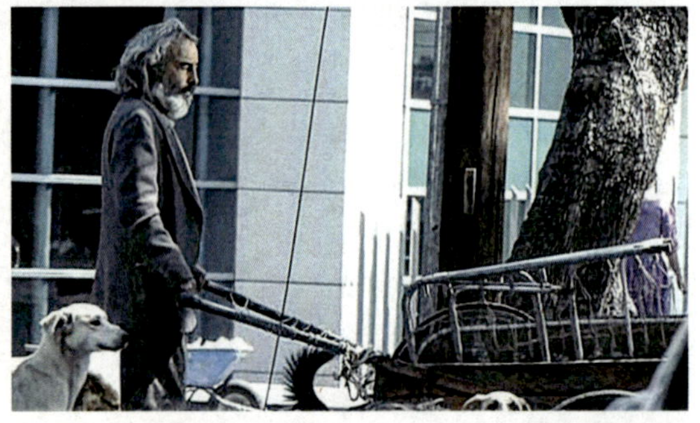

Fig. 3
El Chivo wandering in striated urban space in Mexico City (*Amores Perros*).

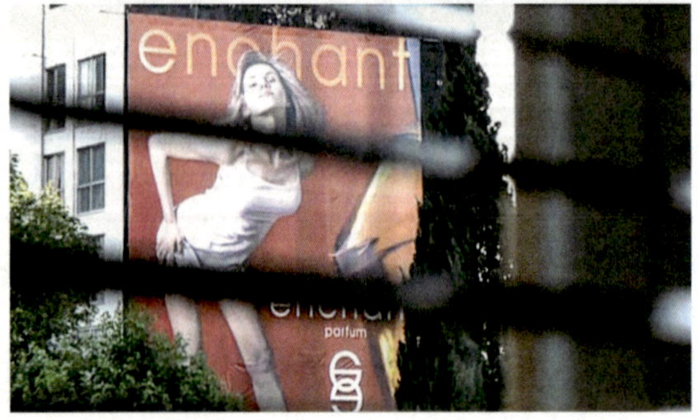

Fig. 4
Valeria's billboard image on Enchant's advertisement campaign seen from her flat (*Amores Perros*).

microcosm of daily life, and an informative social text with its temptations and opportunities, according to Henri Lefebvre's theories of space.[34] For Michel de Certeau, it is through "walking acts", inspired by the linguistic theory of speech acts, that individuals subvert the unnamed control, challenge the established order, and transform the geometrical city spaces into "a mobile organicity of the environment"[35]. In Iñárritu's films, however, driving acts substitute for De Certeau's walking acts, through which Octavio transgresses the boundaries between mosaic pieces and challenges established social order in a microcosm of daily urban life. In fact, it is the car, the symbol of private life in cosmopolitan Mexico City according to Jeff Menne,[36] which enables the meeting and clashing. As cars are the epitome of bourgeois life in the global city through their mobility, which is forbidden to those who cannot afford cars, El Chivo, the anti-bourgeois figure, dissembles the bourgeois value system by intruding into the protected private car space and disintegrating the cars into pieces. He kidnaps the businessman Luis by cuffing him to the steering wheel and later sells both the luxury cars of Luis and Gustavo to a garage. Cars, within which the bourgeois businessmen segregate and protect themselves from the underprivileged people, are later demolished and disintegrated into parts of the multiplicity: car wheels, metal pieces, and engines, which are captured by the camera in a sequence of close-ups. They thus cease being the metal fort of private space, and become splinters and shreds.

As Menne points out, the car crash serves "as [a] plot device [...] for public life in the increasingly global dimensions of Mexico City"[37]. Through car crash, the globalised Mexico City manifests itself as the point of clashing between disparate groups from diverse spatial configurations. This cinematic mosaic is thus resonant with the theories of the globalised space illustrated by Featherstone, who argues that the world city is an important site where the various flows of people, images, information, and goods intermingle. People from the

34 Henri Lefebvre: The Social Text. In: Id.: *Key Writings*, ed. by Stuart Elden / Elizabeth Lebas / Eleonore Kofman. London: Continuum 2003, pp. 88–92, here pp. 90–91.

35 Michel de Certeau: *The Practice of Everyday Life*, trans. from French by Steven Rendall. Berkeley / Los Angeles: University of California Press 1984, pp. 97, 99.

36 Menne: A Mexican Nouvelle Vague, p. 76.

37 Ibid., p. 75.

centre and the periphery, the rich and the poor, the new middle-class professionals and the homeless, are "brought together to face each other within the same spatial location"[38]. This is also where Appadurai's financescapes, ethnoscapes, mediascapes, technoscapes, and ideoscapes intersect and negotiate in a complex way.[39] In the globalised Mexico City, all the characters are influenced by the change brought by free markets, the private enterprise of neoliberalism, and global interdependence, but their social polarisation comes from different degrees of access to global resources. During the uneven process of globalisation, some become white-collar bourgeois, dressed in smart suits working in finance and commerce, like Daniel and Gustavo. Some, lacking the savoir-faire in a global network, become easily replaceable at lower ends of labor market and marginalised in the working class district, like Octavio and Ramiro. Through the portrayals of individuals with different relationships to the global flows of wealth and information, *Amores Perros* foregrounds the social divides between wealth and resources under the unequal process of gobalisation.

As a matter of fact, in the globalised Mexico City, only the privileged ones who have access to international resources and benefit from global interdependence, like the model Valeria, are able to flow from one segment to another through media broadcast. The first appearance of Valeria, instead of her presence in the actual space, is on the TV screen in Octavio's room right before the final dogfight. The grainy image of Valeria on the TV talk show *Gente de Hoy* revealing her private life is initially unframed, unexplained, and unsolicited in the section of "Octavio and Susana". This broadcasted image then cuts to Jorge and Octavio counting money for their last dogfight bet with the TV playing in the background. This is when the audience realises the context of Valeria's appearance as virtual, transmitted by media and shared in the imagined community's image consumption. When the film cuts back to Valeria on the TV, the images are clearly reframed within Octavio's black TV screen margins, showing the context of consumption by Octavio in his bedroom right before the last dogfight. Another example of global flows of images and information entering local spaces can be seen in the billboard image of

38 Featherstone: Localism, Globalism, and Cultural Identity, p. 65.

39 Appadurai: *Modernity at Large*, pp. 32–35.

Valeria for the perfume *Enchante*'s campaign (Fig. 4), which appears very early on in the segment "Octavio and Susana", looked at by El Chivo when driving by in his old truck. Among the three central characters, it is only the wealthy Valeria, the Spanish model working in Mexico, whose virtual images are empowered to move freely between segregated socioeconomic milieus. The working class Octavio and tramp El Chivo, because of their marginalised position lacking global connections, can only consume, and are unable to embody virtual images. Valeria's engagement in the global flows of advertisement for the perfume company with a French name, however, is lost after the car accident which scars the assets of her beautiful long legs and disconnects her from her modeling career. Her bigger-than-life poster in front of her window is taken off and the contract with *Enchante* is discontinued. Néstor García Canclini and Christof Parnreiter have noted that media circuits offer new modalities of encounter and recognition beyond national spaces through virtual, rather than physical, means[40]; but actually, within imbalanced global flows with disjunctive order, only the privileged with global commercial values can have their images diffused and disseminated for these one-way encounters.

In fact, the representations of individuals with different levels of access to global flows reveal the meeting of local spaces in the global on screen. The subject matter of *Amores Perros* is both specifically local/Mexican as well as global, foregrounding the issues of social divide, urban violence, corrupt politicians, political assassination, extreme urbanisation, dysfunctional families, and imbalanced regional and economic development. This urban cityscape and its problems, though specific to Mexico, are not unknown to the large amount of urban audiences in the global space, who also share a common experience in the post-industrial capitalist world as city-dwellers in different corners of the world. City-dwellers all live with or are surrounded by cars, experience alienation and lack of identity to different degrees, and are overwhelmed by mediatised images on television. As Featherstone says, "the locality is no longer the prime referent of

40 Néstor García Canclini: From National Capital to Global Capital: Urban Change in Mexico City, trans. from Spanish by Paul Liffman. In: Appadurai (ed.): *Globalization*, pp. 253–259, here pp. 258–259; Christof Parnreite: Mexico: The Making of a Global City. In: Saskia Sassen (ed.): *Global Networks, Linked Cities*. London: Routledge 2002, pp. 145–182, here p. 145.

our experiences"[41]. The specific and distinctive smell and essence of Mexico City have been used to portray a globally-shared urban reality, which is not the same across Mexico but reflects some universal themes and concerns which can be easily translated to spectators from other cultures in the global space.[42] On the one hand, the Mexican audiences, and especially those who live in Mexico City, would recognise Valeria's fashionable residential area, Colonia Condesa, in the film and feel like they have been represented on screen.[43] The film "captures the smell and essence of the city" which only local residents would grasp, and Iñárritu claims it to be "very Mexican".[44] On the other hand, Iñárritu deliberately avoids tourist shots of the Zocalo and the Historic Centre, as well as skyscrapers and modern business districts,[45] and hence foregrounds a globally recognisable urban space easily consumed in a wide range of geopolitical spaces. Unlike many Latin American films depicting urban reality, which favour an establishing shot of densely housed hills or a helicopter shot of the layout of cities, such as *Midnight* (USA 1998, D: Woody Allen), *And Your Mother Too* (*Y tu mamá también*, ES 2001, D: Alfonso Cuarón), *City of Men* (*Cidade dos homens*, BR 2007, D: Paulo Morelli), *City of God* (*Cidade de deus*, BR 2002, D: Fernando Meirelles / Kátia Lund), *Carandiru* (BR 2003, D: Hector Babenco), *Déficit* (MX 2007, D: Gael García Bernal), *The Zone* (*La zona*, MX 2007, D: Rodrigo Piá), *Rudo and Cursi*, *Linha de passe* (MX 2008, D: Walter Salles / Daniela Thomas), *Sin nombre* (MX 2009, D: Cary Joji Fukunaga), and *Traffic* (USA 2010, D: Steven Soderbergh), no sky-line aerial shot of the city provides a visual overview of the cityscape in *Amores Perros*. In addition, the boulevards where the car chase in *Amores Perros* takes place are like other boulevards in the world, divided into lanes of standard width with trees lining the middle. Through blending the local, culturally specific subject matter in Mexico City, and the global, common experiences shared by city-dwellers in the global space, *Amores Perros* creates a marketable space which connects with communities of movie-goers across national borders.

41 Featherstone: Localism, Globalism, and Cultural Identity, p. 63.

42 Wood: *The Faber Book of Mexican Cinema*, p. 88; Marvin D'Lugo: *Amores Perros/Love's a Bitch*. In: Alberto Elena / Marina Díaz López (eds): *The Cinema of Latin America*. London: Wallflower 2003, pp. 221–230, here p. 221.

43 Smith: *Amores Perros*, p. 52.

44 Wood: *The Faber Book of Mexican Cinema*, pp. 87–88.

45 Smith: *Amores Perros*, p. 51.

In *Amores Perros*, Valeria moves from being connected to being secluded from flows of global mediated images, information, and finances, whereas El Chivo is the character who is capable of smoothing the striated across horizontal mosaic pieces and opening up to new connections. According to Deleuze's framework of the intensive and the extensive, deterritorialisation and reterritorialisation, the nomad is the person who constantly creates spaces through the trajectories of their journeys from one place to another across mosaic pieces.[46] Being the only character who has experienced violent conflicts in the national past, El Chivo becomes the best negotiator between mosaic pieces in the contemporary global city. In his smoothing of the striated as a nomad, he transcends social classes and the confinement of mosaic pieces by starting new paths beyond his original self and 'travelling' across boundaries. The back story from the dialogue between the corrupt policeman and Gustavo informs the spectator that, after having abandoned the striated life as an elite college teacher with his wife and daughter for leftist idealism, he wanders into the smooth as a guerrilla fighter. He is later forced to return to the striated when he is put in jail, and subsequently dwells in the shanty house as a tramp and contract killer. By the force of chance encounter with the mongrel Cofi after the car accident, he deterritorialises himself from his role as assassin and creates spaces beyond the immediate mosaic pieces. This transformation starts from his transformation of body, resonating with Jack's body transformation by erasing his crucifix tattoo with a heated knife after being released from the prison in *21 Grams*. After locking the feuding brothers Luis and Gustavo next to each other, he cuts his nails, shaves, gives himself a haircut, showers, wears his taped glasses, and dresses himself in business attire taken from Gustavo. El Chivo's body, through a change in hair, beard and clothing, is transformed from a vagabond to a bourgeois figure, a conventional image which he wants to present to his daughter Maru. At the same time that he crashes bourgeois etiquette by rejecting Luis and Gustavo's value system and discarding their cars, he re-embodies a bourgeois figure. In a close-up of Maru's graduation photo, we see El Chivo using his now clean and trimmed fingers to remove his tramp image, pasted earlier by himself, and to glue his bourgeois image on top of Maru's stepfather's face. Yet after

46 Tom Conley: Space. In: Adrian Parr (ed.): *The Deleuze Dictionary*. Edinburgh: Edinburgh UP 2005, pp. 257–259, here pp. 258–259.

putting the modified photo back in Maru's room, his trajectory is towards the wilderness and the void. Thus, *Amores Perros* ends with the backs of El Chivo and the mongrel dog, having sold Gustavo and Luis' cars, walking side by side across a landscape which is dried out and broken into segments. The long shot shows them walking in the sunset, side by side, towards the wilderness. The landscape is open, unrestricted, uninhabited and smooth. Yet the ground that they step on is so dry that it breaks into striated fragments and chunks, with wide gaps which demarcate the boundaries. It is in the coexistence between, and juxtaposition of, the open smooth and the fragmented striation, which translate each other in a circuit and interweave into a mosaic, that the film ends.

We can see Iñárritu's horizontal mosaic of wealth divides as a result of globalisation. Along with the weaving of narrative threads from different characters' perspectives, the film assembles their socio-economic spaces, ranging from bourgeois to working class to homeless, with different levels of access to global resources. The global and the local are blended in terms of representations of Mexico City, subject matter, and character portrayal. It is only by smoothing the striated segregation of El Chivo that one is able to transform demarcation and transcend the boundaries of mosaic pieces. The dynamic terrain between the global and the local, and the smooth and the striated, within the mosaic space of socioeconomic and geopolitical varieties, will continue to be discussed in *Babel*.

5. *Babel*

Babel, Iñárritu's third feature film, extends the meeting between different socioeconomic spaces and different access to global resources to a larger geopolitical scope, exploring the encounter, be it conflictive or benign, between North and South, and West and East. As the characters from the USA, Mexico, Morocco, and Japan have an impact on one another's lives through a rifle shooting in Morocco, their perspectives, as well as the spaces that they carry, are interwoven into a mosaic. *Babel* will demonstrate how Iñárritu's characters experience dynamic relationships with the striated and the smooth, and the local and the global, in the age of global interdependence and interconnectedness, as well as the imbalanced development of globalisation.

Paul Kerr posits that the specific global connections in the media industry determine *Babel*'s form, rather than, or as well as, the national cultural context, which "finds echoes in the locations of its financial backers"[47]. He attributes this transnational mode to what David Bordwell terms "package-unit production", which assembles "circulating objects: commodified, casualized labourers or, for those names above the title, 'brands'" in the international network of agencies with global capital.[48] *Babel*'s integration of financial resources, film professionals, and distribution routes across continents, including the use of brand names will also be foregrounded here. Yet, in my framework of mosaic space and authorship, I am arguing that *Babel*'s establishment of global connections in its transnational filmmaking mode correlates with, instead of determining, its film content, not only in terms of narrative structure but also spatial assemblage. We can look at its transnational filmmaking context from its production, distribution companies, and its cross-cultural communication in the making of the film. Through the connection of Iñárritu's US agent John Lesher, it was produced by Paramount Vantage, the branch of Paramount Pictures which focuses on low budget films (headed by Brad Grey), as well as Iñárritu's own Zeta Films, the American company Anonymous Content (with whom Iñárritu collaborated regularly for music videos and commercials such as *Power Keg* for BMW advertisement), and the French film company Central Films.[49] It was distributed in Japan by Gaga Communications and in Latin American by UIP.[50] With its big budget of about US$ 25 million, the film relied largely on the profits from global distribution instead of domestic box office. In the end, it grossed US$ 135 million globally at the box office, of which only about a quarter was from the US.[51] Dragging the whole crew around the world for almost a year, like a "global travelling circus"[52] in Iñárritu's own words, the filmmaking process itself is a story of transcultural and multilingual communication. Seven languages (English, Spanish, Arabic, Japanese, French, Berber,

47 Kerr: *Babel*'s Network Narrative, p. 41.

48 Ibid., p. 39.

49 Hagerman (ed.): *Babel. A Film by Alejandro Gonzalez Inarritu*, p. 263; Kerr: *Babel*'s Network Narrative, pp. 44–45.

50 Kerr: *Babel*'s Network Narrative, p. 45.

51 Ibid.

52 Alejandro González Iñárritu cited in Hagerman (ed.): *Babel: A Film by Alejandro Gonzalez Inarritu*, p. 72.

and Japanese sign language) are spoken on and off screen among the team of 150 people.[53] The most prominent example of the difficulties embedded in this transnational project occured during shooting in the little town of Taguenzalte in Morocco, when six languages were spoken amongst the crew of 120, composed of Italians, French, North Americans, Mexicans, and Moroccans (speaking Arabic or Berber). In order to direct the scene of the old Berber woman offering Susan a smoke, Iñárritu's English words would have to be translated into Arabic by the Palestinian actress Hiam Abbass, and then into Berber, and wait for her answer to be translated back again through two linguistic mediations.[54] This shows an interesting correlation between the extradiegetic film context and the diegetic film content. In the same way that the Berber woman comes to Susan's aid without understanding the surrounding voices in the diegesis, she is also at a loss in the doubly-mediated translation process extradiegetically. In addition, whereas the American couple Richard and Susan fly from the US to Morocco, and Amelia and Santiago drive across the Mexico-USA border, the film crew makes exactly the same journey extradiegetically. At the same time that the film shows children in a rural Moroccan village chasing foreign tourists who appear with the tour bus like exotic attractions in the diegesis, the villagers who have participated in the filmmaking experience exactly the same cross-cultural encounter during the filmmaking process extradiegetically. From the filmmaking process to the film content, dialogues are polyphonic where multiple translations are needed.

Therefore, corresponding to the transnational filmmaking context, which weaves together global flows of finances and people, *Babel* assembles the narrative threads of four characters in four distinct geopolitical contexts around the world into a mosaic. Portraying the intangible connection between these characters from different corners of the globe, the film keeps zigzagging from one snippet to another, from one continent to another. The film opens with a shepherd family's purchase of a rifle in the smooth open space of Morocco (Fig. 5), where vast unmarked hills spread across landscapes without demarcations. After the two boys' playful shooting from a hill towards a tour bus driving along a meandering road among hills, the film cuts to the bright, clean, organised, and sizeable bourgeois

53 Mike Goodridge: Mike Goodridge in Cannes.

54 Hagerman (ed.): *Babel: A Film by Alejandro Gonzalez Inarritu*, pp. 72, 94, 260.

space in San Diego, where the Mexican nanny Amelia plays with two blond kids. This segment is followed by the American couple Susan and Richard sitting under a tent in a tourist area of Morocco. Then we see a volleyball match between two teams of deaf-mute girls in Tokyo, Japan. This jumping between different storylines with characters of different ethnicities, socioeconomic status, age groups, and against different spatial features, which initially seem unrelated to one another, continues throughout the film. Despite the segregation of segments, these mutually unacquainted characters and local spaces are in fact interconnected through the circulation of a rifle from Japan to Morocco. The rifle of a Japanese businessman, whose deaf-mute daughter Cheiko is alienated and emotionally unavailable because of her mother's suicide, is given to his Moroccan guide Hassan as a gift. Hassan sells the rifle to a goatherd, Abdullah, to shoot jackals. Abdullah's two sons, Yussef and Ahmed, later fire at a tour bus and inadvertently wound Susan, an American tourist vacationing with her husband Richard in an attempt to reconcile with each other. They are thus stranded in Morocco and unable to return to San Diego on time. Failing to find a substitute, their illegal immigrant nanny Amelia opts to take their kids, Mike and Debbie, with her to her son's wedding in Mexico. On their return from Mexico, Amelia's nephew's behaviour results in a dangerous situation in the desert and her eventual deportation.

Sometimes the interweaving of narrative is done through a literal "editing-together" of all these pieces, through graphic matches, which juxtapose and compare the images of different locales. In this way, the seemingly separate mosaic pieces of different locations and characters are edited together into visual continuity. When the tour bus stops in the middle of the road in Morocco after Ahmed's shooting at the beginning of the film, we see Ahmed and Yussef exchange fearful looks and run away from the edge of the hill, captured by a medium shot framing their backs against the background of a blurry hill. This scene immediately cuts to Richard's son Mike in San Diego running away from the camera to hide beside the sofa on the left side of the frame in a game of hide-and-seek. Within split seconds, space jumps from the rural Moroccan grazing hills to a modern suburban house in San Diego, thousands of miles apart. In this jump, the mood of the scene changes dramatically, while the action of the children maintains continuity. Another cutting and matching between individuals' body movement happen after we see Susan, her mouth open and face distorted, shouting in pain when a local veterinarian in Tazarine stitches up her gun wound on the shoulder without anesthesia. A series of fast-cutting close-ups between Susan's wound being stitched up, her feet kicking and wrinkling the carpet on the floor, and her distorted face and open mouth, shouting from the pain, cuts to a close-up of an Asian girl's mouth moving in silence on the right half of the frame. The camera then zooms out to show the visual context: a dentist's receptionist against a clinically white background, from the deaf-mute Cheiko's perspective. Similarly, the scene in which blood splashes from a chicken's neck, which Santiago breaks in front of children before the wedding, cuts to Susan bleeding in the bus. Through graphic montage, protagonists who have never met, and will never meet, are brought to occupy adjoining screen space and connected together. They are connected through the mapping of body movement, body parts, and blood, which are parts of shared human experiences across local boundaries. In seconds, the spectator is taken to the other side of the world to view seemingly continuous images of completely different mise-en-scène. Through matching body movement, body parts, and blood on screen, these disjunctive cuts between spaces, instead of emphasising differences, create visual approximation between individuals from different backgrounds and connect these individuals into a visual mosaic.

In this assemblage of characters and perspectives through narrative structure and graphic matching, geopolitically distinct spaces which the characters inhabit in the nation-states of Japan, USA, Morocco, and Mexico, East and West, North and South, urban and rural, dryland and humid places, developed and developing areas, and wealthy and poor are interwoven into a mosaic. This is thus a more global picture of horizontal mosaic than his first two feature films, as wealth divides and social inequality are extended from Latin America in *Amores Perros* and North America in *21 Grams* to a cross-continental scale. The contrast between wealthy and deprived citizens is mapped onto the contrast between globalised and local, developed and developing, regions in the world. These characters dwell in different kinds of spaces; the bourgeois and the working-class spaces are mapped into the striated and the smooth, respectively. Susan and Richard are wealthy bourgeois in the developed West. Their house in the suburban San Diego is spacious, bright, orderly, and clean, regulated and striated by the boundaries of wooden cupboards, balcony, swimming pool, kitchen, and children's room according to their separate functions. Cheiko and her father are the wealthy bourgeois in the East, dwelling in a guarded skyscraper with polished marble floors, black painted wooden furniture, and white walls. Their space is marked by even stronger striation, which defines identities and interpersonal relationships, compared to Richard and Susan's space in San Diego. Long shots of intersecting metro lines, roads with traffic jams, and skyscrapers, and medium shots of teeming teenagers in the city centre compose the cramped images in the Tokyo segment with funky colours and neon lights. In Cheiko's routine life, she is confined to cells separated by striated lines, such as the enclosed gym, her father's car, a café-restaurant, and the dental clinic. These urban, cosmopolitan, and metropolitan spaces of glossy and sleeky Tokyo and sunny San Diego are contrasted to the smooth open space in the poor regions, such as the desert around the Mexico-USA border and the dry hills in Morocco, which can hardly be measured or demarcated. Amelia's working-class family in Tijuana also resides in an underdeveloped dryland covered in dust, but their household is decorated with bright and saturated colours, compared to the brown tone of Abdullah's house. Covered in dust and blown by wind, the Quarzazate mountains in Morocco[55] are inhabited by the shepherd Abdullah's family with limited wealth. Both spaces of developing areas are open and smooth, but Abdullah's space is smoother than Amelia's, for they live in isolation from other houses in the desert where there is no demarcation of space, no boundaries of limits, and no striated line to regulate the traffic. Dried hills with occasional appearances of grass and bushes are linked with another chain of dried hills. Shepherds wander with their flocks on land without street names, and women covered from head to toe in black carry water on their heads. Occasionally, a couple of travellers on camels pass by the desert in front of the camera, moving slowly and silently. Mapping between wealth divides and degrees of spatial striation, *Babel* interweaves the poor geopolitical locations, which are characterised by open space and unobstructed vision, with the wealthy regions of striated and regulated space.

The film's conscious reflection on the interweaving of local spaces into a mosaic can be understood through the works of Sassen, Appadurai, and Hardt / Negri. The world, what Hardt / Negri call "Empire",

55 Hagerman (ed.): *Babel: A Film by Alejandro Gonzalez Inarritu*, p. 258.

is becoming more mobile and fluctuating, in which more and more people consume images and objects from remote locations, widely travel, encounter immigrants, and follow global trends in terms of fashion and culture.[56] With the invention of communication and transportation tools, people are no longer restricted in the physical space of here and now. Hence, the global space, with its complex, overlapping, and disjunctive order, is brought into local spaces with a snap of the fingers, and local spaces are no longer fragmented units entirely distinctive and exclusive from one another.[57] Yet this exchange and interconnectedness between global flows of people, information, finances, and images (and even the physical bodies and organs) are far from being balanced and equal. In fact, the divides between the rich and the poor, and North and South, are very often reinforced instead of evened out.[58] The privileged benefit from their more available access to the global flows and more resources for border-crossing, whereas the underprivileged become easily marginalised and disconnected from the networks of the global space, which is exemplified in *Babel*. Their differences, instead of disappearing with the encounter, are reinforced. Whereas the bourgeois American couple Richard and Susan can easily afford a trip in Morocco to consume the packaged experiences of North African desert, their tour guide and his fellow villagers could hardly do the same in reverse. After Richard transmits the information of the gunshot to the US through a local public phone, the information flows between several locales: their family members in the US, the American and Moroccan governments, the US embassy, press, and local police office in Morocco. Immediately afterwards, the incident and their images are broadcasted and consumed in the global arena. (Fig. 6) Thanks to the circulation of resources between nations and embassies, which is accelerated by the exchange of information and images, Richard and Susan are able to leave the local space with a helicopter from the USA. On the other hand, Abdullah, Yussef, and Ahmed, without the privilege to be connected with the global flows of information, images, finances,

56 Hardt / Negri: *Empire*, p. 39.

57 Davie Morley: *Home Territories: Media, Mobility and Identity*. London: Routledge 2000, p. 9; Appadurai: *Modernity at Large*, pp. 33–41; Sassen: Spatialities and Temporalities of the Global, p. 265; Sassen: *Territory. Authority. Rights*, pp. 402–403.

58 Michael J. Shapiro. *Cinematic Geopolitics*. London: Routledge 2009, p. 91.

and resources, can only resort to the local by trying to hide within the neighbouring hills. The contrast between well-off Richard and Susan from a wealthy country, and the poor Abdullah, Yussef, and Ahmed from a developing country, demonstrate this imbalanced and unequal globalised space.

In the globalised world where people are able to move between mosaic pieces across continents, like Richard and Susan's trip in Morocco and Amelia and Santiago's return back to Mexico, the task of realising different degrees of striation and adapting to them can be complicated. For example, Richard and Susan are used to their well-striated bourgeois life in the USA, where standards of hygiene and housing are regulated and national borders are strictly guarded. Upon their arrival in Morocco, Susan tries to maintain the same degree of striation in the smooth space of the Moroccan desert. Travelling in a packaged tour with a group of white middle-aged tourists from the US and France, Susan and Richard have their lunch served in the standardised western manner. First comes their canned coke. Then their meals arrive in a formulated procedure of starter-main-dessert, delivered by a well-trained waiter in white apron. By insisting on the Western table etiquette while in an open desert land, they striate the smooth. Susan is further striating the surrounding by following strict hygiene rules and insisting on throwing the ice away from the glass. By organising their existence according to their Western grid, despite being out of the original context, Susan fails to accept the open space and adapt to the nomadic space. As the camera stays very close to their faces and cuts them off from the surrounding space, the desert seems a mere background which is irrelevant to their ontological existence. It is only through the traumatic aftermath of the shooting that they gradually succumb to the smooth and adapt to local customs. When Susan accepts local food and even experiences wound-sewing while lying on the carpeted floor of a local house surrounded by the Moroccan guide and the village veterinarian, she finally melts into the smooth local space. The pivotal moment of her smoothing the striated happens when she smokes the Berber woman's opium. A close-up of the Berber woman's serenely carved and tanned face inhaling and exhaling the tobacco wrapped in blue paper while lighting it with her wrinkled hand is followed by Susan's weeping face smoking, then gradually relaxing at the hand of the Berber woman. At the moment that the Berber woman strokes Susan's hair and utters comforting words incomprehensible to non-Berber speakers, Susan and the Berber woman share the same frame in harmony; Susan's pale face with softened expression on the right half of the frame and the Berber woman's profile in the unlit left frame. Although there is a contrast in the colour schemes between left and right, the image composition is still and tranquil. Through the process of rapprochement with her surroundings, Susan finally loosens up her boundaries of body territory and goes closer to the unknown and the foreign.

In contrast to Susan, the Mexican nanny Amelia is used to far less striation, and the unawareness of differences in striation across the globe leads to her eventual deportation from the USA. As she fails to understand and adapt to the more rigidly defined striation in her host country, where interpersonal relationships are strictly regulated by laws which protect children's welfare in legal terms instead of community consensus, Amelia crosses the border with Mike and Debbie to Mexico and subsequently allows her nephew Santiago to drunk drive back towards California. When Santiago leaves them in the New Mexican desert after panicking at the border control, Amelia is also unable to cope with the completely smooth desert space. Walking aimlessly with the children in the absolutely smooth space, without any demarcation of signs, boundaries, and landmarks, she is completely disoriented. (Fig. 7) Her high-heeled shoes are not for walking in the desert, and her red embroidered dress is torn apart by dried spiky bushes. At the same time that she fails to conform to intense striation, she does not have the means to survive in the absolute smooth either. Hence, from the examples of Susan and Amelia, we can see two different tasks of adapting to divergent degrees of striation while crossing over to another mosaic piece in the globalised space. Susan eventually manages to smooth the striated, whereas Amelia, stuck at a striation level between the highly striated North American society and the complete smoothness of the desert, is unable to cross between mosaic pieces at ease.

The soundtrack in *Babel*, composed and produced mainly by Gustavo Santaolalla, also creates an audial mosaic composed of transnational elements. Santaolalla's use of a single instrument, an oud, which is an ancient Arabic string instrument, to imply the folkloric instruments of three cultures is the key to the audial mosaic. As Iñárritu notes, the sound of the oud, though profoundly Afro-Mediterranean, "has the additional quality of recalling to us the wail of the flamenco

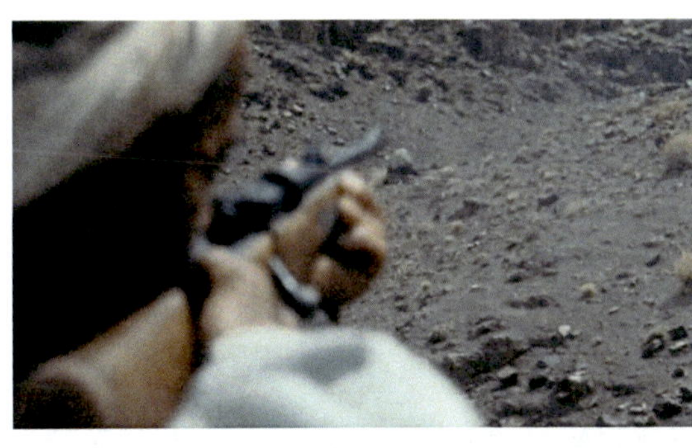

Fig. 5
Abdullah testing the rifle in the smooth open space of Morocco (*Babel*).

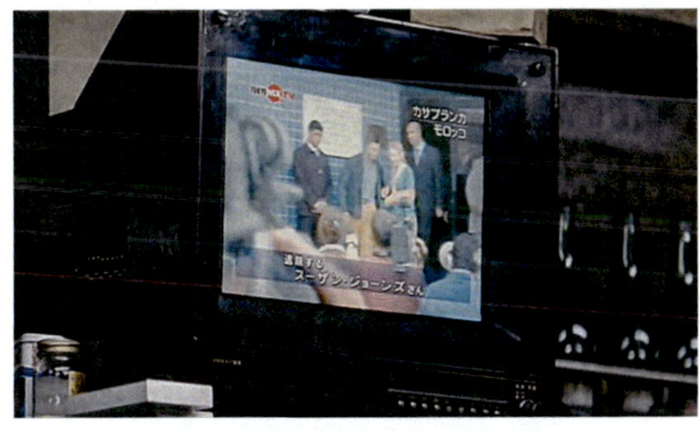

Fig. 6
On a television set in a local restaurant in Tokyo, a news channel broadcasts the incident of Susan being shot in Morocco (*Babel*).

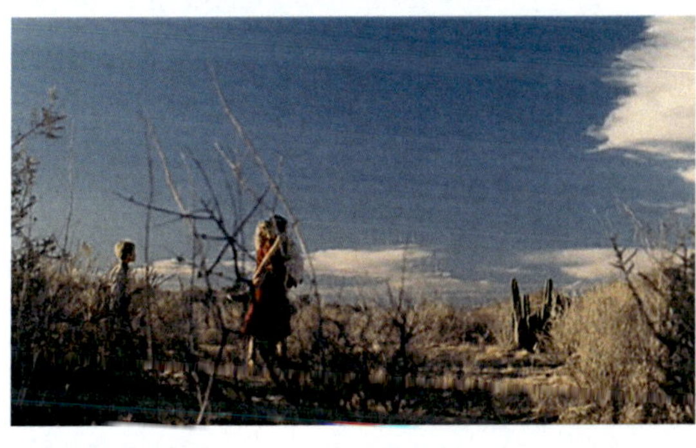

Fig. 7
Amelia walking aimlessly with Mike and Debbie in the absolutely smooth space by the US-Mexico border (*Babel*).

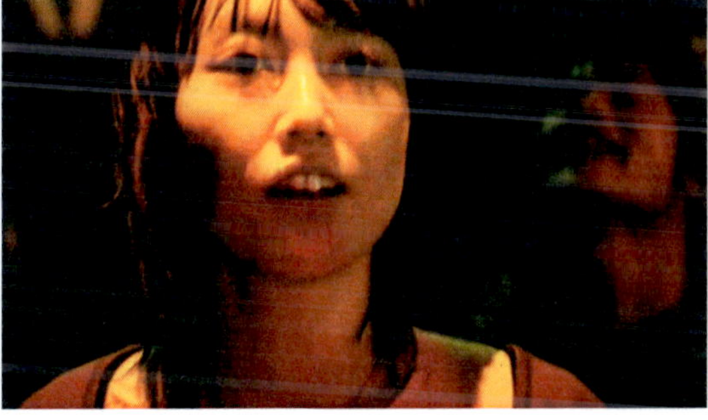

Fig. 8
Close-up of Chieko bathed in neon lights and funky colours in a night-club in Tokyo (*Babel*).

guitar, and hence the Mexican, together with a touch of the scent of the Japanese *koto*"[59]. Apart from the main tune itself carrying a transnational quality, throughout the film, music elements are composed of a balanced mixture between East and West, North and South, and popular music trend and classical genres. Ranging from folk to hip hop, the soundtrack includes works from Chavela Vargas (a Mexican folklore singer), David Sylvian (an English music writer and singer), Ryuichi Sakamoto (a Japanese composer), Nortec Collective (a Mexican electronica group), Rip Slyme (a Japanese hip hop group), and Control Machete (a Mexican hip hop group). For the music accompanying the segment of Morocco, Iñárritu and Gustavo Santaolalla recorded various gnawa music bands, while he recorded music from norteño groups, especially Los Incomparables, in Tijuana for the story shot in Mexico.[60] As Marvin D'Lugo suggests in his essay on *Amores Perros*, a global approach to the soundtrack "shatters the impression that this is one more exotic Third World narrative by suggesting a more universal urban experience"[61]. The visual mosaic is thus complemented and emphasised by the musical mosaic in many different ways. In the Mexican segment, for example, the first drive across the US-Mexico border is emphasised by music. A lively Mexican song by Celso Piña plays while the camera tracks the car's movement, observing the fleeting images of vendors on the road, national flags flying in the air, wooden crosses on a wall, and densely-built houses on a hill. These images are presented from the perspective of Mike and Debbie in Santiago's car, crossing the border and experiencing the route to Tijuana for the first time: saturated colours, prostitutes on the street, dusty roads, and traditional kiosks. All these experiences of the senses are reinforced by Celso Piña's music, which brings out the local dynamic atmosphere, warm colours, and the lively rhythm of cinematography capturing the space. On the other hand, as we can see in the Tokyo segment, the juxtaposition and remixing of music interweave the local and the global, and emphasise the transnational dimension of film images. The song *September*, by the American band Earth, Wind & Fire, remixed into the British Fatboy Slim's song

59 Hagerman (ed.): *Babel: A Film by Alejandro Gonzalez Inarritu*, p. 259.

60 Ibid., pp. 150, 258.

61 D'Lugo: Amores Perros/Love's a Bitch, p. 227.

The Joker,[62] is juxtaposed with the images of nightlife in Tokyo, full of neon lights, funky colours, and a unique sense of fashion. (Fig. 8) It is a song which is written, produced, remixed, and consumed in diverse contexts, imaginable or unimaginable by the original creator. Disparate spatial planes in global space are thus connected and brought together through the transformed version of *September*.

Amores Perros and *Babel*, as well as Iñárritu's other works until *Biutiful*, demonstrate a horizontal mosaic of wealth, geopolitical and socioeconomic divides, in which global connections, along with their uneven power relations, are brought into local spaces. These spatial planes are juxtaposed and connected visually and audially, which bring disparate perspectives and spatial configurations together. Music is also used to portray the mosaic space of the global and the local, in which flows of people, images, and information are brought together. At the intersection between these flows, the characters have the task of adapting to different degrees of striation embedded in respective local spaces, which is not always easy. In the following chapter, I will explore the different form of spatial assemblages in Egoyan's vertical mosaic, in which character-territory and spectator-screen space relationships are embedded with historical concerns.

62 Hagerman (ed.): *Babel: A Film by Alejandro Gonzalez Inarritu*, p. 236.

Part II

Vertical Mosaic

Chapter 2
Atom Egoyan: The Diasporic and Cinematic Mosaic of Deterritorialisation/Reterritorialisation and Actualisation/Virtualisation

1. Introduction

In Part II, "Vertical Mosaic", I group together Atom Egoyan's diasporic and cinematic mosaic of deterritorialisation/reterritorialisation and actualisation/virtualisation, and Hou Hsiao-hsien's historical mosaic of multilayered mise-en-scène. Their mosaic spaces delve into historical causes and effects in relation to collective trauma, in contrast to Alejandro González Iñárritu's horizontal mosaic, which assembles contemporary spaces of socioeconomic and geopolitical divides. In this chapter, I will demonstrate how Egoyan's mosaic foregrounds the continuous and dynamic negotiation between deterritorialisation and reterritorialisation at both the levels of the diegesis, in terms of the bond between diegetic characters and territories, and formal aesthetics, in terms of the relationship between the spectator and screen space. On the one hand, the characters, whose separate and fragmented storylines are interwoven by mosaic narrative, negotiate the territory of residence and the territory of origins or adopted origins, as well as between the territory of the present and the territory of the past. Their physical deterritorialisation for socio-political, historical, or personal reasons situates them in the seer position, unable to react to the post-trauma and/or post-displacement any-space-whatever with media saturation. As they are deterritorialised in the actual space and are incapable of reacting to the territory actively and directly, they strive to reterritorialise through virtual means such as recording and projecting machines which stand in for memories and actual connection. From this emerges the dynamic mapping between deterritorialisation/reterritorialisation (their distanciation from and reappropriation to a certain territory) and actualisation/virtualisation (entering and leaving the doubly-mediated virtual media enabled by the technical innovation of TV, video, and digital media). On the other hand, formal cinematic properties visually portray the shifting relationship of deterritorialisation and reterritorialisation between the spectator and screen space. By initially truncating human bodies and objects through framing them in close-ups, film images disorient the spectator and detach them from the screen space. The spectator is then reterritorialised when the camera zooms out to provide the full visual context of the images. Through deterritorialisation and reterritorialisation, the assembled mosaic images enable the spectator to feel rootless and dislocated during the viewing, and replicate the experience of migration and displacement, correlating to Egoyan's experience as a mosaic auteur. I would thus argue that the interweaving diasporic and cinematic mosaic of deterritorialisation and reterritorialisation, and actualisation and virtualisation in Egoyan's films corresponds to his multiple identities as a Canadian auteur with Armenian descent and his continuous circuit of deterritorialisation and reterritorialisation, and displacement and emplacement. Thanks to his multiple identities and sufficient financial resources, he is privileged to be able to cross borders with more freedom than most accented auteurs, and is hence able to integrate filmmaking resources from different geopolitical locales and distribute his films internationally.

This chapter will first examine Egoyan's status as a mosaic auteur incorporating Canadian and Armenian identities and combining international filmmaking resources. His assemblage of mosaic space, correlating to the transnational filmmaking contexts, will then be investigated from both the thematic and formal aspects. Gilles Deleuze's framework of deterritorialisation and reterritorialisation as well as Hamid Naficy's and David Martin-Jones' contextualised readings of it, will be used to demonstrate the unique relationship between diegetic characters and their territories and between spectators and screen territories in Egoyan's mosaic. Deleuze's any-space-whatever will also be contextualised in the particular filmmaking contexts of Egoyan as the post-trauma and/or post-displacement media-saturated any-space-whatever, with which the character-seers are only empowered to interact through mediated means. Detailed analyses of *Next of Kin* and *Calendar* will follow the theoretical discussion.

2. Atom Egoyan and Myriad Identities

Moving between Canada, Armenia, Lebanon, UK, and USA constantly in his filmmaking,[1] Egoyan integrates language zones and cultural heritages across continents and constantly negotiates his role as a Canadian citizen with Armenian ancestry throughout his career. The dual/multiple identities and privileged ability to cross borders, thanks to his Canadian passport and sufficient financial support, enables him to integrate filmmaking resources in terms of cast, crew, funding, and distribution routes from different local spaces and develop a transnational filmmaking mode.

Egoyan's incorporation of filmmaking resources from different contexts originates in his multiple identities. Atom Egoyan was born in Egypt, like his Armenian parents, but was brought up in Victoria on the west coast of Canada, where very few Armenian diasporic families reside.[2] Compared to Iñárritu, Hou, and Haneke, Egoyan crosses the boundaries between a wider cultural and geographical gap, between a North American developed country and a war-ridden postcommunist deprived country, and integrates a constantly shifting "Canadianness" with deep cultural diversity and an "Armenianness" continuously under redefinition. Although included in the national cinemas of both Canada and Armenia, he both challenges the notion of Canadian cinema, which struggles to be recognised despite the dominance of north American film industry, and that of Armenian cinema, which is hardly active enough to be called a national cinema. Egoyan's multiple identities and the resultant transnational filmmaking mode are referred to as "accented cinema" by Naficy. As discussed in the introduction, according to Naficy, accented auteurs are distanced from their places of origin by choice or for survival, and are hence infusing the issues of displacements into their authorship and films.[3] Though also a journeyman who oscillates between displacement and emplacement, Egoyan is a lot freer in relation to national borders than other accented auteurs. He is privileged to be able to move freely between two sides and two continents, like other mosaic auteurs. As deterritorialisation and reterritorialisation work side by side in a circuit in terms of his relation to the territory, Egoyan

1 Emma Wilson: *Atom Egoyan*. Urbana/Chicago: University of Illinois Press 2009, p. x.

2 Ibid., p. 2.

3 Naficy: *An Accented Cinema: Exilic and Diasporic Filmmaking*, p. 34.

understands the dual situation from a more comprehensive and less limited point of view, instead of working in an either/or situation as in the case of accented auteurs. Rather than embarking upon the quest for one root, Egoyan embraces multiple identities.
While Egoyan struggled to achieve a sense of belonging in Canada as a child, he came to terms with his Armenian identity at a later stage of his life. Egoyan went to Canada with his parents at the age of three. As an immigrant child in the WASP community of Victoria, British Columbia, he experienced peer pressure to assimilate at school, and in order to 'belong' to the circle completely, he even refused to speak Armenian at home. He did not start to reconsider his ethnic origins as an important part of his identity until he left home to study at the University of Toronto, where he actively participated in the political Armenian movement through the campus Armenian Society and started taking lessons in the Armenian language.[4] Instead of embracing his Armenianness without question, the Armenian heritage was only gradually espoused by Egoyan and measured against his Canadian/Anglo-Saxon culture after his departure from home.[5] This gradual process of reterritorialisation to the ancestral land, and integration between the dual identities of Canadianness and Armenianness, is reflected in Egoyan's film works. As Egoyan's trope of Armenianness was implicit in the beginning of his filmmaking career, hiding in the ethnic identity of the Deryans in *Next of Kin*, for example, it was only in *Calendar* and *Ararat* (CA / FR 2002), the two films which explicitly address the issue of Armenian Genocide and diaspora, that Egoyan became recognised and credited as an Armenian director, side by side with his Canadian identity.

Egoyan's status as a Canadian filmmaker is far more overt from the beginning of his career than as an Armenian filmmaker, often being referred to as "the most important Canadian filmmaker of his

4 Lisa Siraganian: Telling a Horror Story, Conscientiously: Representing the Armenian Genocide from *Open House* to *Ararat*. In: Jennifer Burwell / Monique Tschofen (eds): *Image and Territory: Essays on Atom Egoyan*. Waterloo, ON: Laurier UP 2006, pp. 133–156, here p. 135; Geoff Pevere: *Exotica*, co-written with Atom Egoyan. Toronto: Coach House 1995, p. 20.

5 Carole Desbarats: Conquering What They Tell Us Is 'Natural'. In: Ead. / Jacinto Lageira / Daniele Riviere / Paul Virilio: *Atom Egoyan*, trans. from French by Brian Holmes. Paris: Dis Voir 1993, pp. 9–32, here p. 29.

generation"[6]. Jim Leach goes even further to claim that Egoyan seems to reflect a distinctively Canadian sense of cultural identity within the domain of art cinema.[7] Being credited as a key figure in Ontario New Wave, or "Renaissance of English-Canadian cinema"[8], Egoyan is often grouped together with filmmakers such as David Cronenberg (*Videodrome*, USA 1983), Peter Mettler (*The Top of His Head*, CA 1989), and Bruce MacDonald (*Roadkill*, CA 1989; *Highway 61*, CA 1991), whose common concerns and influences include interests in video images, communication breakdowns, dubious identities, the overwhelming power of media, the interaction between different screens, and repressed sexuality.[9] These concerns can be observed in a wide range of Canadian films such as *Love and Human Remains* (CA 1993, D: Denys Arcand), *Jesus of Montreal* (*Jésus de Montréal*, CA 1989, D: Denys Arcand), *Sex, Lies and Videotapes* (USA 1989, D: Steven Soderbergh), *Double Happiness* (CA 1994, D: Mina Shum), *Last Night* (CA 1998, D: Don McKeller), and *Possible Worlds* (CA 2000, D: Robert Lepage), as well as most of Egoyan's films. However, the complexity of the cinema of Canada is tied with the fluctuousness of the notion of the nation state of Canada, described as an ethnic mosaic with deep diversity and plurality by John Porter, Roberta Hamilton, and Leo Driedger.[10] It is also affected by Hollywood dominance in the postcolonial era, as Canadian film production, like other aspects of production and consumption, relies heavily on foreign capital and goods.[11] At the same time that its socio-political reality is intrinsically complex and multifaceted, Canada faces the threat of cultural invasion and under-representation of its identity. Academic works such as *The Cinema of Canada*[12], edited by Jerry

6 Pevere: *Exotica*, p. 16.

7 Jim Leach: *Film in Canada*. Oxford: Oxford UP 2006, p. 114.

8 André Lavoie: I've Heard the Mermaids Singing: Patricia Rozema, 1987. In: Jerry White (ed.): *The Cinema of Canada*. London: Wallflower 2006, pp. 195–203, here p. 139.

9 Ibid., p. 139; Marc Glassman / Wyndham Wise: Ontario's New Wave. In: *Take One* 12 (Summer 1996), pp. 34–37.

10 Jerry White: Introduction. In: Id. (ed.): *The Cinema of Canada*. London: Wallflower 2006, pp. 1–10, here pp. 1–2; Leo Driedger: Introduction: Ethnic Identity in the Canadian Mosaic. In: Id. (ed.): *The Canadian Ethnic Mosaic: A Quest for Identity*. Toronto: McClelland & Stewart 1978, pp. 9–22, here p. 10.

11 Ted Magder: *Canada's Hollywood: The Canadian State and Feature Films*. Toronto: University of Toronto Press 1993, pp. 4–6.

12 White: Introduction.

White, *Canada's Hollywood: The Canadian State and Feature Films*[13], by Ted Magder, and with a different discourse of the nation, *Quebec National Cinema*[14], by Bill Marshall, have all discussed the complexity of Canadianness. Here, it suffices to note that Egoyan's understanding of the complex mosaic of the shifting, diverse, and myriad Canadian identity which demonstrates rapidly multiplying possibilities and expressions, as displayed in his preface for *The Cinema of Canada*[15], reflects his own embodiment of multiple identities, which are accumulative and additive instead of mutually exclusive.

Thanks to Egoyan's awareness of multiculturalism coming from the perpetual negotiation between the complex Canadian national identity and the ancestral Armenian cultural identity, many of his films juxtapose the spaces of film funding, cast, crew, settings, and distribution routes across national borders. With his myriad identities, Egoyan is thus a mosaic auteur in art cinema at the same time local (Canadian or Armenian, Canadian and Armenian) and global (who embraces the global art cinema form and its circulation within festival circuits) in terms of both production and distribution. We can see that his funding comes from both the local resources of Canada (local councils, Serendipity Point Films, Alliance Atlantis Communications, and Egoyan's own Ego Film Arts) and the Soviet Union (which Armenia belonged to until 1990), and global resources from the USA (such as Miramax), France (such as Studio Canal, ARP Sélection) and Germany (such as ZDF). Although his early feature films *Next of Kin* and *Family Viewing* (CA 1987) are filmed in Canada and produced by Egoyan's own Ego Film Arts, the Canada Council, and the Ontario Arts Council, from *Speaking Parts* (CA 1989) onwards, Egoyan expands his filmmaking networks. The shooting location remaining in Canada, *Speaking Parts* was made with Egoyan's income from directing of USA television series such as the episode "The Wall" in *The Twilight Zone* (USA 1989) and the episodes "There Was A Little Girl..." and "The Final Twist" in *Alfred Hitchcock Presents* (USA 1987–1988), along with

13 Magder: *Canada's Hollywood*.

14 Bill Marshall: *Quebec National Cinema*. Montreal: McGill-Queen's UP 2000.

15 Atom Egoyan: Preface. In: White (ed.): *The Cinema of Canada*, pp. xii–xv, here p. xiv.

Wim Wenders' \$ 5,000[16] prize for the Best Feature award for *Wings of Desire* (*Der Himmel über Berlin*, DE 1987, D: Wim Wenders) at the Montréal Festival of New Cinema and Video, which was given to Egoyan to show Wenders' appreciation for *Family Viewing*.[17] Subsequently, *Exotica* (CA 1994, D: Atom Egoyan), *Felicia's Journey* (CA / UK 1999, D: Atom Egoyan), and *Ararat* were co-produced by the Canadian Alliance Atlantis, Serendipity Point Films, American Miramax, and Icon Entertainment International, respectively, with the footage shot in Canada, Ireland, England, and Turkey.[18] *Calendar* is another interesting case of Egoyan's transnational film production, which is strongly linked with the drastic political change in the global map of nation states. Its original budget came from the one million roubles that Egoyan's previous film *The Adjuster* (CA 1991) won at the 1991 Moscow Film Festival, but because of the disintegration of the Soviet Union, this fund was dramatically devalued. It was only after securing funding from the German television station ZDF and the Franco-German television station Arte that *Calendar* could eventually be made.[19] *Calendar* is also co-produced by Armenian National Cinemathèque, and was shot half in Canada and half in Armenia. In terms of distribution, Egoyan's films are mainly circulated in arthouse cinemas and consumed by the global spectator of art cinema as well as the local Canadian and Armenian spectator. Travelling between international film festivals, they were nominated in major ones such as Cannes Film Festival and won prizes at São Paulo, Locarno International Film Festival, and Toronto International Film Festival. They have also gained more visibility on the global cinema scene by being nominated for Academy Awards and having won FIPRESCI prizes.

16 Various resources, including Hamid Naficy: The Accented Style of the Independent Transnational Cinema: A Conversation with Atom Egoyan. In: George E. Marcus (ed.): *Cultural Producers in Perilous States: Editing Events, Documenting Change*. Chicago: University of Chicago Press 1997, pp. 179–232, and Yoram Allon / Del Cullen / Hannah Patterson: *Contemporary North American Film Directors: A Wallflower Critical Guide*. London: Wallflower 2002, p. 152, do not specify whether it is in US dollars or Canadian dollars.

17 Naficy: The Accented Style of the Independent Transnational Cinema, p. 179.

18 Naficy: *An Accented Cinema: Exilic and Diasporic Filmmaking*, p. 57; Jonathan Romney: *Atom Egoyan*. London: British Film Institute 2003, p. 125; Wilson: *Atom Egoyan*, p. xi.

19 Romney: *Atom Egoyan*, p. 96; Wilson: *Atom Egoyan*, p. x.

In addition to funding resources, shooting locations, and distribution routes, some of Egoyan's cast also demonstrates transnationality through their multiple identities. The actor Elias Koteas, who has played variegated roles including a Turkish actor and ethnically indiscernible Canadian characters in three of Egoyan's films, is a Québec-Canadian of Greek descent. Egoyan's wife, the Lebanon-born Armenian-Québecois Canadian actress Arsinée Khanjian, on the other hand, traverses Canadian cinema and French cinema through her ethnically unmarked roles in Haneke's *Code Unknown* and Catherine Breillat's *Fat Girl* (*A ma soeur*, FR 2001), and her participation in all of Egoyan's films apart from *Chloe* (US / CA / FR 2009) as ethnically marked or unmarked characters. Other regularly casted actors and actresses in Egoyan's films include the Canadian-American Maury Chaykin, the Canadian Gabrielle Rose of English descent, British David Hemblen, and Canadian actors Bruce Greenwood and Don McKellar.

In section 2, Egoyan's complex mosaic authorship will be demonstrated in terms of multiple identities and transnational filmmaking networks. This contextual mosaic corresponds to the interweaving between different territories and different relationships with the territory in his films.

3. The Diasporic and Cinematic Mosaic of Deterritorialisation/Reterritorialisation and Actualisation/Virtualisation

Egoyan's diasporic and cinematic mosaic of deterritorialisation and reterritorialisation is in fact coupled with actualisation and virtualisation, in terms of the spectator's viewing process and diegetic spatial configurations. An integrated understanding of Deleuze / Guattari's ahistorical notion of deterritorialisation in combination with the contextualised view of deterritorialisation of Naficy and Martin-Jones will help elaborate these points. Deleuze's any-space-whatever will be contextualised to look at the seer position of Egoyan's deterritorialised characters, who are unable to react to the post-trauma and/or post-displacement any-space-whatever with media saturation.

At the same time that Egoyan integrates spaces in his multiple identities and transnational filmmaking mode, his films jump between different characters' perspectives and juggle several narrative lines, which are not necessarily chronologically organised, to interweave into a mosaic. This mosaic, founded on the profound disbelief in unifying principles, deliberately interrupts the narrative flow by interweaving narrative threads following several characters whose paths crisscross by chance encounter. Carole Desbarats and Emma Wilson use the trope of a layered build-up of "Chinese boxes" and "puzzle pictures" to describe Egoyan's multilayering images and narratives[20]; Linda Ruth Williams calls this a "layered narrative" and "time-travel film" to describe the jumping back and forth between different time zones and multiple perspectives,[21] while Richard Porton calls *Exotica* an "elaborately mounted puzzle film"[22]. The metaphors of Chinese boxes, mazes, or puzzles all point to the nature of narrative fragmentation in Egoyan's films, in which layers of narratives are embedded inside other layers, which alienates spectators from the subject matter. However, the understanding of this narrative structure in the framework of mosaic space here is not temporality-focused like Williams' "time-travel films", nor is it seen as a psychological mind game like Porton, Desbarats, and Wilson's analogy of a puzzle. Rather, this narrative strategy of Egoyan is analysed as one of the tools available to construct a spatial mosaic with different relationships to the territory, and as a spatial compilation corresponding to the transnational production mode. While Egoyan's characters are brought to the same spatial plane through interweaving narrative, they bring their respective spaces with them, along with the historical spaces shared by certain communities, by zigzagging between the narrative present and the recollection-images[23], which are often substituted with recorded and displayed virtual images of various textures. The decomposed and fragmented images, being played and replayed, weave into a shifting patchwork. The narrative thus unfolds from the efforts of the spectator to reorder the fragments and allows a deeper look at the process, rather than focusing solely on the lurid event and its outcome. Compared with Iñárritu's mosaic narrative demonstrated in the previous

20 Desbarats: Conquering What They Tell Us Is 'Natural', p. 24; Wilson: *Atom Egoyan*, p. xi.

21 Linda Ruth Williams: Songs for Swinging Lovers. In: *Sight and Sound* 15,12 (December 2005), pp. 32–35, here p. 32.

22 Richard Porton: Family Romances: An Interview with Atom Egoyan. In: *Cineast* 23,2 (December 1997), pp. 8–15, here p. 8.

23 Deleuze: *Cinema 2*, pp. 47–50.

chapter, Egoyan uses mosaic narrative to disorient the spectator by cutting between temporalities, spatialities, and virtualities, whereas Iñárritu uses mosaic narrative to foreground the interconnectedness between individuals across the globe.

Take the mosaic of *Ararat*, for example. The film starts with a close-up of an old button attached to a string. As the camera follows the string upwards, it reveals the background of a faded black-and-white photo of a mother and a son, dressed in folk Armenian clothing, looking straight into the camera. With the camera's movement right and then downwards, we see a pencil drawing of exactly the same photo in close-ups, an Armenian artifact of Jesus on a cross, brushes of different sizes, jugs of oil, and tubes of paint. When the camera moves upwards for the second time, it scans an oil painting in close-ups; first scrutinising the mother figure on the right hand side and then the son on the left. It then keeps panning left and finally stops at the profile of a dark-haired man with a moustache leaning by a window frame. At this moment, we do not know who he is and what his narrative role is. This is followed by blurry images of passers-by later brought into focus to show a close-up of an elderly man, played by the renowned French singer of Armenian descent, Charles Aznavour, who subsequently melts into a grainy handheld image of Mount Ararat. This is cut to the same elderly man being questioned by the customs officer David for a pomegranate in his bag, and then Celia barging into an Armenian gathering in the house of the art historian Ani, who is also her stepmother, and Raffi, who is her stepbrother. The sequence is followed by a lunch scene in another troubled household, composed of David, his son Philip, Philip's lover Ali, and Philip's son. It is only after ten minutes of jumping between seemingly unrelated fragments with different mise-en-scènes that we realise that what we see in the opening sequence is the Armenian-born painter Arshile Gorky working on the oil painting in his studio in New York City. In medium shots, we can see the stringed button and the black-and-white photo contextualised and surrounded by pencil drawings sketched by Gorky in preparation for the oil painting. After Gorky walks away from the frame, the camera zooms slowly towards the initial black-and-white photo to connect it with the disorienting opening sequence.

Decontextualised close-ups create a similar effect of suspense in *The Adjuster*, which also weaves together several characters' fragmented narrative threads: the adjuster Noah, his wife Hera, her sister Seta, the young censor Tyler, and the rich couple Bubba and Mimi, who fail to find any goal in life. In the very beginning of *The Adjuster*, the camera moves to the right very slowly to reveal an extreme close-up of the abstract form and texture of an immobile hand, indistinguishable at first because of its dissociation from the visual context. The camera first contemplates the palm and a square-shaped ring on the wedding ring finger, and then moves right and down to show the fingers, whose upper parts are immersed in darkness and whose bottom shines in a red hue. The camera returns to complete darkness after it moves away from the neatly trimmed, translucent fingernails. Until this moment the camera stays so close to the object that the image is rendered abstract. The image's origin remains unknown until the camera pulls away to a medium shot, revealing a man's lower body sitting on the edge of a bed. His left hand is put on top of a torch held by his right hand. The camera then moves upwards to reveal the body's head. It is only then that the spectator realises that what we just saw, instead of an abstract object, is the male protagonist Noah, sitting in an unlit room contemplating his hand illuminated by a torch, which renders his hand red and translucent. The ending of the film also ties back to the decontextualised close-up of Noah's hand. The camera tilts down from the smoke in the sky to capture Noah standing in front of his burning house in the middle of the wasteland. At the moment that Noah looks at his right hand contemplatively, it cuts back to the starting point of a similar tilting of the camera down from the sky foregrounded by tree branches with very few leaves, to a medium shot of Hera holding a baby standing beside her sister Seta, both in despair. Noah, this time with mid-length hair, delivers his self-introduction as someone who would "adjust it". This Noah then contemplates his hand for a few seconds before placing it on Hera's shoulder. At the cue of this gesture this scene cuts back to the initial Noah at a later temporal point after the departure of Hera, Seta, and the boy, in front of the burning house. It is only at this point that the spectator realises that the fragment containing Hera is in fact the recollection-images of Noah, who is reminded of his encounter with Hera by the sight of the burning house and his hand rendered translucent and red by the light of fire. The close-up of Noah's lit hand in the beginning, and his contemplation on his hand illuminated by real flames of fire, bring the film full circle. The intercutting between the two Noahs and the two right hands, one which starts to make a connection with Hera and the other which has lost it forever, is further linked back to the beginning of the film, which disorients the spectator with the extreme close-up of Noah's hand lit by a torch. The ending of *The Adjuster* shows the beginning of Noah's marriage, whereas the whole film is about the end of it, as the marriage falls apart throughout the film. The initial deterritorialisation of the abstract image of Noah's hand is transformed into a reterritorialisation of the narrative time and space in the end. Although the ending is open, and it remains unknown what Noah and Hera would end up being and doing, loose ends from different fragments are tied up, resolved, and reterritorialised into a complete mosaic.

From these examples we see the working of Egoyan's formal mosaic, which not only jumps between several storylines but also foregrounds the spectator's shifting understanding of the screen territory through framing and camerawork. Egoyan's use of false cues and misleading threads results in the initial indeterminacy and arbitrariness of images, which are tied back to the original track at a later point. The close-ups and selective framings first truncate and fragment screen space by revealing only some parts of the mosaic, and then they are grounded by the zooming out or other movement of the camera which reveals the big picture. William Beard remarks that some arbitrary images become determined and even overdetermined with the unfolding of fragments throughout Egoyan's films.[24] While discussing Egoyan's short film *Diaspora* (CA 2001), Marie-Aude Baronian states, "the film 'exiles' us from certain worn trajectories and lets us find ourselves in a different kind of representational space"[25]. She further argues that:

> Egoyan's filmic style produces a very tight and closed image space, emphasizing the delimitation of the screen and the multiplication of repetitive images. In so doing, the film expresses the very experience of being in diaspora – the tension between the open, infinite, timeless, and boundless aspect of the homeland and its inheritance through closed constructed images of repressed memories. The deconstructive and reconstructive structure of the film's images, which Egoyan reshapes and reshoots in different formats and which he decomposes and multiplies, underlines, in a way, the myth of the possible unproblematic, transparent reconstitution of history.[26]

24 William Beard: *Exotica*: Atom Egoyan, 1994. In: Jerry White (ed.): *The Cinema of Canada*. London: Wallpaper 2006, pp. 195–203, here p. 196.

25 Marie-Aude Baronian: History and Memory, Repetition and Epistolarity. In: Monique Burwell / Jennifer Tschofen (eds): *Image and Territory: Essays on Atom Egoyan*, pp. 157–176, here p. 169.

26 Ibid., p. 168.

Here, I am combining both Beard's formal folding and unfolding of images, and Baronian's mapping between cinematic deconstruction and reconstruction of film images, with the experience of diaspora, while adding a stronger spatial focus. Egoyan's films are thus understood as a mosaic at the same time demanding a constant active process of negotiation and reterritorialisation on the part of the spectator and reflecting the experiences of displacement. In this way, the images, like the individuals in displacement, are at first deterritorialised from their immediate contexts, and subsequently reterritorialised to render a comprehensible whole picture. In contrast to the psychological process implied in what Porton calls an "elaborately mounted puzzle film" when talking about *Exotica*,[27] the understanding of Egoyan's mosaic of deterritorialisation and reterritorialisation here focuses on the assemblage of spatial representations and the spectator's spatial construction in relation to displacement and/or diaspora; negotiation of space happens both at the levels of physical territory and screen territory.

The theories of Deleuze / Guattari, Martin-Jones, and Naficy thus come into the picture in regard to the understanding of the relationship with the representational territory and screen territory. In the model of Deleuze / Guattari, every territory presupposes a prior deterritorialisation, and every deterritorialisation presupposes a correlative reterritorialisation.[28] In talking about the ungrounding and grounding force of deterritorialisation and reterritorialisation, Deleuze / Guattari state that:

> Movements of deterritorialization are inseparable from territories that open onto an elsewhere; and the process of reterritorialization is inseparable from the earth, which restores territories. Territory and earth are two components with two zones of indiscernibility – deterritorialization (from territory to the earth) and reterritorialization (from earth to territory). We cannot say what comes first.[29]

Everyone, in their search for a territory, can be seen as being caught in the eternal circuit of being detached from the territory and being reattached to it; reterritorialisation can take place on almost

27 Porton: Family Romances: An Interview with Atom Egoyan, p. 8

28 Gilles Deleuze / Félix Guattari: *What Is Philosophy?*, trans. from French by Graham Birchill / Hugh Tomlinson. London: Verso 1994, p. 68; Deleuze / Guattari: *A Thousand Plateaus*, pp. 332–338.

29 Deleuze / Guattari: *What Is Philosophy*, pp. 85–86.

anything – fetish, image, recollection, or dream. In *Anti-Oedipus: Capitalism and Schizophrenia*, fetish is the terrain of reterritorialisation, which frees schizophrenic desire from pre-established zones and objects.[30] Displacement and alienation of language and identities in Kafka's *The Metamorphosis* are described as absolute deterritorialisations in *Kafka: Towards a Minor Literature*.[31] In *A Thousand Plateaus*, one becomes minoritarian in deterritorialisation whereas "a becoming-minoritarian exists only by virtue of a deterritorialized medium"[32].

The multiplicity of the concept "deterritorialisation" has been contextualised by Naficy and Martin-Jones. In Naficy's genre of independent transnational cinema, exilic transnationals, residing in perpetual limbo between old home and new home, dystopia and utopia, and thus being freed from old and new relations, constraints, and modes, are deterritorialised. They travel in the interstitial zone of fusion and admixture, becoming "liminars suffused with hybrid excess"[33]. On the other hand, revisiting Deleuze / Guattari's model, Martin-Jones maps the process of deterritorialisation and reterritorialisation with Deleuze's time-image and movement-image, and argues that the former, implying the unruly presence of the plane of consistency of the time-image, "enables a displacement of narrative into multiple labyrinthine versions", whereas reterritorialisation "entails a constraining of a narrative into one linear timeline"[34], suggesting the presence of the plane of organisation of the movement-image. He argues that this process formally foregrounds the negotiation of national identity in cinema.[35]

Here, I incorporate Deleuze / Guattari's ahistorical notion of deterritorialisation under different forms, and the contextualised view of deterritorialisation by Naficy (in terms of the homeland territory)

30 Gilles Deleuze / Félix Guattari: *Anti-Oedipus: Capitalism and Schizophrenia*, trans. from French by Robert Hurley / Helen R. Lane / Mark Seem. Minneapolis: University of Minnesota Press 1983, p. 212.

31 Gilles Deleuze / Félix Guattari. *Kafka: Toward a Minor Literature*, trans. from French by Dada Polan. Minneapolis: University of Minnesota Press 1986, pp. 13–17.

32 Deleuze / Guattari: *A Thousand Plateaus*, pp. 321–322.

33 Hamid Naficy: Phobic Spaces and Liminal Panics: Independent Transnational Film Genre. In: Ella Shohat / Robert Stam (eds): *Multiculturalism, Postcoloniality, and Transnational Media*. New Brunswick, NJ: Rutgers UP 2003, pp. 202–226, here p. 208.

34 Martin-Jones: *Deleuze, Cinema amd National Identity*, p. 4.

35 Ibid., pp. 4–5, 26.

and Martin-Jones (in terms of the mapping between screen territory and film narrative), and argue that the mosaic of Egoyan lies on the interactive relationship between deterritorialisation and reterritorialisation, which take both a cinematic form through framing (relationship between the extradiegetic spectator and the territory of screen space) and a narrative form (characters' relationship with territories in the diegesis) in terms of diaspora. In both aspects, detachment and dislocation occur in deterritorialisation, whereas stability and order are re-established in reterritorialisation.

In terms of the cinematic deterritorialisation and reterritorialisation, the images, which are detached from the whole territory, are deterritorialised; when they are contextualised or related back to the integral territory, they are subsequently reterritorialised. The misleading cues and deceptive turns in Egoyan's films, created by close-ups and camerawork, henceforth result from the deterritorialising power of certain images which are framed in such a way that their entirety is unrooted; these images are later reterritorialised for the sake of narrative integrity once the camera pulls back to the bigger picture. Through this deterritorialising force, Egoyan's images are set free from their fixed position and removed from their original referents. This creates space outside metric relations and spatio-temporal coordinates, simultaneously casting the spectator out of the illusion of the whole and leaving the spectator the freedom to wander in the multilateral turns and twists of the images to decipher the ensemble of mosaic pieces. Consequently, the spectator goes through the process of deterritorialisation and reterritorialisation, and disorientation and re-engagement, with the screen space while assembling the decomposed images into a mosaic picture; some guesses that the spectator makes according to the initial information turn out to be false and need to be modified in relation to the information that subsequent fragments carry. The realisation of the images' context, though delayed, always reterritorialises the spectator upon completion of Egoyan's mosaic, at the same time that Egoyan attempts to resolve the misleading threads and provide detailed psychological backgrounds for all of his characters, including minor roles with only ephemeral appearances. For example, according to Egoyan's commentary on the DVD special features of *The Adjuster*, even the fleeting appearance of a wandering crazy billboard guy had been originally designed as a destitute bankrupt builder of Noah and Hera's house, trying to be close to the world that he lost.

In fact, the initial difficulty for the spectator to decipher the deterritorialised fragments imitates the inceptive disorientation experienced by individuals in displacement or diaspora, extending from the suggestion of Baronian.[36] In both the examples of *Ararat* and *The Adjuster*, everything is puzzling in the beginning, and it is only after a prolonged process of negotiation and reterritorialisation that the mosaic of voyaging, in-betweenness, and multiplicity emerges. At the same time that the spectator is going through the mosaic during the visual experience of deterritorialisation and reterritorialisation in the film-viewing process, Egoyan's diegetic characters on screen undergo a similar kind of negotiation, being unrooted from the physical or metaphorical territory and then re-establishing it. Embedded with Egoyan's experience of displacement, many of Egoyan's characters are deterritorialised (literally separated from their territories) for socio-political or personal reasons. As Damian Sutton and Martin-Jones' example of colonialisation demonstrates that the process of deterritorialisation and reterritorialisation can be unequal and violent,[37] Egoyan's characters' reterritorialisation is also not completely benign and balanced. During their negotiation with the territory, some are deprived of many capacities and some are re-empowered after deterritorialisation. For example, the sisters Hera and Seta in *The Adjuster*, both deterritorialised from Armenia (which is subtly hinted by the Armenian sign on one of their photos sent from home) and relocated to the WASP Canadian society, can be seen as two different kinds of reterritorialisation, one being empowered and the other being deprived of some capacities. In her reterritorialisation, Hera possesses the power to rate films on a portable control panel according to official guidelines of censorship. She is usually situated close to the camera, sitting in the first row of the projection room on the left side of the frame with a blue beam of projector's light shining from the operator's booth in the background. Seta, on the other hand, deprived of speech acts in the sense of Michel de Certeau (appropriation or reappropriation of language in a particular situation of exchange under a certain cultural context)[38] because of

36 Baronian: History and Memory, Repetition and Epistolarity, p. 169.

37 Damian Sutton / David Martin-Jones: *Deleuze Reframed: A Guide for the Arts Student*. London: Tauris 2008, pp. 7–8.

38 De Certeau: *The Practice of Everyday Life*, pp. 19, 33.

her incapability to speak the language of the host territory, is isolated from the world outside the house. A silent and almost immobile character, she is often framed in medium shots sitting on a sofa front-on, in profile examining photos sent by their brother back at home, or watching tapes with extreme violence and explicit sex scenes, secretly recorded by Hera from work. Maintaining a neutral and calm demeanour, she sees the photos and watches the films without emotional reactions.

Seta's seer position links the negotiation between deterritorialisation and reterritorialisation, theorised in *A Thousand Plateaus*, with Deleuze's any-space-whatever and seer theorised in *Cinema 2*, which helps unlock the structural mosaic space. As discussed in the introduction, Deleuze observes postwar Europe as giving rise to any-space-whatever, a "deserted but inhabited" space where we "no longer know how to react".[39] This is where the direct time-image proliferates in contrast to the movement-image characterised by sensory-motor situation. The characters in the disconnected and emptied any-space-whatevers are immersed in purely optical or sound situations and no longer know how to react as *actants*; they become *seers*.[40] Although the postwar crisis in Western Europe may cease being part of our immediate perception of space, the concept of any-space-whatever regains new meanings in some contemporary situations through contextualisation. For example, Laura Marks argues against the Eurocentric position of Deleuze's any-space-whatevers and reflects upon the postcolonial and diasporic seers in Western metropolises, who are aware of the violent colonial history but physically unrooted from the territory of their origin. She posits that these any-space-whatevers of postcolonialism emerge with the migratory flow of non-Western people into Western metropolitans, for the new populations in Europe and North America displaced from the formerly repressed culture in the developing world become seers. They reside in the emptied and hollowed any-space-whatever of the West, while being aware of violent histories to which its dominant population is blind. They carry their homeland's ruins with them and "possess what Fatimah Tobing Rony (1996) calls a third eye, which allows them to perceive the dominant culture from both inside and outside"[41].

39 Deleuze: *Cinema 2*, p. xi.

40 Ibid., p. 5.

41 Marks: *The Skin of the Film*, pp. 27–28.

Approximating Marks' argument, any-space-whatevers populated by seers in this book also contextualise historical and geopolitical circumstances beyond the scope of Deleuze, instead of being restricted to the post-Second World War situation in Europe. While Hou's and Haneke's different kinds of any-space-whatevers will be illustrated in chapter 3 and 4, what is different between Marks' any-space-whatevers and any-space-whatevers in Egoyan's films here is their different reasons for displacement; the former comes from postcolonialism whereas the latter is established on the context of the Armenian Genocide. In addition, Egoyan's post-displacement and/or post-trauma any-space-whatevers are dominated by an abundance of images and mediation. The any-space-whatever of "post-displacement" reflects Egoyan's own experience of travelling, multiple identities, and negotiation with territories, and "post-trauma" refers to Egoyan's understanding of the post-Armenian Genocide through collective memories which is implied in *Next of Kin*, *Family Viewing*, and *Calendar*, and explicitly represented in *Ararat*. We can also see post-trauma at a more personal level, such as the aftermath of the school bus accident in *The Sweet Hereafter* (CA 1997) and the death of Francis' daughter in *Exotica*. In Deleuze's post-Second World War any-space-whatever, the survivors of the war in Europe were left face to face with ruins, crumbled buildings, and deserted warehouses, but the physical land remains. In contrast, the expatriate-survivors of the Armenian Genocide, like the post-displacement and post-trauma Hera and Seta in *The Adjuster*, no longer have the ruins; many have become people in diaspora scattering around the world, having physically been uprooted from their native land for survival. Their original land of Armenia before genocide, since then existing only in their collective memories, has disappeared and become unreachable. Worst of all, the genocide is at the risk of being forgotten and obliterated because of the Turkish government's persistent denials. Therefore, the seers become the silent witnesses seeing the unfolding of the chain of events but unable to come to terms with them verbally, for "they've been traumatized into silence"[42]. In this post-displacement and/or post-trauma any-space-whatever, the seers in exile, who are distanced from their original territory, possess the third eye, like Marks' seer in

42 Baronian: History and Memory, Repetition and Epistolarity, p. 162; Egoyan: Preface, p. 222.

the postcolonial any-space-whatever. They are aware of the atrocities committed in Armenia, which most of the dominant population in Western metropolis is unconcerned with. Unable to relate to the real land and to react, they resort to virtual means mediated by images to engage with their lost ones and lost territories.

To return to the example of Seta in *The Adjuster*, she is the deterritorialised and reterritorialised seer with the third eye in the media-saturated post-trauma and/or post-displacement any-space-whatever. Deterritorialised from the actual territory of the homeland, she attempts to reterritorialise herself through virtual means, going in and out of the doubly-mediated images. In fact, we can see the dynamic mapping between deterritorialisation/reterritorialisation and actualisation/virtualisation in the way she engages with the virtual in substitution for the actual in order to reterritorialise the deterritorialised self. She immerses herself in the black-and-white photos from her hometown, sent by their brother, and the recorded tapes of censored films, brought back by Hera. Having lost physical contact with Armenia, Seta's only contact with the space of her past is through photographic representation, whereas her only contact with the space of her present is through the filmic representation mediated by two cameras, one to shoot the films and the other to film the projected images on screen in the censors' projection room. Withdrawing from the actual of the surrounding environment and submitting to the world of representations, Seta reterritorialises herself in the virtual space of explicit sex and violence consumed in the territory of her host country. In her interaction with both photos and films, she is a seer, who does not know how to react with the actual space and is caught in the virtuality. We can also see the media-saturated any-space-whatever in her physical dwelling in the suburban area. Abandoned but inhabited, it is a model house for a building project which later goes bankrupt. Standing alone in the middle of the vast deserted wasteland, it is overwhelmed with images which imitate life, such as hollowed out prop books with only hard covers on the bookshelf. The advertisement billboards, erected in an empty space, are painted with the image of a typical happy middle-class WASP family of three in front of a house, representing the image that the builder wants to sell along with the houses. Instead of being rooted in the actual, the dwelling is the deserted but residential space, mediated by virtual images of different kinds. As Egoyan himself says in an unusual kind of "interview" conducted in the form of video exchanges with Paul Virilio, "It becomes difficult to distinguish between natural patterns of behavior which represent our true intentions and patterns of behavior which we create to represent our intentions as we believe will best serve our image."[43] This indistinction has been integrated in Egoyan's films in terms of the mosaic of reframed images, layered representations, and imitated behaviour. As the spaces in the end of the 20th Century are overloaded with consumable commodities and images on all channels of media, the virtual means of communication becomes similar to what Deleuze calls "deserted but inhabited"[44] platforms which record, express, or project the suppressed desire. Instead of reacting to the images in an active way, Egoyan's protagonists are instead sucked into the virtuality of images and trapped in their roles as seers. Being trapped in the image-saturated world that they create for themselves, they record, erase, rewind, and fast-forward the manipulable images, whereas they have very little control over the actuality. It is through image reconstruction and virtualisation that they attempt to reterritorialise. They resort to the process of reliving through viewing and/or through virtual mediation – pretending in a role play or viewing screen reflections and representations – in order to come to terms with the questions of their deterritorialised existence in a certain territory. As if seeing with one's own eyes is not enough to perceive, they have to see through layers of virtual images. Jonathan Romney, in his monograph on Egoyan, says, "Throughout Egoyan's work, people maintain their sense of self through recorded memories and projected fantasies, a bulwark against forgetting and self-loss. Of course, images can be projected onto a wall, but they will not stick."[45] They will not stick because, no matter how lifelike the mediated images are, they remain virtual. As virtualisation does not bring the deterritorialised characters back to engagement with the actual, it does not result in reterritorialisation. They are thus caught in the mosaic between deterritorialisation and reterritorialisation, coupled with virtualisation and actualisation, within multiple layers of mediation through TV or computer screens of different sizes, two-way mirrors, camera lenses, or paintings.

43 Atom Egoyan / Paul Virilio: Video Letter. In: Desbarats / Lageira / Riviere / Virilio: *Atom Egoyan*, pp. 105–117, here p. 107.

44 Deleuze: *Cinema 2*, p. xi.

45 Romney: *Atom Egoyan*, p. 23.

We can see how the characters are caught within different layers of mediation in the media-saturated any-space-whatever in *Family Viewing* and *Exotica*. In *Family Viewing*, the over-presence of media has numbed the characters and transformed them into seers as they review and revisit their recollection-images of the past through the virtual medium of celluloid, in which threads of subjectively manipulated images compose the narrative.[46] In the beginning of *Family Viewing*, the zapping of TV is transformed into the zapping of recollection-images and the main protagonists' portraits. Images of different natures are edited together into a mosaic of virtualities: TV programmes on polar bears and ecology, CCTV surveillance videos, home pornography, action films on a film channel, family video tapes of a random sunny day, and that of a funeral. In the constantly reframed and virtualised space, the son Van and his father Stan both look straight into the camera of their own installation, which is also Egoyan's installation, at different moments; that is, they look into the eyes of the spectator. In the beginning of the film, Van visits his Armenian grandmother Armen in an old people's home. In his attempt to switch the channels on the TV situated high in the corner, Van raises his head and looks straight into the camera, which is positioned where the TV is supposed to be. The projection device is transformed into a recording device, whose recording is projected on screen; by looking straight into the camera, Van is looking straight at the spectator. Stan, on the other hand, looks into the camera consciously knowing that it is a camera. Having the habit of recording instead of experiencing and remembering, Stan records family videos, and, subsequently, home pornography with his second wife over the previous family images. With the camera fixed on a tripod, Stan switches on the camcorder and stares at it for a few seconds. Both Van's and Stan's gazes see through instead of seeing. They are looking into the eyes of the unknown and unspecified spectator behind the doubly reframed virtuality; they are unable to react to their actual space because the layer of mechanic device blocks them from having direct contact with their immediate physical environment.

In *Exotica*, the act of looking straight at the spectator has a different dimension. In the very beginning, we see two customs inspectors behind the double-sided mirror; the more experienced, played by David Hemblen, tells the less experienced, played by Calvin Green,

46 Ibid., p. 54.

that the task of a customs officer is to observe the passengers' gestures and facial expressions while checking their bags because the look of the passenger tells more stories than their bags. A medium shot shows Thomas, the petshop owner who traffics blue hyacinth macaw eggs into Canada, looking at himself into a mirror, which is a disguised one-way glass. A reverse shot shows the opposite side of the glass/mirror through which Thomas is in fact looking right into the eyes of the two inspectors hiding behind the mirror, and also right into the camera lens and, hence, the spectator. The direct gaze into the camera, unlike the gaze in Haneke's *Funny Games* (AU 1997) and *Funny Games U.S.* (USA / FR / UK / AT / DE / IT 2007), which intentionally breaks the fourth wall to remind the spectator of their moral responsibilities during image consumption, is fully-justified in the narrative framework. Without breaking the illusion of cinema, they are the gazes which surpass the actual layer of space and penetrate the mediated layer, be it a recording machine or a mirror. Thomas and the inspectors seem to be seeing and facing each other, but Thomas' gaze bypasses the inspectors'. The same can be said about the gaze between Thomas and the spectator, who are spatially and temporally apart but meet each other thanks to the recording and projecting machines. In a way, this is a metaphor which sums up the mosaic space of Egoyan, in which human relationships are often mediated through virtual layers. The characters look at each other, but they don't really look at each other. They look at the spectator directly on the surface but they don't actually meet each other. Instead, they gaze through the actual space and into the mediated virtual layer. As discussed earlier, this is also why Egoyan's deterritorialised characters' efforts of reterritorialisation through virtualisation in the mosaic do not always work; the gazes across doubly-mediated screen bypass each other without meeting and without being reterritorialised in the actual.

In the mosaic of the actual and the virtual, in *Exotica* as well as *Family Viewing*, *Speaking Parts*, and *Calendar*, seeing is not really seeing, and "vision is not insight"[47], since experiencing is often mediated. These seers, overwhelmed by images in Egoyan's films, see through instead of seeing, and wander in the media-saturated any-space-whatevers. Media becomes their only mode of expression and their means to salvation. Unlike the uncontrollable and haunting presence of media

47 Jacinto Lageira: The Recollection of Scattered Parts. In: Desbarats / Lageira / Riviere / Virilio: *Atom Egoyan*, pp. 33–82, here p. 54.

in Haneke's *Caché* and *Funny Games*, Egoyan's multilayered virtual space is not necessarily represented as an evil being. It seems that through mediation, the diffracted redoubling of images, "the image extracted from ourselves materializes, becomes incarnate, and now begins to regard us – no longer as fantasy, but as a witness to the movements whereby we drift away from the censorship of bodies and images"[48]. Both Naficy and Baronian have noted Egoyan's use of epistolary technologies as a means of mediation, translation, and double-framing, and as a tool to conquer the difficulties of communication and connection, which are often inadequate in verbal forms.[49] It is also a way to hide behind the doubly-mediated layers. Naficy explains:

> [Video] instigates unverifiable identities, slippery relations, and absence – all because of the performativity that it encourages and the slippage it induces between self and other, here and there, and now and then. It also fans a crisis of representation by undermining the viewer's confidence in the video's reality effect. On the other hand, the live ontology, the copresence, and the immersive subjectivity of videoconferencing counter these crises of identity and verifiability.[50]

The virtual thus becomes a hiding place for Egoyan's characters. Geoff Pevere suggests that Egoyan's characters confront the confinement of their space, which is represented by mediated images, and thus look for alternatives in the manipulation of images.[51] For Egoyan's characters, memories and experiences generate the virtual and come to be mediated by technology. The deterritorialised characters are unable to directly deal with the past in general, and with the Armenian Genocide specifically, and to reterritorialise themselves, so they rely on recording technologies, such as tape recorders, video recorders, answering machines, telephones, and video conferencing to stand in for memories and engage in a process of mediation.[52] In the mosaic of deterritorialisation and reterritorialisation coupled with actualisation and virtualisation, the doubly-mediated virtuality also provides

48 Daniele Riviere: The Place of the Spectator. In: Desbarats / Lageira / Riviere / Virilio: *Atom Egoyan*, pp. 83–104, here p. 97.

49 Baronian: History and Memory, Repetition and Epistolarity, p. 161; Naficy: *An Accented Cinema: Exilic and Diasporic Filmmaking*, p. 139.

50 Ibid., p. 139.

51 Pevere: *Exotica*, p. 36.

52 Baronian: History and Memory, Repetition and Epistolarity, p. 161.

a safe distance when looking at the tragic history of Armenia, and the unspoken and unspeakable pain of genocide. As Lisa Siraganian illustrates in her analysis of *Ararat*, the way Egoyan assembles fragments of events instead of directly portraying the action in its whole reflects the difficulty of representing Armenian Genocide, which can only be implied and can hardly be told.[53] As the genocide can never be understood as a whole because of the Turkish government's denial, and no representation could be faithful enough to give justice, it can only be represented in fragments and behind virtualities. It is a safe distance from which trauma is not rendered melodramatic and historical authenticity is less likely to be challenged. This is also the understanding of deterritorialised exilic transnationals who travel in the interstitial zone of fusion and admixture,[54] who are free from established relations and able to comprehend behind layers of virtualities. For example, *Ararat*, the film with the most explicit portrayal of the Armenian Genocide, represents the genocide in the fictional director Saroyan's filmmaking process embedded within the diegesis. The film-within-the-film serves as a strategy to dismiss the charge of falsification or propaganda, while at the same time the film tackles the unspeakable horror and the Turkish government's constant denial.[55] Hence, all the unbearable atrocities depicted in *Ararat* have been placed inside the film-within-the-film frames of the mosaic narrative. The scene when the young Gorky and the photographer's son Sevan are captured by the governor of the Ottoman Empire, Cevdet Bey, starts with a slow panning of the camera which follows the torturers carrying Sevan away. Accompanied by the sound of an offscreen scream from Sevan, who is tortured and then killed by Turkish soldiers, the camera establishes Bey on the right side of a desk and Gorky on the left. After a series of shots and reverse shots of close-ups showing Gorky's muddy and frightened face and Bey's malicious and distorted expression, the camera turns clockwise while advancing at the same time until it finally reveals the diegetic filmmaker Saroyan sitting on a director's chair surrounded by the camera crew, Raffi the production assistant, a sound engineer, a big Dedo light, and the painting of Mount Ararat in the distant background of the studio.

53 Siraganian: Telling a Horror Story, Conscientiously, p. 148.

54 Naficy: Phobic Spaces and Liminal Panics: Independent Transnational Film Genre, p. 208.

55 Siraganian: Telling a Horror Story, Conscientiously, p. 148.

The seemingly actual images of Gorky's misfortune are revealed as reframed within the virtual images reenacted by a film crew. Furthermore, the entire scene is inserted between mosaic pieces of the custom officer David interrogating Raffi. Through the device of the doubly-layered virtuality, the film representation of Gorky's painful childhood experiences do not linger on. In a later sequence, which depicts a group of Armenian women being forced to dance nakedly in a circle before they are burned to death by Turkish soldiers, the film-within-a-film representation of the iniquity is juxtaposed with a close-up of the German woman recounting the sight to the doubly-mediated character Clarence Ussher (played by the diegetic character Martin, who is played by Bruce Greenwood), a two-shot of Raffi's reading of the German woman's lines in front of the customs officer David, and the fragments showing Saroyan and Raffi on set. This creates a multiple and multiplying mosaic in which the traumatising event is embedded within several layers of recounting. Instead of confronting the bloody past directly, Egoyan reframes these historical events through camerawork and editing within layers of virtuality, and puts them between mosaic pieces of different temporalities and spatialities. In the process of jumping back and forth in time, in space, and in virtualities, Egoyan achieves a kind of *mise-en-abyme*, which swirls down the depth of history and creates a mosaic of diverse time frames, spaces, and virtualities, between the ungrounding deterritorialising force and the grounding reterritorialising force.[56] The projection of images is where the actual is virtualised and where the narrative is deterritorialised, which implies "the unruly presence of a strong time-image"[57], according to Martin-Jones. This is a circular and endless movement, contrary to linear movement, and characterises the mosaic of the *mise-en-abyme* in history and the repressed trauma embedded inside. The scattered and fragmented mosaic pieces in Egoyan's films chase one another in an interchange between private and public, actual and virtual, and deterritorialisation and reterritorialisation, when the characters seek their identities and re-approach their territories.

In correlation with his multiple identities as a mosaic auteur, Egoyan's films form a mosaic of deterritorialisation and reterritorialisation in terms of the formal spectator-screen relationship and the thematic

56 Martin-Jones: *Deleuze, Cinema and National Identity*, p. 26.

57 Ibid., p. 4.

character-territory relationship. Some diegetic characters become the seer in the post-displacement and/or post-trauma any-space-whatever of media saturation, in which the seers 'see' through the doubly-mediated media. As the deterritorialised characters strive to reterritorialise in the virtual, they are further detached from the actual and are sucked into the *mise-en-abyme* of deterritorialisation and reterritorialisation, actualisation and virtualisation. The virtual becomes the seers' strategy to tackle any-space-whatevers and the filmmaker's strategy to tackle the collective trauma, which is impossible to be represented in its whole. We can see different manifestations of this circular relationship between deterritorialisation and reterritorialisation in the splitting images of Peter and Bedros in *Next of Kin*, and the photographer and Arsinée in *Calendar*.

4. *Next of Kin*

Next of Kin is Atom Egoyan's first feature film and the starting point of his exploration of the diasporic and cinematic mosaic of deterritorialisation and reterritorialisation, and actualisation and virtualisation. The Armenian element is implicit here, but through Peter's reverse direction of reterritorialisation, the film examines the act of migration in a broader sense. During the process of assimilation into the Deryans, Peter splits into an actor and an audience: Peter in a WASP family and Bedros in an ethnic family. While his past as Peter becomes doubly-mediated virtual images which only appear at intervals, his Bedros identity, taking over the screen space, becomes real, actual, and grounded. *Next of Kin* thus forms a mosaic assembled by spaces of Peter and Bedros, WASP bourgeois space and ethnically marked diasporic space, and the actual and the virtual. As discussed earlier, deterritorialisation and reterritorialisation also work at the level of the spectator-screen relationship. Whereas Peter/Bedros is deterritorialised from the biological family and reterritorialised into the adopted root, the spectator is initially deterritorialised by the use of framing and subsequently reterritorialised into the visual context.

Atom Egoyan's filmmaking career until *Calendar* appears to be an ongoing process from implicit ethnic identity to overt affiliation with Armenian culture. At the same time that Egoyan's characters interweave a mosaic of deterritorialisation and reterritorialisation,

Egoyan's filmmaking career is a mosaic which gradually assembles pieces of identities and territories. In the beginning of the process, as in *Next of Kin*, the Armenian element is rather implicit but nonetheless present in the mosaic of deterritorialisation and reterritorialisation. Like his short film *Open House* (CA 1982) and his later feature films *Family Viewing* and *The Adjuster*, the Deryans' Armenian origin is hinted at through the mise-en-scène of the family house, the language use, and diegetic folklore songs flowing in the background. The veiled signifiers of Armenianness are prevalent in the Deryans' house with traditional Armenian artifacts, food, folklore music, and the name "Deryan", but the word "Armenia" is never pronounced.[58] In fact, the signs of Armenian culture and language can work both ways for Egoyan. They can be explicitly labelled for the purpose of showing cultural specificity but they can also be disguised as an unidentifiable identity. On the one hand, Armenian names, language, and culture can be used in such an imperceptible way that they designate foreignness in a general sense and open up to a broader discussion of immigrant community and culture. On the other hand, these ethnic signs can be explicitly pronounced as a link to historical events such as the Armenian Genocide. Compared to Egoyan's later films such as *Calendar* and *Ararat*, which address the specifically signposted Armenian context, *Next of Kin* uses the foreignness of the Deryans at a metaphorical level, which embodies all immigrant families of ethnic minorities as a counter-example to WASP families. Instead of addressing the specific Armenian community with their particular historical path, Egoyan inquires into the experience of immigrants from an unusual perspective, that is, from the endeavour of a WASP Canadian boy to be assimilated into an ethnically accented family.

Written, directed, and edited by Egoyan, *Next of Kin* was produced with a budget of merely US$ 37,000, funded partially by the Canada Council and the Ontario Arts Council.[59] In this film, the WASP Canadian only child Peter, living in a spacious luxury suburban house with his wealthy parents, goes through family video therapy sessions in order to re-establish his relationship with the parents and to regain motivation for life. After watching the Deryans' therapy videos

58 Romney: *Atom Egoyan*, p. 26.

59 Watson: *Atom Egoyan*, p. x.

accidentally, Peter leaves his family to pretend to be the Deryans' son Bedros, who is adopted upon their arrival in Canada. The film is interwoven with fragments of luggage moving with a conveyor belt, Peter's unhappy family life with his wealthy parents, his happy family life with the ethnic Deryans as Bedros, actual diegetic images of therapy sessions, and the virtual doubly reframed blue images of them. The film starts with a right-to-left tracking shot, which shows chest-down truncated human bodies leaning on walls with luggage on the floor or being dragged around. This sequence is followed by a 360 degree panning revealing the panoramic view of an airport hall. It cuts to Peter lying on a king sized bed, first listening to his parents' quarrels offscreen and then putting on guitar music and mimicking guitar-playing. From the segment at Peter's home, we jump back to the setting of the airport. This time the camera is placed on a conveyor belt and moves steadily with the belt while framing a beige piece of luggage in a close-up. It is followed by a close-up of Peter's feet tapping water in their home swimming pool and a long shot of him coming out of the water and lying beside his parents' chaise lounge. Juxtaposed with the image of Peter stretching out on the diving board, we hear the extradiegetic voice-over starting with "my name is Peter" which narrates the story; the disembodied voice actually comes from a later temporal point when he becomes Bedros and records himself for a previous task assigned by the family therapist. It is only the third time we see the luggage scene that we are given the full picture of the unknown human bodies in the airport lounge being framed in long shots. (Fig. 9) After another sequence jumping back and forth between the luggage sequence and Peter's home space, we see a slow tracking rightwards capturing a therapist, Peter, his mother, and his father in close-ups in a therapy room wired with recording cameras. The camera then zooms out to reveal its position across a big window pane dividing the therapy and the recording rooms. It slowly moves right to show four monitors projecting the live virtual images of the family's therapy sessions from different cameras. (Fig. 10) Finally, the camera zooms into a big monitor which plays the flickered virtual images cut between close-ups of Peter (Fig. 11), his father and mother, and three-shots. A few sequences later, Peter picks up his luggage from the conveyor belt and walks out of the airport. This starts a new mosaic assembled by the snapshots of Peter/Bedros' interaction with the Deryans family: the father George, the mother Sonya, and the daughter Azah, accompanied by the soundtrack of Armenian tunes.

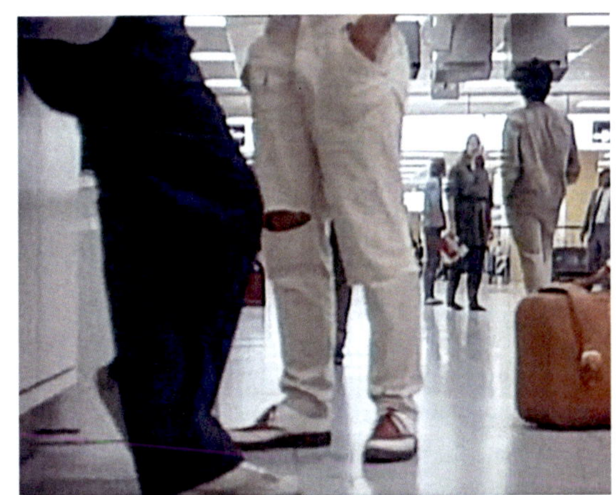

Fig. 9
A shot from the perspective of a conveyor belt. (*Next of Kin*).

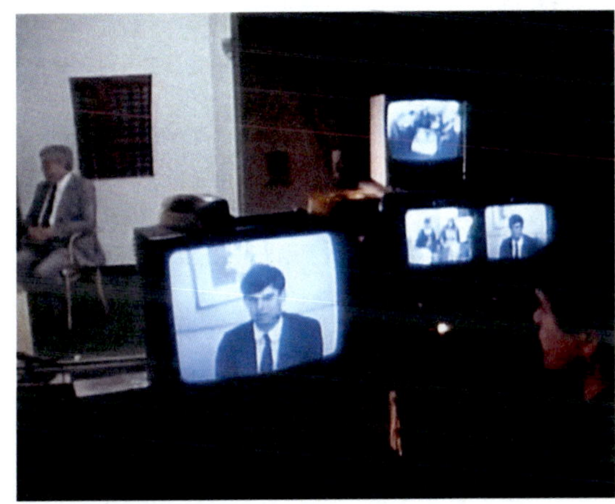

Fig. 10
Four monitors projecting family therapy sessions across a glass pane right next to the therapy room (*Next of Kin*).

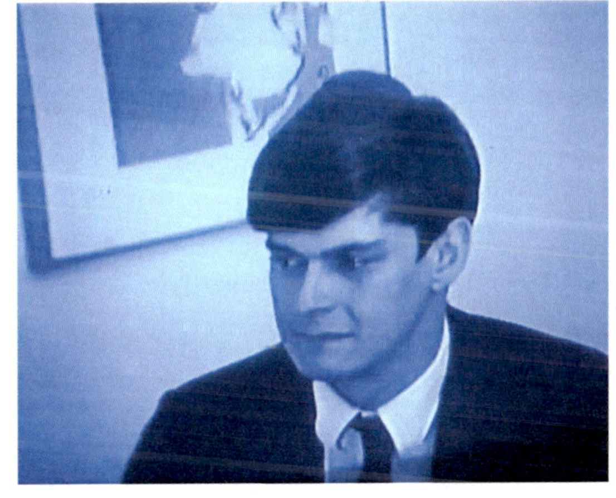

Fig. 11
Close-up of Peter after the camera zooms into a monitor (*Next of Kin*).

From the opening sequence, we can observe the cinematic mosaic of deterritorialisation and reterritorialisation in terms of the relationship between the spectator and screen space. The spectator is constantly dislocated and relocated, deterritorialised and reterritorialised, through mosaic narrative and framing. The spectator's initial feelings of disorientation approximate the feelings of people in diaspora, who arrive in a territory with totally unfamiliar signs and rules. Instead of giving an establishing master-shot, the film starts with the disorienting images of close-ups of luggage, which intentionally confuse the spectators. On the one hand, the spectator is deterritorialised from the screen image because of the cutting back and forth between seemingly unrelated sequences in the airport lobby and in Peter's spacious house; from the baggage carousel to Peter's double bed, back to the baggage carousel, and then to legs in the swimming pool. On the other hand, the spectator is deterritorialised in the opening tracking shot because the camera disembodies the mechanised and numb bodies of passengers and reveals only the legs truncated from the upper bodies. For Batia Boe Stolar, this baggage carousel scene signifies "a disembodied gaze that evokes a feeling of cultural, social, linguistic, and geographical dislocation"[60]. It defamiliarises the camera's gaze and disorientates the spectator through the use of unintelligible background noise and the alienating space of the airport. Watching these fragments, the spectator is denied the route of identification with the lower bodies because images of legs accompanied by images of luggage and the conveyor belt do not convey emotions like faces. However, the spectator, after the initial deterritorialisation from the screen space, is further reterritorialised through the dozen fragments afterwards. In the reterritorialising snippet, we see the first high angle shot so far, which captures Peter picking up his two suitcases from the carousel. The deterritorialised images of body parts are subsequently revealed to be either nameless passengers in the airport or Peter in the swimming pool once the camera zooms out to reterritorialise the initial images into a bigger territory.

Next of Kin is also a diasporic mosaic of deterritorialisation and reterritorialisation in terms of the characters' relationship with the

60 Batia Boe Stolar: The Double's Choice: The Immigrant Experience in Atom Egoyan's *Next of Kin*. In: Monique Tschofen / Jennifer Burwell (eds): *Image and Territory: Essays on Atom Egoyan*, pp. 177–192, here p. 189.

territories. It is interwoven by Peter being Peter in the original upper middle class WASP family and Peter being Bedros in the middle class Armenian family. The former family is portrayed as a machine-like, ordered, icy, and ahistorical world in comparison to the warm, colourful, spontaneous, and history-laden world of the latter. Reversing the usual WASP-centred position, in this mosaic Peter 'emigrates' from his WASP family and 'immigrates' into an Armenian family. At the intertwining and doubling core is the relationship between WASP Canadian culture and Armenian-immigrant culture in Canada, represented through Peter and his embodied Bedros, which can be seen as the "split subject"[61] as termed by John Orr and adopted by Stolar. The split subject Bedros/Peter is situated in between the two distinct cultures, "simultaneously inside and outside both cultural constructs"[62]. Emma Wilson also remarks that *Next of Kin* is a film intertwining two narratives and two culturally distinct spaces, which are the two different cultural practices in contemporary Canada.[63] Through Peter's splitting roles, Peter's biological family and his adoptive ethnic family interweave into a mosaic of Peter's past and Peter's present, Peter's emotionally unavailable and disconnected family background, and his refound connection in the ethnic family. In fact, the split subject is a double; simultaneously, the outsider Peter who observes and remarks, and the insider Bedros, who is allowed to the deepest family secret and who is empowered to act. As Peter says in the beginning of the film, one part of him is the audience looking at the unfolding of his life and the other part takes on different roles like actors. Peter/Bedros is thus at the same time the split subject between two cultures, and between Peter/Bedros the spectator and Peter/Bedros the actor. We can see his splitting in the recorded video footage of psychological therapy sessions, in which Peter obediently answers the therapist's questions and observes the therapist working with patients from the detached position of a spectator.

In this mosaic of deterritorialisation (from the WASP family and from the role as Peter) and reterritorialisation (into the Armenian family and the role as Bedros), the act of viewing as a spectator and

61 John Orr: *Contemporary Cinema*. Edinburgh: Edinburgh UP 1998, p. 119; Stolar: The Double's Choice, p. 178.

62 Ibid., p. 178.

63 Wilson: *Atom Egoyan*, pp. 14–15.

acting as an actor is Peter/Bedros' way of demarcating territories. The spectator Peter/Bedros uses the deterritorialising force to alienate himself from the original territory; the actor side of Peter/Bedros enables him to camouflage himself and reterritorialise himself into the new territory of residence. Therefore, at the same time that he deterritorialises himself from his WASP bourgeois family, he reterritorialises himself by inserting himself into an ethnically accented family. When Peter/Bedros is reterritorialised into the Deryans during the second half of the film, he becomes attuned to Armenian dishes and emotionally attached to the family. Meanwhile, the fragments of Peter/Bedros in the Deryans overtake those of Peter in his biological family, and appear under the form of actual diegetic images at length. The images of Peter's original family, however, are inserted into the diegesis only very briefly as the reframed virtual images. As a result, the splitting Peter/Bedros' deterritorialisation and reterritorialisation maps with the images' actualisation and virtualisation. As Stolar puts it, "The immigrant other is thus invested with the autonomy of the real, whereas the normative WASP Canadian is reduced to the level of mimic or copy."[64] In the mosaic of deterritorialisation and reterritorialisation, Peter's deterritorialisation from his original WASP family is virtualised, whereas his reterritorialisation in the Deryans family is actualised. At the same time that Peter is reterritorialised into the Deryans, Peter's role as a WASP boy ceases existing as actual diegetic images and appears only as the bluish doubly-mediated virtual images. In the sequence when Peter/Bedros and Azah have a siblings' talk on swings in a park outdoors, filmed with a high-angle shot, their conversation is intruded upon by very brief snapshots of the bluish virtual images of Peter in close-ups, taken from the footage filmed in a psychiatric session. The intercutting between the static medium two-shots (the shots which encompass a view of two people) with natural colours and the fleeting mediated blurry image with a blue tone projected on small TV screens outside the therapy room jumps between Peter's past life in his original WASP family and his new reterritorialised life as Bedros. The past life with his biological family, which is supposed to be real and actual, is in fact trapped in the virtual image which is doubly-mediated, framed, modified, and shaded with unnatural colours. The images of his past life are manipulated by the camera's position in the therapy room, and subject to

64 Stolar: The Double's Choice, p. 178.

the camera's zooming and the editing of the footage. These snapshots are only inserted very briefly, like a cursory recollection-image which haunts Peter subconsciously. The images of Bedros, on the other hand, are the ones with natural colours and without mediation or virtuality, for Bedros' identity provides Peter with a more autonomous image with a more substantial existence and a more grounding power of reterritorialisation. When Peter the passive son in his wealthy WASP family becomes a dynamic young man through his assimilation into the ethnic Deryans family, his reterritorialised life also occupies an image in the open air, which is no longer reframed by mediation. The grounding force of the real and the process of actualisation, which are generated in the process of reterritorialisation in the Armenian family, are further demonstrated in the closing scene. Contrary to an opening sequence in which Peter pretends to play the guitar to the tunes of Albéniz's *Asturias* from the radio (which is, in fact, a recording of Egoyan), in the closing scene, under the reterritorialised identity of Bedros, he plays *Asturias*, though at a slower pace, for real. The camera slowly pans from Bedros playing the guitar on the bed rightwards to Azah pasting Bedros' photo on a family album by the window. In the shared flat with Azah, Peter, instead of being a simulacral image of pretension, actualises the act of pretending and gains his real existence in the reterritorialisation. Peter's reterritorialisation into Bedros is the reverse of the homecoming reterritorialisation, because Peter is, in fact, dissociated from his original social status and his biological parents, while being integrated in a family with whom he shares no cultural or blood bonds. The reversed direction of reterritorialisation is expressed formally in the fragments of the luggage conveyor belt. As *Next of Kin* starts with a right-to-left tracking shot from the angle of a luggage on a conveyor belt, accompanied by humming noises of machines, it works in opposition to the left-to-right Western orthographical conventions, and cinematically portrays Peter/Bedros' reverse reterritorialisation.

The mapping between deterritorialisation/reterritorialisation and actualisation/virtualisation of diegetic images is further complicated by the physical or audial entry into, and exit from, the screen frames of the director Egoyan, who has a self-conscious relationship with his autobiographical background as the second generation of Armenian diasporic immigrants. Audially, Egoyan's presence enters the frame by his own recording of the Spanish guitar piece, Albéniz's *Asturias*, which Peter listens to while his parents argue downstairs in the beginning of the film. The scene of Peter mimicking guitar-playing to the music played by the director Egoyan hints at a veiled mapping between Egoyan the director and Peter the character.[65] Whereas Egoyan is reterritorialised in his natural root of Armenian culture after entering the University of Toronto, Peter is reterritorialised in the adopted root of the Deryans at about the same age. At the birthday party for Peter/Bedros in the end of the film, Egoyan, along with real members of the Armenian community in Toronto, acts as an extra.[66] He appears side by side with Peter/Bedros' mother Sonya singing, cheering, and clapping when the camera turns counter clockwise 180 degrees from capturing the reaction of the surprised Peter/Bedros to the partygoers. He appears for the second time during Peter/Bedros' lengthy speech, when the camera scans the crowd again, this time 360 degrees clockwise. On both occasions, Egoyan's face is framed in close-ups for several seconds and can be easily recognised. This unambiguous presence of the filmmaker in front of the camera mixes up the diegesis with the world of the extradiegetic filmmaking process, and blends the world behind the camera and in front of the camera. Even at the moments when Egoyan is not within the screen frame physically or audially, the juxtaposition between different sides of the camera is foregrounded through the doubly-mediated images which signal the presence of someone behind a camera. As described earlier, during the sequences of family therapy, the camera zooms out of the actual therapy room, pans right to the monitors, and zooms into the grainy bluish doubly-mediated images on screen. Later on, immediately after Peter watches the Deryans' therapy videos, we can see a swift and unexpected cut to a bluish grainy doubly-mediated close-up of Peter. The camera subsequently zooms out from the close-up and pans left to look at the therapy room across glass panes, and then downwards to focus again on the double images projected on a monitor. In fact, this sequence, which starts with the close-up of the virtual images, works in reverse direction compared to the earlier sequence of family therapy, which starts from the actual and zooms in to the virtual bluish image. Through constantly going in and out of the virtual images, the mosaic is interwoven by the director's images

65 Romney: *Atom Egoyan*, p. 28.
66 Wilson: *Atom Egoyan*, p. 19.

and the images captured by someone else behind another camera. Seeing the mingling between the actual diegetic images and the reframed images shot by another camera, the spectator is rendered aware of the presence of someone behind the camera.

Next of Kin, carrying the implicit Armenianness of Egoyan as well as the implication of migration and assimilation in general, thus demonstrates a diasporic and cinematic mosaic of deterritorialisation and reterritorialisation, coupled with actualisation and virtualisation, through the splitting identities of Peter/Bedros. In the unusual direction of diaspora, whereas Peter/Bedros is deterritorialised from his original WASP family and reterritorialised into the Armenian Deryans, his screen presence in the former context is virtualised and in the latter instance is actualised. We only see Peter/Bedros with his biological family in brief snapshots of doubly-mediated images, but Peter/Bedros in the Deryans becomes sustaining actual images shot both indoors and outdoors. The filmmaker Egoyan's visual and audial presences also add an extra layer of extradiegetic space into the mosaic. Cinematically, this mosaic is experienced through the spectator's deterritorialisation from the screen space, through truncation of images by framing, and reterritorialisation back in it, through visual contextualisation of the formerly truncated images.

5. *Calendar*

Calendar, the turning point in Egoyan's career, is the first film in which he clearly foregrounds Armenianness and his diasporic multiple identities, encompassing both the ancestors' culture and the host culture. It was filmed in the transitional phase when Armenia had just become an independent nation after the disintegration of the Soviet Union, which enabled the realisation of the film. Whereas Armenian national identity underwent a period of redefinition during the filmmaking, Egoyan went through the process of negotiating his role as an assimilated Canadian director of Armenian descent. As the endeavours of the diegetic Canadian photographer of Armenian heritage, played by Egoyan himself, to reconcile with his roots in Armenia fail, the Armenian bond that he shares with his wife, played by his real-life spouse Arsinée Khanjian, breaks down. His initial thought of reconstructing national history and personal bonds through framing calendar-looking images is forced to be modified when it becomes clear that images speak on their own. In this section, I will demonstrate the mosaic space of multilayered circuits of deterritorialisation and reterritorialisation, in relation to both personal and collective territories, and actualisation and virtualisation.

In the film, Atom Egoyan himself plays the main character, a photographer who is entrusted with the task of photographing churches in Armenia for a calendar. His relationship with his wife Arsinée, who translates for him, falls apart as a mutual attraction grows between the wife and their Armenian driver, Ashot. Their marriage bond, which is closely connected with their shared identities as second-generation Armenian immigrants, becomes more and more fragile as they visit churches and listen to stories recounted by the driver. As the film progresses, it becomes obvious that the photographer and his wife Arsinée represent two different degrees of assimilation and two different approaches to their ancestors' land. The former, like Egoyan himself before he entered university, is fully assimilated into the host culture and holds lukewarm attitudes towards the ancestors' land, where he never resided and whose language he does not speak. The latter, however, like Arsinée Khanjian, is brought up in the minority community in Canada bilingually and biculturally. She feels at once at ease with her Armenian origin and her image in Armenia. As the film jumps between film footage shot in Armenia and Canada, shaky bluish grainy Super-8 video footage, and diegetic film in natural colours, snippets of different time frames, spaces and virtualities permeate each other into an undecipherable mosaic of images, circling around deterritorialisation and reterritorialisation, and actualisation and virtualisation.

Calendar's mosaic is composed of the shooting of twelve churches for twelve images on a calendar, edited together with snippets which capture the photographer back in Toronto having dinner with twelve escort girls. In the first shot, we see an immobile frame of Gabdavank on the hill against the sky, with a car driving up the zigzagging path. This initial actual image later appears as a still photo for the month of January on a calendar hanging next to a phone by a water cooler. Several sequences later the image of February on the same calendar leads to a moving image shot from exactly the same angle with a static camera. The interplays and mutual transformations between the still photos on the calendar and the moving images shot in films compose the whole film. On-location shooting of landscapes in Armenia framed by static camera is repetitively fossilised into a calendar image of a month. In return, the still image on the calendar is animated into a moving film footage, shot from exactly the same camera angle. For each month, there is thus a carefully framed photo of a church in Armenia, apart from one pagan temple (Garni in June), which projects national imagery for people in diaspora. Still images, hung on the wall of the photographer's house in Canada, and the moving images, which are at once recollection-images and recorded film footage, are neither identical replicas of one another nor separate entities. Each pair of images leaks into each other's presence and enables the spectator to travel in and out of the photographer's present that is passing and past that is being preserved.[67] Whereas images alternate between visual mosaic pieces of different temporalities, spatialities, and virtualities, the sound, including the music component and Arsinée's voice translating back and forth between Armenian and English, traverses in-between these pieces and constantly leaks into neighbouring images from a different space and time frame. Here, the interweaving of the actual and the virtual, present and past, Armenia and Canada, can be understood through Deleuze's time-image. In *Cinema 2,* Deleuze describes time as in the constant process of splitting into the present that passes and the past that is preserved.[68] No objective recording of the past is possible as the past is preserved among several virtual images that exist simultaneously and confront each other. He calls the continual exchange of actual and virtual images, which are constituted around the splitting of time, "time-image". As Marks reiterates, "the original point at which actual and virtual images reflect each other produces, in turn, a widening circuit of actual and virtual images like a hall of mirrors"[69]. Seen in this light, *Calendar* is a visual rendering of the Deleuzian crystal, encompassing the past that is preserved and the present that is passing.[70] Memories of a nation and of a person fuse together into something distinct and yet indiscernible. Jumping back and forth between the actual and the virtual, and between Armenia and Canada, the present in Canada keeps progressing whereas the past keeps being recalled back. Images

67 Deleuze: *Cinema 2*, p. 123.

68 Ibid.

69 Marks: *The Skin of the Film*, p. 65.

70 Deleuze: *Cinema 2*, p. 123.

in *Calendar* simultaneously project the breakup of the relationship, which is about to happen, which is happening, and which has happened. Simultaneously and inexplicably, the photographer is about to be deterritorialised in his ancestors' land, he is being deterritorialised, and he has been deterritorialised. The narrative thus unfolds in the coexistence of different sheets of the past.[71] This is how *Calendar* is the turning point of Egoyan's career, when Egoyan's attention on ethnic minorities is manifestly embodied in his fully recognised Armenian origins; it is not by chance that *Calendar* reaches the summit of time-image, mingling the virtual and the actual into a mosaic about territory, memory, and loss in life.

The segments set in Armenia all take place around the photographing of calendar images carrying the projected national symbols, which are collectively remembered by the Armenians in diaspora. As Wilson reminds us, "The calendar is one of those that, in the diaspora, represents the beauty of a homeland for a dispossessed and dissembled people"[72]. This is valid for those who are physically distant from the actual land but remain emotionally attached to it. For the photographer, however, the calendar reminds him of the painful memories of the shooting process, which at the same time mark both his physical and emotional deterritorialisation from the ancestors' land and from his wife. In contrast to other seer characters, such as Seta in *The Adjuster* who is deterritorialised from the homeland and does not know how to react to her destination of reterritorialisation, the photographer in *Calendar* is deterritorialised from his ancestral land because of his reterritorialisation and thorough assimilation; it is in fact the supposed homeland Armenia that becomes the post-displacement any-space-whatever for the photographer. At the same time that Armenia becomes the post-displacement any-space-whatever, which the deterritorialised photographer does not know how to react to, the images are also cinematically deterritorialised from their anchorage on actuality. We can see that the statically framed images shot in Armenia, replicating the camera angle of still photos on a pre-existent calendar, are indiscernible from 'real' recollection images and mechanical memories, that is, between the virtual images on the brain as a screen and the doubly-mediated

71 Deleuze: *Cinema 2*, pp. 96, 101.

72 Wilson: *Atom Egoyan*, p. 61.

virtual images recorded by the camera. Unlike free-flowing recollection images, the frame is fixed and one-directional. Unlike mechanical memories, the film footage, with film quality far better than the images produced by a V-8 camcorder, does not seem to be recorded from the equipment they brought along, which is composed of a photographic camera and a V-8 camcorder. The images' origins are thus indiscernible because they are at the same time the diegetic photographer's recollection-images and the extradiegetic director's images; they imitate the photographer's camera angle and also imply the director Egoyan behind the photographer. There are thus several crossovers between the actual and the virtual, because both of them fail to define these images which are on the borderline in-between. With the juxtaposition between various layers of virtualities and the mapping of the virtual double with the actual, it becomes impossible to pinpoint the actual images of Armenia. In addition, what appears on screen in the Armenian parts is at the same time the diegetic couple the photographer and Arsinée, and the extradiegetic couple Atom Egoyan and Arsinée Khanjian. The calendar on the wall is at the same time the calendar of twelve months and the process of filming these twelve images. The audience, in their turn, are immersed in the indiscernibility between the virtual and the actual to the extent that some wrote to Egoyan feeling sorry for his separation from his wife, which happened on screen and was taken for real.[73] In the mosaic of the virtual and the actual throughout *Calendar*, virtual sheets of the past keep intruding in de-actualized peaks of present.[74] As Deleuze writes:

> An actual particle has its virtual double, which barely diverges from it at all; an actual perception has its own memory as a sort of immediate, consecutive or even simultaneous double. [...] [T]here is coalescence and division, or rather oscillation, a perpetual exchange between the actual object and its virtual image: the virtual never stops becoming actual. The virtual image absorbs all of a character's actuality, at the same time as the actual character is no more than a virtuality.[75]

73 Pevere: *Exotica*, pp. 65–66.

74 Deleuze: *Cinema 2*, p. 126.

75 Gilles Deleuze: *Dialogue II*, trans. from French by Eliot Ross Albert / Barbara Habberjam / Hugh Tomlinson. London: Continuum 2006, pp. 113–114.

In fact, the photographer and Arsinée have exchanged roles in the actual and the virtual in relation to their deterritorialisation and reterritorialisation and their screen presences are interwoven into a mosaic of *mise-en-abyme*. The photographer and Arsinée have completely reversed presences in Armenia and in Canada, and their growing alienation is reflected in their presence in different layers of virtualities. They become each other's virtual double, both caught in the circuit between the present that passes and the past that is preserved, the actual and the virtual, and deterritorialisation and reterritorialisation. Contrary to his wife Arsinée's perception, Armenia, from which the photographer is deterritorialised, is the virtual space of the past and Canada, to which he is reterritorialised, is the actual space of the present. Images filmed in Armenia take the spectator in and out of memories and time from the photographer's perspective. During their photo-shooting trip, the physical body of the photographer, always behind the viewfinder of his camera, is visually absent from the landscape of Armenia (Fig. 12), apart from his finger, which occasionally points at certain objects, and his shadow across the façade of the church, captured on the super-8 bluish images. His voice, often in a grumpy and commanding tone, manages to enter the diegetic world and penetrates the images, but the incomprehensibility of his language in the surroundings of Armenia disempowers him; his voice can only be understood and acquire meaning through Arsinée's translation. In Canada, however, the photographer is framed head-on in medium shots in the middle of the screen, with his voice well understood and connected with the visual presence. (Fig. 13) Arsinée, on the other hand, is visually present in Armenia, into which she is reterritorialised, but only audially present in Canada, from which she is deterritorialised, with her voice transmitted by an answering machine. Whereas the photographer is an outsider in his own homeland who only occupies space vocally, Arsinée becomes an outsider in their home in Canada. In the setting of Armenia, the photographer lives in the offscreen virtual space, whereas in Canada it is Arsinée who lives in the offscreen virtual. Armenia for the photographer and Canada for Arsinée are the spaces of the past, which are preserved for them as virtual beings but from which they are physically and emotionally deterritorialised. Meanwhile, the photographer is reterritorialised and actualised in Canada, whereas it is in Armenia that Arsinée is reterritorialised. In fact, their physical and auditory

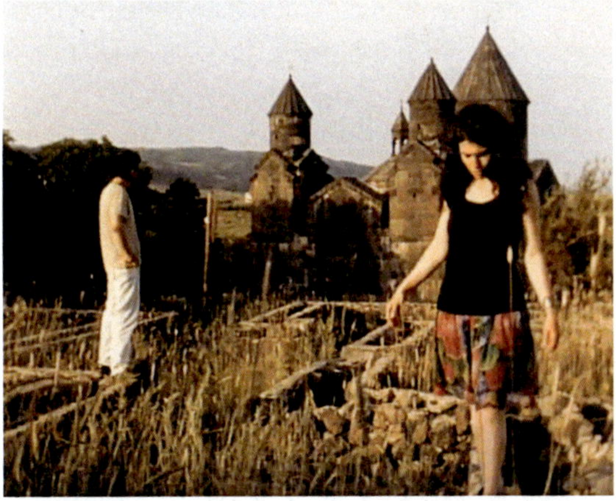

Fig. 12
The physical body of the photographer is absent from the landscape of Armenia captured by his camera (*Calendar*).

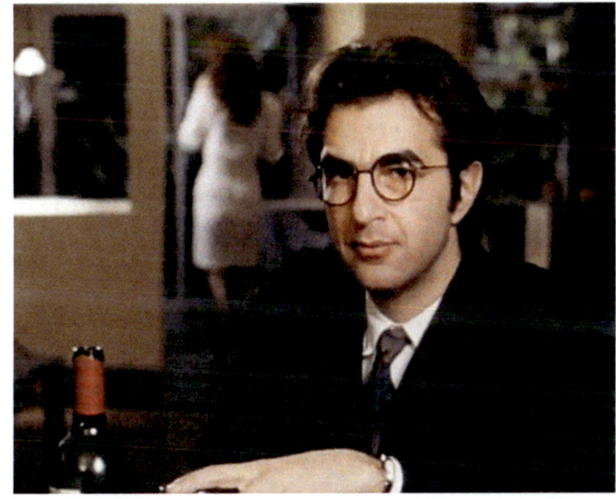

Fig. 13
In Canada the photographer dominates the screen both in terms of visual and audial presence (*Calendar*).

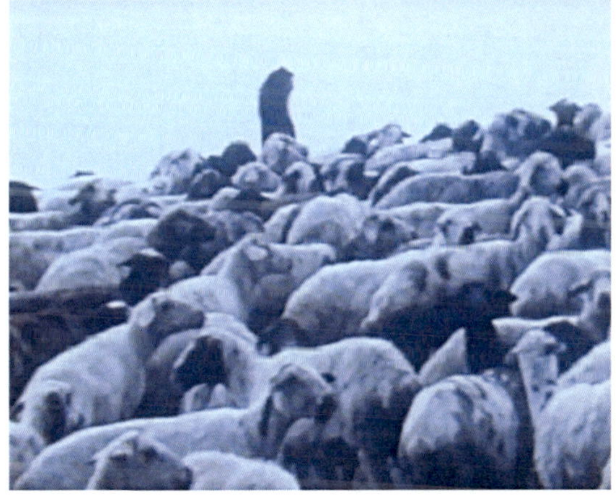

Fig. 14
The video footage with Arsinée chasing flocks of sheep is rewatched by the photographer (*Calendar*).

presences, instead of being synchronized and integrated, are dislocated and disjointed; images and sound work as separate planes of virtuality and criss-cross each other.

Marks has also remarked on the juxtaposition between the actual, which is the present that passes which can never be recalled, and the virtual, the past that is preserved within the institutionalised representation of the moment, in *Calendar*. Yet her argument focuses more on the processes of memory; the conflict between virtual images and the recollection-images which are not preserved through virtual means, which is, the clash between official recorded representation and private memories and unofficial history.[76] Here, the virtual and the actual within the mosaic are understood in relation to the territory, and the photographer and Arsinée's reverse presences in the virtual and the actual are in fact linked with deterritorialisation and reterritorialisation, their approaching or distancing from the territory. Whereas Arsinée's physical presence lies in the virtual space of photographed or filmed Armenia from the past, which is doubly-mediated from reality, she is willingly reterritorialised in the smooth Armenia. Through this reterritorialising force, Arsinée actualises Armenia, despite being preserved in virtual images of the past. The photographer, alienated and deterritorialised in Armenia, endeavours to reproduce this process of deterritorialisation in his return to striated Canada by hiring escort girls with different ethnic origins and languages. During the dinner shared by the photographer and twelve escort girls, in twelve snapshots, we see them trying in vain to connect with each other. When the photographer distributes the last drop of wine in two glasses, an escort girl leaves the table and pretends to be talking on the phone in an 'exotic' language (such as Arabic, Italian, German, Hebrew, and Russian) and erotic tones. Meanwhile, the photographer tries to write a letter to his wife. It is only through repetitive role-play, which replicates his feelings of incomprehension as an outsider, that he is able to reconstruct and express what he has experienced in Armenia. As Wilson phrases it, his ritual "restages his wife's departure and its conflicting motivations"[77]. The photographer, on the surface dwelling in the actual 'present' Canada, relives deterritorialisation through repetitive role-play under the gaze of the

76 Marks: *The Skin of the Film*, pp. 40–41.

77 Wilson: *Atom Egoyan*, p. 71.

projected national images of Armenia on the calendar. Caught in this perpetual circuit surrounding the projected nation and the projected self, the photographer is unable to reconcile with the splitting of time, which maps with the splitting of Canadian and Armenian identities. It is only at the end of the film when he finally abandons role-play and engages with the escort girl of November as actual individuals that he is able to break from the eternal circuit and embark upon another splitting circuit. This is achieved through his jumping out of the circuit of reliving the process of deterritorialisation and opens up to reterritorialisation.

As the characters and the images wander in and out of virtualities within the mosaic space, Armenia and Canada have become two distinct spaces, the former fluid, smooth, and virtual, and the latter formulaic, striated, and actual. Armenia can be seen as a smooth space with continuous variation, where one occupies without counting and where the points are subordinated to the trajectory, according to Deleuze and Guattari's term in *A Thousand Plateaus*.[78] Canada, on the other hand, becomes a striated space with fixed elements and distinct forms where one counts in order to occupy and where lines and trajectories tend to be subordinated to points. They become two kinds of images in the mosaic. The former is a nomadic space and "A Body without Organs"[79], while the latter is a sedentary space and an organism.[80] Furthermore, the smooth and the striated can be seen through Egoyan's cinematic portrayal of these two spaces. Armenia is shot exclusively outdoors and in the open, where Arsinée and the driver stand in the knee-high grass, sit on random rocks, and walk on ruins of ancient dwelling. Although in the film footage the camera is static and frames the churches and landscapes in such a way as to recreate the images on the calendar, Arsinée and the driver are fluid entities inside the frame. Their presence, being spontaneous and unstructured, faces the camera but addresses the invisible photographer behind the camera. Bodies are free to wander and occupy any corner of the screen frame. Video footage shot by Egoyan the director during his trip to Armenia further interrupts the static moving images and breaks the neat division between the film footage in Canada and that

78 Deleuze / Guattari: *A Thousand Plateaus*, pp. 523–551.
79 Ibid., pp. 165–184.
80 Ibid., pp. 525–528.

in Armenia. We see Arsinée chasing a huge flock of bleating sheep, and dancing with the singer in an errant band. Video footage thus brings in a new dimension to the image and another sheet of the past. It appears as the footage shot by the character the photographer, but in fact is shot by Egoyan the director, during his 'real' first visit to Armenia. In video images the camera tracks, wanders, and meanders. It collects bits and pieces of memory-images without focusing on any movement. The video footage with Arsinée chasing flocks of sheep is also subject to rewinding and rewatching by the photographer, who clings to memory-images of the process of the breakdown of their relationship. (Fig. 14)

On the other hand, the only setting in Canada is the dining room and the room with a calendar on the wall and a phone on a water cooler in Egoyan and Khanjian's real-life house. It is a confined and demarcated space where objects and furniture have their fixed position. People also have their fixed positions. The physical body of the photographer is always shown sitting at the dining table, and his escort girls are either shown at the table or standing by the wall when they make erotic phone calls in foreign languages. There are only three camera angles when shooting the house. The camera either faces the wall and the hanging calendar, captures the photographer with or without escort girls in front of the dining table with the phone visible in the background, or gives a reverse shot of the previous one by focusing on the escort girls holding a phone with the back of the photographer in the background. In the striated space of Canada, Egoyan and his escort girls' bodies are puppet-like and formulaic, as if on a theatre stage, their movement having been rehearsed and contrived.

The complicated multilayered and multilayering mosaic space of deterritorialisation and reterritorialisation in *Calendar* is interwoven with the spatial configurations of the actual and the virtual and the smooth and the striated in relation to the territories in Armenia and Canada. It becomes a Deleuzian crystal, which assembles the past in Armenia that is preserved in the doubly-mediated virtual images and recalled back, and the present in Canada that is passing and progressing. During the creation of twelve calendar images, the photographer and his wife Arsinée, physically occupying the striated Canada and the smooth Armenia respectively, are splitting images of the virtual and the actual, mapped with their distanciation from a land and reappropriation of a land. Having been fully reterritorialised and assimilated in Canada, Armenia becomes the photographer's post-displacement any-space-whatever from which he is deterritorialised. By recreating the feelings of language incomprehension in Canada, he relives deterritorialisation and the process of separation from Arsinée. Arsinée, on the other hand, as his virtual double, is reterritorialised back to the ancestors' land by actualising the virtual, and occupies a fluid existence in the smooth space of Armenia. In the following chapter, I will demonstrate that Hou, though also engaging with a vertical mosaic laden with historical concerns, builds a very different mosaic through the multilayered mise-en-scène on screen corresponding to the architectural features in the East Asian context.

Chapter 3
Hou Hsiao-hsien: Historical Mosaic of Multilayered Mise-en-Scène

1. Introduction

This chapter on Hou Hsiao-hsien continues the exploration of vertical mosaic, which composes a mosaic by digging deep into history. However, the mosaic of Hou, instead of deterritorialising and reterritorialising images like Atom Egoyan, layers the space of the mise-en-scène in correspondence to the historical depth of the subject matter. In fact, Hou's mosaic of the layered mise-en-scène is constructed through both temporal and spatial distance. When the subject matter delves deeper into history, we see more partial obstructions of the mise-en-scène in front of the camera and, hence, the space is more layered. In fact, the layers of screen space are facilitated by fluid and flexible East Asian architecture, which has been explored by the 'half-outsider half-insider' position of Hou's camera right outside the architectural threshold between two rooms. The camera at the 'half-outsider half insider' position keeps a certain distance from the filmed object so that it both captures it and allows partially obstructing layers to come between them. This liminal position is at the same time the position of the camera and the position of some politically disenfranchised Taiwan-born characters in Hou's films, who are seers in the postwar postcolonial any-space-whatever in Taiwan. They see the unfolding of historical events but are not *actants*. It is also the liminal position of the spectator who understands Taiwanese history and is conscious of the seer position of the politically disenfranchised characters. This kind of mosaic space correlates with Hou's multiple belongings as a mainlander by birth and nativist by demeanor, and transnational filmmaking mode as a Taiwan-based mosaic auteur who integrates transnational funding, cast, crew, and distribution networks from Chinese-speaking areas, Japan, and France through travelling.

Hou's status as a mosaic *auteur* will first be examined in terms of his multiple identities and filmmaking milieus. Hou's construction of a mosaic of multilayered spatial planes in the mise-en-scène will then be analysed in relation to the 'half-outsider half-insider' seer position of the camera, which enables the screen space to fold with the depth of history. Instead of comparing it with multifocal Chinese paintings, as discussed by Hao Dazheng and Ni Zhen in *Cinematic Landscapes*[1], I will argue that the unique context of East Asian architecture has provided Hou with a different method for constructing mosaic space, which differs from Atom Egoyan, Alejandro González Iñárritu and Michael Haneke. Finally, detailed analyses of *Good Men, Good Women* and *Three Times* will follow an examination of Hou's oeuvre as a whole.

2. Hou Hsiao-hsien, Multiple Identities and Border-crossing

Hou is a mosaic auteur who started border-crossing from an early age and possesses multiple identities because of historical consequences. As an infant, he experienced forced migration from mainland China to Taiwan with his Cantonese family because of the retreat of the Nationalist government KMT (Kuomindang). As a filmmaker, he has made films in five language varieties (Southern Min, Mandarin Chinese, Suzhou Dialect, Japanese, and French) and constantly pulls funding from multinational resources. Although Hou's films have often been analysed in terms of 'Chineseness' and his portrayal of historical events,[2] his filmmaking milieus in fact reach beyond the Chinese-speaking world to Japan and France, and his films are widely consumed in international arthouse cinema circuits.

Born in Guangdong Province, a southern coastal province of Mainland China, Hou moved to Kaohsiung in the south of Taiwan

1 Hao Dazheng: Chinese Visual Representation: Painting and Cinema. In: David Desser / Linda C. Ehrlich (eds): *Cinematic Landscapes: Observations on the Visual Arts and Cinema of China and Japan*. Texas: University of Texas Press 1994, pp. 45–62; Zhen Ni: Classical Chinese Painting and Cinematographic Signification. In: Ibid., pp. 63–80.

2 For example: Kuan-Hsing Chen / Paul Willemen / Ti Wei: Editorial Introduction. In: *Inter-Asia Cultural Studies* 9,2 (2008), pp. 169–172.

in 1948, at the age of two. At that time, his parents retreated from Mao's communist China (People's Republic of China aka PRC) with the defeated Nationalists KMT government led by Chiang Kai-chek (Republic of China aka ROC) at the end of the Civil War, post-Second World War. Due to these historical circumstances, Hou experienced enforced border-crossing because of rotations of political power. New immigrants from the mainland, like Hou's family, formerly resisted Japan during the Second World War. Often referred to as 'mainlanders', they have gone through very different historical trajectories from the residents in Taiwan. The latter, often called 'nativists', are the Chinese immigrants who already lived in Taiwan for several generations before the fifty-year Japanese colonisation began in 1895. These two major groups in Taiwan were segregated in different dwelling villages[3] and were divided by political, ideological, linguistic, and cultural barriers. Mainlanders aspired to 'recover' the mainland from Mao's Communist Party in order to return to their hometown; nativists' initial excitement about being free from Japanese colonisation was substituted by disappointment and discontent with the shattered and corrupted KMT military government, who spoke unfamiliar dialects and behaved in a 'foreign' way. Linguistically, the nativists, who are predominantly from the south of China,[4] spoke Hokkien,[5] Hakka, or aboriginal languages in family settings and used Japanese for education and administration during the Japanese occupation. Their lingua franca was Japanese, the language imposed by the colonising Japanese government. The mainlanders, having immigrated

3 The mainlanders are assigned accommodation in a community called juan-cun, where new immigrants from different provinces with different dialects, cuisines, and habits mix and mingle. The unique juan-cun culture has been popular materials for TV drama and theatre in Taiwan in recent years. Some examples can be seen in many of Wang Weizhong's productions such as the theatrical play *Bao Dao Yi Cun* (2008).

4 Early immigrants are mainly composed of people from Fujian and Kuantong provinces because these two regions, plagued with political instabilities and food shortages, have easier access to Taiwan by boat, thanks to their proximity.

5 Hokkien, literally meaning "Fujian", which is a province where people use the dialect bearing its name, is called Southern Min in sociolinguistics, "Taiyu", literally "Taiwanese", in Taiwan, and Minnanyu (Minnan dialect) or Xiayu in the PRC; Jeremy E. Taylor: From Transnationalism to Nativism? The Rise, Decline and Reinvention of a Regional Hokkien Entertainment Industry. In: *Inter-Asia Cultural Studies* 9,1 (2008), pp. 62–81, here p. 63. It is the dialect used by the majority of the population in Taiwan (70 %) and its use very often connotes political and ideological meanings.

from diverse Chinese provinces instead of predominantly from the South, carried with them numerous varieties of dialects which are mutually incomprehensible. They use Mandarin Chinese, the dialect in the north, as a common language. The situation is further complicated by the presence of aboriginal tribes, which were never taken as a cinematic subject in Hou's films and very rarely represented in Taiwanese cinema until Wei Te-sheng's *Seediqbate* (TW 2011). Given the complicated ethnic, linguistic, cultural, and political situation, the KMT government took stringent measures to maintain control on this island, which was foreign to them. The accumulated tension and misunderstanding resulted in serious conflicts, such as the February 28 Incident in 1947, triggered by a dispute between a black market cigarette vendor and a police agent. It consequently evolved into violent encounters between the nativists and the mainlanders, followed by the Nationalist government's repression and some thirty thousand deaths.[6] It is in the aftermath of the 28 February Incident, the White Terror, and the antagonism between the Nationalists and the nativists that Hou grew up. Despite his mainlander family background, Hou fully assimilated himself in the nativist culture in Southern Taiwan, characterised by the predominant use of Hokkien dialect. His family background and grassroots demeanour thus become the two paradoxically contradictory yet integral elements of his character, and Hou becomes someone who cannot clearly be categorised as belonging either to the mainlander group or the nativist group, but as possessing multiple identities.

However, most analytical works on Hou, instead of stressing Hou's multiple identities across categories, focus on Hou's status as a national filmmaker within the bigger framework of Chinese cinema. As Emilie Yueh-Yu Yeh and Darrell William Davis point out, the two prevalent ways of reading Hou are as an Oriental director to be studied in contrast to Western directors, and as a 'critical sphere' for debates on representation and politics within Taiwan[7]. In the first instance, Hou is considered "great" and different because he is "Chinese", nurtured by different aspects of Chinese civilization.[8]

6 Kuan-Hsing Chen: Taiwan New Cinema, or a Global Nativism? In: Valentina Vitali / Paul Willemen (eds): *Theorising National Cinema*. London: British Film Institute 2006, pp. 138–147, here p. 138.

7 Emilie Yueh-Yu Yeh / Darrell William Davis: *Taiwan Film Directors: A Treasure Island*. New York: Columbia UP 2005, p. 133.

8 Chen / Willemen / Wei: Editorial Introduction.

Rosemary Haddon, as one example, describes Hou's discursiveness as "edifying" and attributes it to Confucian doctrines on *ren* (humanity) and *yi* (righteousness), which help differentiate Hou's works from Hollywood films.[9] Ni Zhen also claims that Hou's cinematic expression incarnates the Confucian spirit of the Orient, such as emotional attachment to one's native land.[10] In a similar vein, Jean-Michel Frodon attributes Hou's rupture from Western tradition of fragmentation through high-speed montage, to the influence of Chinese civilisation which does not have the concept of montage.[11] These Orientalist views not only fail to recognise the heterogeneity of Chinese civilisation, for which it is very difficult to define 'Chineseness', and wrongly assume that it lacks a concept of montage, but also fail to account for Hou's practical reasons during film production, such as the material constraints experienced by filmmakers of Hou's generation in Taiwan. In the second instance, Hou's representation of political events is often read in a politicised way. As a matter of fact, the political issues such as undetermined identities, language diversity, colonisation of different forms, the conflicts between the early-comers and the late-comers, the occupiers and the natives, and the conflicts which resulted from drastic modernisation and transformation are often discussed in Hou's films.[12] As these politically laden issues have always been sensitive, and remain unsolved until now, Hou's lack of explicit and direct representations of historical events often causes debate among critics and scholars both within and outside Taiwan. For example, *A City of Sadness* (*Bei Qing Cheng Shi*, TW / HK 1989, D: Hou Hsiao-hsien) uses the traumatising February 28 Incident as a historical backdrop against which individual life stories unfold, instead of directly portraying the violent event. It triggered fierce reactions from critics who were disappointed by Hou's lack of a direct handling of political and historical issues in a 'correct' way which would correspond to the spectator's expectation; that is, a severe and direct condemnation of the ensuing massacre

9 Rosemary Haddon: Hou Hsiao Hsien's *City of Sadness*: History and the Dialogic Female Voice. In: Chris Berry / Feii Lu: *Island on the Edge: Taiwan New Cinema and After*. Hong Kong: Hong Kong UP 2005, pp. 55–65, here p. 58.

10 Zhen Ni: Classical Chinese Painting and Cinematographic Signification, p. 75

11 Jean-Michel Frodon: *Hou Hsiao-hsien*. Paris: Cahiers du Cinéma 1999, p. 25.

12 Gary Needham: Ozu and the Colonial Encounter in Hou Hsiao-Hsien. In: Dimitris Eleftheriotis / Gary Needham (eds): *Asian Cinemas: A Reader & Guide*. Edinburgh: Edinburgh UP 2006, pp. 369–383, here p. 376.

authorised by the KMT government of that time that would render justice to the victims and their families cinematically. An example of criticism of this sort can be found in an article written by Ching Shu, published in the Hong Kong magazine *Cinema* on the 14th of December 1989. Even critics and scholars who praise Hou's works display the same tendency, suggesting politicised readings of Hou's works. For example, Yingjin Zhang argues that, in *A City of Sadness*, Wenqing's muteness reflects the muted masses under the regime of Nationalists who are unable to voice their disagreement because of the regime's repression[13]; Haddon proposes that Hou's condemnation of the February 28 Incident is made clear in Kuanmei's dialogic female voice and that Hou's "integrity of his identity as an émigré from the Mainland" was not compromised.[14]

In fact, Oriental and political readings of Hou's films are both concerned with the 'Chineseness' and/or 'Taiwaneseness' of Hou's works. These concepts, underlying the articulation of ethnicity as agency, are not self-evident but demand questioning.[15] In the aforementioned frameworks, Hou is restricted to a director who has the social responsibilities of 'truthfully' representing historical events (although what is a 'truthful' representation remains debatable). There is thus a serious lack of research which recognises Hou's multiple identities, which include both his nativeland, where he was born, and his homeland, where he spends his life. Contrary to categorising Hou as either a supporter of the KMT regime or a nativist at heart, I propose to take Hou's multiple identities and border-crossing into account, because instead of either/or, I argue that his cultural belonging is both/and.

In addition to his multiple belongings under the complex cultural and historical backgrounds in Taiwan, Hou draws production and distribution resources together from a diverse range of spaces in his transnational filmmaking mode, by crossing the boundaries between two sides of the Taiwan Strait (Taiwan, Hong Kong, and mainland China), between two sides of island chain (Taiwan and Japan), and between two continents (Asia and Europe) to make films. Through the incorporation of filmmaking resources, Hou juxtaposes all these

13 Yingjin Zhang: *Chinese National Cinema*. London: Routledge 2004, p. 249.

14 Haddon: Hou Hsiao Hsien's *City of Sadness*, p. 56.

15 Rey Chow: *Primitive Passions: Visuality, Sexuality, Ethnography, and Contemporary Chinese Cinema*. New York: Columbia UP 1995, p. 88.

spaces in the transnational filmmaking network. At the beginning of his career, he mixed Taiwanese and Hong Kongese stars by casting the Hong Kong film and recording star Kenny Bee and the Taiwanese popular singer Fong Fei Fei in commercial romantic comedies *Cute Girl* (*Jiu Shi Liu Liu De Ta*, TW 1980), *Cheerful Wind* (*Feng Er Ti Ta Cai*, TW 1981), and *Green Green Grass of Home* (*Zai Na He Pan Qing Cao Qing*, TW 1982), to ensure a wide audience appeal in the region. During the movement of New Taiwan Cinema (which approximately spanned from 1983 to 1987), he was involved in Taiwan-based projects funded by Central Motion Pictures Corporation of the KMT government, with strong local concerns and an entirely Taiwan-based cast and crew, such as *The Boys from Fengkuei* (TW 1983), *A Summer at Grandpa's* (TW 1984), *The Time to Live, The Time to Die* (TW 1985), *Dust in the Wind* (TW 1987), and *Daughter of the Nile* (*Ni Luo He Nu Er*, TW 1987). These films were widely circulated in international film festivals, such as Nantes Three Continents Festival, Berlin International Film Festival, Rotterdam International Film Festival, and Torino International Festival of Young Cinema, and secured international release in some parts of the world, through distribution companies such as International Film Circuit in the USA, ASC Distributions in France, and ICA Projects in the UK. In 1989, the success of *A City of Sadness*, both critically, by winning the Golden Lion at Venice Film Festival, and commercially, at the box-office,[16] opened up Hou's production and distribution networks further. Not only did it embrace the markets of Hong Kong, thanks to the casting of the Hong Kong star Tony Leung, and Japan, because of the portrayal of the post-Japan Taiwan, it was also released internationally through Ciclop Films in France, Artificial Eye in the UK, and Rizzoli Corriere della Sera Home Video in Italy, among others. Since then, Hou's film production has been well connected with the French film festival and art cinema circuit, to the extent that the only place that the subtitled DVD of his under-appreciated *Good Men, Good Women* can be bought in the West is on Amazon.fr. Afterwards, *Flowers of Shanghai* (TW / JP 1998) further strengthened Hou's connection with the Japanese filmmaking network by casting

16 With its record NT$ 35 millions box-office, *A City of Sadness* remained the most commercially successful Taiwanese film in Taiwan until *Cape N. 7* (2008) broke its record with an overwhelming NT$ 5.2 billions in 2008.

the Japanese star Michiko Hada, using the music of Yoshihiro Hanno (the Japanese composer who has also composed for Jia Zhangke's films *Platform* (*Zhantai*, CN 2000) and *24 City* (*Er Shi Si Cheng Ji*, CN 2008), and co-producing with the Japanese Shochiku Company. *Café Lumière*, which is a tribute to Yasujirō Ozu, was entirely produced by Japanese companies: Shochiku Company, Asahi Shimbunsha, Sumitomo Corporation, Eisei Gekijo, and Imagica Corporation. It was also entirely shot in Tokyo. This film forms a strong link between Taiwan and Japan by casting the singer/actress Yo Hito, who has a Taiwanese father and a Japanese mother, to play the main protagonist who tries to track down the trajectory of the Taiwanese composer-baritone Jiang Wen-Ye, who has worked in Tokyo and Beijing. *Café Lumière* thus brings various spaces together in many layers. At the same time that a Taiwanese filmmaker is recruited for a Japanese project to pay tribute to a classic Japanese filmmaker, the Taiwanese-Japanese actress is investigating the traces of an exilic Taiwanese musician in Tokyo. From the beginning of the 21st century, Hou was more involved in the French filmmaking scene for the production of *Millennium Mambo* (*Qian Xi Man Po*, TW / FR 2001) and *Three Times*, which were co-produced by 3-H Productions and Sinomovie in Taiwan, and Orly Films and Paradis Films in France, and distributed through a wide network, such as Filmmuseum Distributie in Netherlands, Bitters End in Japan, Océan Films in France, Palm Pictures and IFC Films in the USA, and Vértigo Films in Spain. This filmmaking network is epitomised in Hou's latest feature film, *Flight of the Red Balloon*. The French-speaking film was originally intended as a short film, which would be juxtaposed with short films by Olivier Assayas, Raúl Ruiz, and Jim Jarmusch in a compilation project of Musée d'Orsay, to pay tribute to Albert Lamourisse's *Red Balloon* (*Le Ballon Rouge*, FR 1956). It later grew into a feature-length film, co-produced by Le Musée d'Orsay, Margo Films, Les Films du Lendemain in France, and 3-H Productions in Taiwan. By bringing his usual crew members such as cinematographer Ping Bin Lee and editor Liao Ching-song to the predominantly French project, the Taiwanese filmmaking context encountered the French one. In the making of *The Assassin* (*Nie Yin Niang*, TW / CN / HK / FR 2015), Hou returns to Chinese-language film industry and assembles resources from Taiwan, Hong Kong, and mainland China.

3. Historical Mosaic of Multilayered Mise-en-Scène: Illustrating the Depth of History

Hou's border-crossing and transnational filmmaking mode correlate with the mosaic space in his films. Whereas Hou has multiple identities and assembles funding, cast, crew, settings, and distribution networks from a diverse range of geopolitical spaces in his filmmaking, his film works assemble the narrative threads of various protagonists and mosaic pieces of the mise-en-scène on screen.

In the example of *In the Hands of a Puppetmaster* (*Xi Meng Ren Sheng*, TW 1993), we can see Hou's multilayered space in the mise-en-scène against the background of East Asian architecture, which is made possible by the 'half-outsider half-insider' seer position of the camera. The film recounts the life story of a renowned puppetmaster in Taiwan, Li Tian-lu. Li's personal ups and downs are interconnected with the backdrop of the rotation of political power in Taiwan throughout the 20th century, from Japanese colonisation, through the Second World War, the KMT government's repossession of Taiwan, to the February 28 Incident, and the subsequent White Terror. The film starts with a dark screen bearing the names of the production team, accompanied by the sound of traditional string instruments and Chinese opera from offscreen. When the first image appears, we see a black wooden round table in the centre of the frame, surrounded by adults and children dressed in the Manchurian dark coloured long gowns, the usual costumes of the late Qing Dynasty, with shaved foreheads and a long queue. Behind them is a shrine decorated with the icons of folk deities, red candles, and offerings against a white wall adorned by Chinese calligraphies written on a red sheet of paper. The stable camera frames them in medium shots. From their conversation, we learn that they are Li's grandfather, family members, and family friends, who are gathered to celebrate Li's birth. Li's father, played by an iconic Taiwanese grassroots actor and singer Tsai Chen Nan, comes into the foreground from time to time to add tea to the guests' cups. While doing so his back obstructs the camera's vision and blocks our visual access to the speaking person on screen. When the newborn Li appears on screen to be congratulated by the guests, the voice-over of the actual Li (who was 83 years old at the time of the shooting) accompanies the image to explain why his surname Li follows the maternal side. The actual Li's voice-over continues when, visually, the film cuts to a stable shot of the muted images of three women surrounding the baby Li sleeping on a wooden Chinese-styled bed decorated with red curtains hung from two bedposts. The mother sits on the bed beside the infant Li and faces the camera, whereas the two other women can only be seen from behind. The film then jumps to a long shot of a live open air puppet show in the countryside. The puppet stage is in the mid-ground against luxuriant foliage. Children run around in the foreground, and the grey silhouette of a mountain lies in the background. When Li's voice-over stops, we are given a closer look at the puppet stage as the camera zooms in to frame nothing but the stage. The puppet show, with synchronised sound and image, is on the one hand documentary footage of a live performance, and on the other hand, a fictional diegetic fragment which represents the puppet show performance that Li grows up with. After another black screen bearing the red Chinese characters of "theatre, dream, life", the Chinese title of the film, we see a long shot of a classroom scene. The classroom is situated on the first floor of a traditional Minnan house with a patio in the middle. Initially, the camera is right outside the knee-high wooden fence of the patio placed in the foreground, framing the children in the mid-ground who recite after the teacher. Light shines in from the background through the side door, which opens to a balcony. A few seconds later, the camera pulls back to reveal a close-up of the silhouette of an elderly man, who sits in the shade in the foreground. At this time, the screen depth increases because the children and the balcony door become further away, and an extra layer of the foreground is added. Without any warning, the classroom scene is cut to a long shot of yellow-green rice fields with a diagonal path in the mid-ground and a brick house in the background. An adult and a child walk together towards the left, whereas a bullock cart goes rightwards.

From this short sequence, we can observe that the film continuously jumps between fragments from different spaces, time frames, and virtualities, and assembles a multiplying mosaic. The storyline is pushed forward by mosaic narrative which weaves together diegetic representations of Li's past life, audial (and at a later point of the film, also visual) presence of the real-life Li at the moment of the filmmaking, and indiscernible and unexplained snippets of the nature and live performance of different kinds of theatrical art. These fragments are pasted together into a mosaic without signposting the causality, spatiality, and temporality of the image. Some of them serve a narrative purpose and provide information about the protagonists, such as the first visual images of *In the Hands of a Puppetmaster*, which represent the celebration of Li's birth and provide information on Li's family structure. Some other fragments, however, seem to be motivated by space rather than by protagonists or actions. The long take of the open air live puppetshow, for example, does not have a direct link to the previous fragments related to Li's birth. It does not push the narrative forward and, furthermore, the long shot renders human figures so small that we cannot recognise any one face clearly. In this scene, the camera seems to be simply attracted by the scenery, and people happen to appear on it. Contrary to Egoyan's mosaic of deterritorialisation and reterritoralisation, in Hou's mosaic, the disorienting indeterminate images, whose origin and function in the narrative are unclear, are never explained by Hou and never reterritorialised into a bigger context. These fragments have the properties of Deleuze's time-images, which record in real time duration instead of subjecting movement to time,[17] as well as what Nick Browne calls the phenomenology of appearance[18]. Hou's scriptwriter, Zhu Tian-wen, refers to the juxtaposition of images with different natures and functions as "yunkuai jianjiefa (cloud patch editing method)"[19], indicating Hou's aesthetics, which simulate the concordant movement of clouds. Yeh remarks that Hou's images are assembled like a puzzle, which is rendered complete, piece by piece, without necessarily following a certain logic.[20] Contrary to Zhu and Yeh's analogies to clouds and puzzles, however, here I argue that Hou's mosaic narrative, weaving discernible and indiscernible images together, functions in combination with Hou's layering of the mise-en-scène with depth of field. Each image in Hou's films is first an autonomous self-standing entity with multiple layers in the mise-en-scène, and it is subsequently connected with the preceding or proceeding fragments through mosaic narrative.

17 Deleuze: *Cinema 2*, pp. xi–xii.

18 Nick Browne: Hou Hsiao Hsien's *The Puppetmaster*: The Poetics of Landscape. In: Chris Berry / Feii Lu (eds): *Island on the Edge: Taiwan New Cinema and after*, pp. 79–88, here p. 87.

19 Emilie Yueh-Yu Yeh: Poetics and Politics of Hou Hsiao-hsien's Films. In: Ead. / Sheldon H. Lu (eds): *Chinese-language Film: Historiography, Poetics, Politics*. Honolulu: University of Hawai'i Press 2005, pp. 163–185, here p. 169.

20 Ibid., p. 163.

We can see this in the long take of a dining room in *In the Hands of a Puppetmaster* at the opening. With the duration of the long take, we can see the shrine is in the background and Li's grandfather and family friends in the mid-ground. When Li's father enters the frame and partially blocks the camera's vision, the mise-en-scène is further layered into the space between the camera and Li's father's body, and between Li's father and the mid-ground. Instead of being given an open and undisrupted view to the frame, we see the screen space in segments, which form layers in the mise-en-scène with great depth of field. In the classroom scene a few fragments later, screen space is further layered by the zooming-out of the camera, instead of by the presence of a moving body in the foreground. Initially we can see the wooden fence in the foreground, school pupils in the mid-ground, the side door in the background, and a glimpse of the outdoor space beyond the side door. Through the zooming out of the camera, an extra layer of the other side of the corridor of the patio is added to the mosaic screen space in the foreground, and the depth of field is deepened. From these two examples, we can see that the screen space in Hou's mosaic is folded and unfolded with the partial obstruction of the camera's vision by different means. A threshold, a wooden door, a sliding screen, a human body, and some glass panes of windows can all be used to obstruct the camera's vision partially and at the same time allow enough space for the spectator to explore the layered mise-en-scène. Sometimes the blocking of screen space and multiplication of layers in the mise-en-scène reflect the power struggle between the empowered and the disempowered. In this way, the occupation of screen space maps with the panoptic power of the representatives of the authority at specific historical moments. For example, a few sequences after the beginning fragments of *In the Hands of a Puppetmaster*, we see a stable long shot of the performance of Beijing opera on stage, a performance which is offered by the Japanese government to the residents in Taiwan while conducting a population census. The camera directly faces the stage in the background, which is the only lit place on screen. The first two rows of spectators are in the first plane of the screen space in darkness. When the Japanese policemen appear, the big black shadows of their backs take over the central screen space and block the visibility of the opera performers. Their presence adds an extra layer of the mise-en-scène to the screen space like the presence of Li's father discussed earlier. Yet the shadows that they create are more dominant and authoritative than the body of Li's father in the earlier fragment, as their voluminous presence determines what remains to be seen onscreen and what is blocked from our vision. Through the deployment of the screen space in the mise-en-scène, the virtual space of theatre, the actual space of common people, and that of politics and history are juxtaposed onscreen into a multi-layered mosaic.

The layering of the mise-en-scène and the exploration of mosaic screen space in depth are made possible by the camera's seer position as 'half-outsider and half-insider'. As the framing of the classroom scene shows, we see screen space layered into the mid-ground of the pupils and the outdoor space beyond the balcony in the background only thanks to the camera position right outside the wooden fence of the patio. In this position, the camera is not a completely detached and indifferent witness; nor does it develop an intimate relationship with characters. At the same time that it peeps into the private domain, it avoids an indiscreet intrusion. In its negotiation between concerns of privacy and visibility, it is an onlooker which avoids physically stepping in others' territory and, hence, allows a certain distance from the object of its gaze; it looks at human bodies but does not stay closely with them. Corrado Neri has pointed out that, in several interviews, Hou claims to share with the novelist Shen Congwen the paradox of portraying the author's intimate feelings with a detached observer's gaze.[21] This gaze makes use of the perspective from high up looking down on trivial matters of the earth.[22] However, as Hou's camera is often placed right outside the threshold or the fence, I would rather argue that the gaze is not completely detached, but rather between detached and attached, insider and outsider, and calm and attentive right outside the architectural threshold in Hou's cinematic aesthetics. It is half obstructed, but still leaves spaces to unfold behind the partial obstruction. This corresponds to Hou's multiple identities, which integrate both mainlander and nativist cultures and enable him to be both insider and outsider, but also half-outsider and half-insider. In fact, it is only with this position that Hou's screen space is able to be layered in the mise-en-scène.

21 Cong-Wen Shen: *Shen Cong-Wen Autobiography*. Taipei: Lianhe Wenxue 1987.

22 Corrado Neri: *A Time to Live, a Time to Die*: A Time to Grow. In: Chris Berry (ed.): *Chinese Films in Focus: 25 New Takes*. London: British Film Institute 2003, pp. 160–166, here p. 162.

This half-detached camera gaze in Hou's films can be seen as occupying a 'seer' position in Deleuze's any-space-whatevers, which sees the unfolding of events without reacting to them by zooming in closely or following the action. It corresponds to the seer position of Hou's characters at the narrative level, who also see the unfolding of historical events in the any-space-whatever without knowing how to react. This any-space-whatever is specifically grounded in the geopolitical and historical context of Taiwan, and is thus significantly different from the European context of Deleuze's *Cinema 2*, Laura Marks' postcolonial diasporic context, or the post-trauma and/or post-displacement context of Egoyan in Chapter 2. In fact, Hou's any-space-whatevers in Taiwan have gone through very different trajectories from the aforementioned contexts, even from the circumstances in mainland China, both before and after the Second World War. Mainland China has gone through the eight-year long anti-Japanese resistance, succeeded by the Civil War between Communists and Nationalists. Taiwan, however, was China's enemy during the Second World War because it was forced to fight for Japan, and the postwar situation is also post-colonial after the Nationalist government repossessed Taiwan. This makes its any-space-whatevers very complex. On the one hand, Taiwan was full of postwar "waste ground, cities in the course of demolition or reconstruction"[23] because it was bombarded by the Allies due to its position as an important strategic point of the Asian battlefield during the Second World War. On the other hand, Taiwan in ruins experienced a major migratory flow, when the diasporic population flooded in before the Communists took over mainland China. In the Taiwanese context, the dismantled colonial power, which drives the emergence of the postcolonial seers according to Marks, is replaced by an outsider regime of the Nationalist government devastated by the Communists. Whereas Marks' postcolonial seers refer to migratory, diasporic, and hybrid populations from non-Western ex-colonies to Western metropolises, who are aware of the violent past and perceive the culture of their residence from both inside and outside,[24] the displaced population of mainlanders who move to postcolonial Taiwan in fact occupy the role of *actants* because they possess political power. It is in fact the formerly

23 Deleuze: *Cinema 2*, p. xi.

24 Marks: *The Skin of the Film*, p. 27.

colonised native residents in Taiwan, remaining in the same space, who are aware of violent histories but have no other position but 'seers' as the Third Eye, instead of the new immigrants, the diasporic Nationalists in this case. Hou's any-space-whatever in Taiwan is thus the reversal of Marks' model of postcolonial any-space-whatever and diasporic seers. Whereas in Marks' postcolonial model, "the repressed memories return to destabilize national histories"[25] with the migratory eruption, in the case of Hou's any-space-whatever, the repressed cultural memories are repressed once again, this time by a different external force of migration. The residents in Taiwan see the any-space-whatever from both inside and outside, because they experience both the postcolonial era and the migratory force which becomes the dominant culture. In addition, unlike Haneke's postwar and postcolonial any-space-whatever, in which non-places proliferate, which will be discussed in chapter 4, non-places do not proliferate in the any-space-whatevers of Hou's films. Rather, Hou's any-space-whatevers are full of 'places' inhabited by seers, such as the family space of Li's grandfather, and the house where the family saga of *A City of Sadness* unfolds. This is the particularity of the East Asian context; historical weight and interpersonal relationship persist behind the layers of space.

We can see Hou's seers, the politically disenfranchised residents in Taiwan who are still deprived of political power at the postwar post-colonial period, in the examples of *In the Hands of a Puppetmaster* and *A City of Sadness*. These seers are the half-outsider and half-insider in relation to the Taiwanese identity, as they are "objectively emptied"[26], always right outside the threshold of the historical course without reacting and without having a say for the historical trajectory. Always going with the flow, Li Tian lu in *In the Hands of a Puppet master* sees the unfolding of the violent history and the rotation of political power as a resident in Taiwan, but does not fight against the Japanese colonisers or the KMT government. When the chance comes, he learns the art of puppetry; when the chance comes, he puts on a propaganda puppet theatre praising brave soldiers sacrificing their lives for Japan without revolting against colonial power. Following the Chinese philosophy of life, Li believes that human beings

25 Ibid.

26 Deleuze: *Cinema 2*, p. 9.

are subject to irreversible destiny, and that everything is fate's will: his grandmother's misfortunes, his youngest son's death, and his lover's mysterious disease and inexplicable recovery after a toad-remedy. Li sees the course of history deploying in front of his eyes, and simply accepts changes of regimes and damages caused by war without questioning or reacting. Near the end of the film, following the documentary footage of Li Tian-lu recounting how the villagers sell aluminum from a dysfunctional airplane to afford his puppet show as an offering to folk gods, we see a long shot and long take of the villagers dismantling a Japanese fighter plane in the immediate aftermath of the war. Several men stand on top of the plane hammering repetitively in the mid-ground, whereas white clouds occupy the sky in the upper half of the frame and golden grass lies in the foreground. The camera's gaze is also Li's gaze, seeing the rotations of power and ephemerality of materials without reacting. The somewhat absurd image of the plane, the symbol of the war, in the process of being dismantled is a visual postwar and post-colonial any-space-whatever. It is a deserted, emptied, and disconnected but still useful postwar ruin "in the course of demolition"[27] in the waste ground. Its disintegration also signifies the end of the Japanese rule and the end of the sight of Japanese planes on the soil of Taiwan. Rambling through the course of history, Li sees the postwar postcolonial space with vacuous logical connection, the ephemerality of man-made machines and the more perpetual existence of the clouds in the background from a position not too distanced and also not too attached; he simply sticks to the half-outsider and half-insider role as a puppetmaster. In addition, while the documentary footage of the actual Li's talking head is included in the diegesis and interacts with fictional representation of his life story, he sees the film *In the Hands of a Puppetmaster* being made and his life being portrayed by a young actor right in front of his eyes. Li's seer position in the diegetic and extradiegetic worlds thus creates a mosaic between many time frames in the history of Taiwan, and between documentary and fiction. Actually, in Hou's postwar postcolonial any-space-whatever, it is the seer position that saves the characters' lives; Li manages to provide food and shelter to his family during the Second World War, thanks to his seeing instead of reacting against the Japanese government. Kuanmei, in *A City of Sadness*, is another example. Her calm voice-over leads the narrative forward

27 Deleuze: *Cinema 2*, p. xi.

as she reads the personal writing on the pre- and post-February 28 Incident from her diary. Uninterested in her brother Kuanrong and his intellectual friends' political discussions and subversive activities against the repressive KMT government, she sees the change of regimes from half a century of Japanese colonisation to the KMT, the February 28 Incident, and the subsequent White Terror without reacting. At a personal level, she sees Kuanrong's active involvement in the leftist movement, his hiding in the mountains, imprisonment, and execution, as well as her husband Wenqing's execution, without reacting. This is how she survives in the postwar postcolonial any-space-whatever, which she cannot recognise and react to. On the contrary, those who refuse to remain seers and react fervently against the surrounding space, such as Kuanrong, are chased down, imprisoned, and/or executed by the Nationalist KMT during the White Terror for their political involvement.

As the seers are those who survive the historical course, they remain within multiple layers of the mise-en-scène until the end of the films. We can see this from an ending fragment in *A City of Sadness*. A long take positions a wooden round table in the mid-ground. The elderly grandfather, also played by Li Tian-lu, and Wenqing's psychologically deranged brother Wenleung, the only two male family members who survive the White Terror thanks to their seer positions, sit behind the table in the dining room and start eating. The room in front of the dining room in the foreground is barely visible on screen as the camera is placed right behind its threshold adjoining the dining room, in Hou's usual 'half-outsider half-insider' seer position. What we can see from this room is two pieces of wooden wall partially blocking our vision from the left and right margins. The backs of two female family members come in the foreground from time to time to bring more dishes to the table. Hence, both the wooden wall pieces and human bodies create extra layers of the mise-en-scène in the first plane. Behind the wooden round table in the background is a wall with translucent square glass panes and an open door dividing the dining room and the room behind it. With great depth of field, we can see another female family member and some children at a smaller table in the background. The elderly grandfather, the psychologically disabled brother, fatherless children, and widows, those who survive the executed or murdered male family members, are the seers who carry on with their daily routine within the layers of the mise-en-scène. They go on seeing without reacting; we do not even see them crying on screen. Hence, the film ends with the remaining seers' point of view against the multilayered mise-en-scène, captured from the camera's seer position. This 'half-outsider half-insider' seer position occupied by the politically disenfranchised characters, such as Li in *In the Hands of a Puppetmaster* and Kuanmei in *A City of Sadness*, can be easily identified by the Taiwanese nativist spectators who have experienced the same seer position in history. They can also recognise the camera's position right outside the architectural threshold, which imitates the position of the disempowered local residents. This identification with the camera's and the characters' seer position on screen does not always happen for the international spectators of arthouse cinema, however, as they do not necessarily understand the postwar postcolonial any-space-whatevers in the Taiwanese context in the same way. Accordingly, the seer position is liminal in terms of their spatial position provided by the camera, as well as cultural, political, and historical, if the spectator chooses and is equipped with enough knowledge to read the seer position of the camera position and the characters.

Furthermore, it is in combination with the spatial configurations of East Asian architecture that the camera's seer position is able to explore Hou's historical mosaic of multilayered mise-en-scène. Due to the historical trajectory, the various East Asian architectural styles which coexist in Taiwan are blended into a fusion, which takes into account both privacy and visibility through a fluid use of space and allows layers of space to unfold on screen, captured by the camera's 'half-insider half-outsider' position. On the one hand, we see Minnan houses like the one where Li resides as a child in the opening sequence of *In the Hands of a Puppetmaster*. They are built by early immigrants of different periods of time from southern coastal China and have the mission of accommodating the whole extended family. Sharing several basic features of northern Chinese architecture, they rely on timber-based frame construction, thatched roofs, and raised platforms, which facilitate opening up to the outside with simple and direct methods. Internal partitions are usually made of timber and not always carried up to the height of the ceiling.[28] Sometimes there

28 Andrew Boyd: *Chinese Architecture and Town Planning 1500 B. C.–A. D. 1911*. London: Tiranti 1962, pp. 23–25, 34.

is a patio in the middle of the building, like the school we see in the beginning of *In the Hands of a Puppetmaster*, or a courtyard house structure which combines several Minnan buildings to form a walled enclosure in the centre.[29] As family members live close together in a courtyard house, with a well-defined hierarchy and relationships, a balance between visibility and privacy becomes the key to harmony and efficient control of the household. Enough visibility makes it easier to supervise and communicate with other family members; yet visibility has to be partially obstructed in order to leave enough privacy. As a result, each small unit of the family lives in a separate *jian* to keep a certain degree of privacy. The embossed and engraved door frames pasted with translucent paper also maintain the balance between privacy and visibility. On the other hand, we see Japanese houses, which are the leftover spatial markers of the colonisation period in Taiwan, in the opening sequence of *The Time to Live, The Time to Die* (*Tong Nien Wang Shi*, TW 1986, D: Hou Hsiao-hsien). Among many fragments of stable shots accompanied by Hou's voice-over, which introduces the dwelling of his childhood, we see a fragment of a long take which fixates on the main living space of the family. Four pieces of tatamis which permit multifunctional and flexible use of space are assembled on the floor and two shirts are hung on the wall facing the camera. Rails of sliding paper screens divide the room laterally and diagonally. The kitchen and courtyard are on the left and right side of the background, respectively. As the use of paper screens and tatamis allow flexible folding and unfolding of the space, several lines reframe the screen space into multiple rectangular shapes to the extent that this long take captures space inside space, space beside space, and space behind space. The only furniture in this frame is a small sewing machine placed in the corner beside two sliding doors and a stool. This long take is succeeded by a view of the house from outside, which reveals the raised platform, vestibule, wood shingle roof, windows of strips of wood, and a tree in the courtyard. This portrayal of fluidity of space efficiently reflects the family's daily use of space and sets the tone for Hou's continuous exploration of space. Within the architectural styles of Minnan and Japanese houses, space is subject to constant reconstruction and

29 Ibid., p. 76; Laurence G. Liu: *Chinese Architecture*. London: Academy Editions 1989, p. 27.

transformation by flexible use of sliding doors, light furniture, and portable tatami pieces, as Kazuo Nishi and Kazuo Hozumi[30], David Young and Michiko Young[31], and Keven Nute[32] point out.

With Hou's 'half-insider half-outsider' seer position of the camera, and the unique fluid spatial configurations of East Asian architecture in mind, we can examine Hou's mosaic space in full. Placed right outside the architectural threshold, the camera looks through the multi-layered space of the East Asian architecture and negotiates between privacy and visibility. This position allows a partial obstruction of vision near to the lens and observes the subject matter at a certain distance, so the screen space extends inwards with greater depth of field. Hence, several layers of space, ranging from the partially obstructing foreground, the mid-ground, and the background are accumulated in the mise-en-scène and assembled into a mosaic. Hou's spatial depth has been remarked on by scholars such as Shen Xiaoyin, who mentions that Hou focuses on "the depth relationship between the front and the back instead of lateral relationship between left and right in his handling of screen space"[33] in *Daughter of the Nile*. Browne, one of the few scholars who pays close attention to the importance of architecture in Hou's films, indicates that Hou's cinema is "an example of a cinema of mise-en-scène and architecture that together trace changes of the family against a backdrop of familiar and repeated daily or annual occurrences and places"[34]. In his analysis of *In the Hands of a Puppetmaster*, Browne argues:

> This action [of big events such as death] is centered on a physical place, chiefly the family's house and the surrounding neighborhood. The decoupage effects a systematic interpenetration and continuity between the two spaces, whether looking into the house, or inversely, from within the house looking out. The perspective, in other words, is transitive. The house is in the Japanese style – with movable screens and partitions – and the framing and composition of shots

30 Kazuo Nishi / Kazuo Hozumi: *What is Japanese Architecture?*, trans. from Japanese by H. Mack Horton. Tokyo: Kodansha International 1985, p. 9.

31 David Young / Michiko Young: *Introduction to Japanese Architecture*. Hong Kong: Periplus 2004, p. 112.

32 Keven Nute: *Place, Time and Being in Japanese Architecture*. London: Routledge 2004, pp. 69–70.

33 Wenqi Lin: Realist Style and Narrative in Hou Hsiao-hsien's Early Films. In: Wenqi Lin / Xiaoyin Shen / Zhenya Li (eds): *Passionate Detachment: Films of Hou Hsiao-hsien*. Taipei: Rye Field 2000, pp. 93–111, here p. 95.

34 Browne: Hou Hsiao Hsien's *The Puppetmaster*. The Poetics of Landscape, p. 80.

> realize at the same time a definition of filmic space that is graphic in its frontal plane (its sense of arrangement of form and color), and three dimensional, creating a space for action that is normally articulated in multiple planes of recession. The approach to mise-en-scène favours the lateral, thus determining the actor's profile and movement. Thus the internal screens that articulate the space sometimes eclipse the action, but only for a moment, when the action is quickly recentered in a legible space.[35]

Browne proposes that Hou's mise-en-scène favours the lateral, and that the obstruction of the frontal plane is only temporary in order to resume the visibility to the action. Yet, here I argue that Hou's screen space, instead of being lateral, is rather longitudinal and the obstruction of vision in fact enables the camera's exploration of screen space in depth and in layers. As we have already seen in the example of the opening dinner table scene in *In the Hands of a Puppetmaster*, visibility is half obstructed by Li's father's back, which enters the middle of the frame from time to time, and the screen space is thus layered in the mise-en-scène. In the middle of the film, when the Li's grandfather falls from the staircase to the off-screen space, the camera, instead of following the movement of the fall for the narrative purpose, remains in its original position. It focuses on the upper part of the room with the off-screen sound of the fall carrying most of the narrative weight in order to invite the spectator to explore the layers of the mise-en-scène. The upper half of the wooden staircase is framed in the right margin, right next to the wall on which hang the black and white photos of the Li family's ancestors sitting straight and wearing formal attire. These photos immediately evoke connotations of obligations and privileges transmitted through family lineage in a visual way. Above the staircase on the upper part of the frame is a bedroom in darkness, and behind and below the staircase on the left side of the frame is the living room in the mid ground, which opens up to the outdoor space in the background by letting light shine in. This Minnan-styled house is framed in such a way that the screen space is a mosaic composed of several sections and fragments: the lower part of the staircase in the foreground, the centre of the room in the mid-ground, and the outdoor light in the background. This sequence reveals how Hou's mosaic space is very much about assembling different layers of planes designed in the mise-en-scène of the East Asian architecture. My framework of mosaic is thus contrary

35 Ibid., p. 80.

to Shen's analysis of *In the Hands of a Puppetmaster*, which claims that the screen space is maintained in the two-dimensional surface in an anti-Welles style.[36] Hou's multilayered screen space, embedded with thresholds between rooms, flexible screens, translucent glass panes, and fixed walls, is looked at by the camera right outside the architectural threshold, whose gaze traverses several compartments and examines the historical events and individual stories. Similar to Egoyan's vertical mosaic, Hou uses distance to avoid direct confrontation with the collective trauma. Although Hou also embeds historical trauma behind the distance created by the virtual, like Egoyan, as we can see in the following analysis of *Good Men, Good Women*, Hou's historical distance predominantly lies in the depth of the mise-en-scène. Whereas Egoyan embeds representations of the painful past within doubly-mediated virtual images, from which the camera zooms out to reveal the visual and diegetic context and to reterritorialise, Hou does not reterritorialise the virtual and looks at the unfolding of historical events through the exploration of the multilayered mise-en-scène without judgment. It is through spatial distance that Hou demonstrates the impossibility of representing historical events with extreme terror, such as the 28 February Incident and the White Terror, that Kuanmei sees in *A City of Sadness*. Lisa Siraganian points out, "Egoyan does not overload the viewer by adding more frightening graphic images, but alludes to scenes that more or less exist in the Armenian diaspora's collective memory"[37]. Like Egoyan's virtual distance, Hou's spatial distance avoids direct portrayal of violence and allows the spectators to fill in the blank according to their collective memory, especially because these events have been left unspoken in public spheres until the 1990s, and no representation can be wholly accurate. Resonant with Egoyan's multiple identities, which allow him to view both the subject matters in Canada and Armenia from multiplying perspectives, Hou's multiple identities as both a diasporic mainlander and an adopted nativist provide him with enough distance to portray the collective trauma with spatial distance on screen and without being radical, politicised, or overly sentimental.

36 Xiaoyin Shen: Meant to be Watched Several Times: Film Aesthetics and Hou Hsiao-hsien [Benlai jiu yingai duo kan liangbian: Dianying meixue yu Hou Xiaoxien]. In: Wenqi Lin / Xiaoyin Shen / Zhenya Li (eds): *Performance that Loves Life: Researching the Cinema of Hou Hsiao-hsien* [*Xilian Rensheng: Hou Hsiao-hsien Dianying Yanjiu*]. Taipei: Maitian 2000, pp. 61–92, here p. 82.

37 Siraganian: Telling a Horror Story, Conscientiously, p. 149.

The exploration of layered screen space indoors can be observed in the examples *Café Lumière*, with its Japanese architecture, and *Daughter of the Nile*, with Minnan architecture. In the former case, the screen space is multilayered through the flexible use of indoor space in Japanese architecture and also through reflection of images on a window. The layers of space are not only composed of onscreen space within the frame in front of the camera, but they also extend to the space behind the camera. When Yoko first enters her home with her father, the camera stably frames Yoko's mother in the kitchen, whose back faces the camera in the furthest plane. Divided by flexible paper screens, two multifunctional rooms lie in the mid-ground of the screen space. The nearest obstruction to one's eyesight is a sliding full-length window pane half covering Yoko's family space. Even this layer is extended to another space by reflecting the offscreen silver family car on the glass pane. Through reflection, the screen space is thus extended to the space behind the camera and opens up to a spatial plane offscreen. In the case of *Daughter of the Nile*, it is the use of light, controlling visibility and invisibility, which has the function of opening up or closing down an extra layer of inner space. Within the interior space of the household, the camera faces the half-open door leading to the study room. When light in the study room is lit, one extra layer of space, which was originally hidden in the darkness, is revealed. When light is off, this layer of space ceases existing onscreen. Whereas sliding paper screen doors in Japanese houses render the space flexible, in these instances, the space can be cinematically folded or unfolded by the use of reflection images and light.

Hou's use of layered mosaic space is not restricted to his shooting of the indoor space of Minnan and Japanese households, but can also be observed in Hou's portrayal of the outdoor public sphere. In *The Time to Live, The Time to Die*, the plaza in front of Cheng-Huang Temple, a temple which is in charge of intellectual activities such as studies and exams, is also spatially layered. This is the space with multiple cultural and geographical meanings and conflicts, according to Li Zhenya.[38] From a series of medium to long shots, we can see that the commercial sectors, with vendors of quotidian utilities on the street

38 Zhenya Li: Historical Space/Spatial History: On Memory and the Construction of Geographical Space in *A Time to Live, A Time to Die*. In: *Chung Wai Literary Quarterly* 26,10 (1998), pp. 48–63, here pp. 53–55.

right in front of the temple, compose the outer layer farthest from the centre. Children playing with a skipping rope are also in a relatively remote layer in the mise-en-scène. A big banyan tree at the front door of the temple, under which a group of elderly people drinks tea, is placed in the centre of the frame. In the immediate outer circle, teenagers play pool or chase people from a different gang. When the girl in school uniform played by Shu-fen Hsin, whom Ah-hao (the representation of the young Hou, played by Ann-Shuin Yiu) admires, passes by the margins of the plaza, she is exposed to partial gazes from all directions, age groups, and social spectrum around the plaza. The whistling and teasing of Ah-hao's friends makes the exchange of gazes between the girl and Ah-hao a public event, scrutinised by the community. When the enemies of Ah-hao's gang pass by the plaza, they are also detected through the partially blocked vision penetrating through the multilayered outdoor space. This is a prototype of pre-industrial community life in rural Taiwan, portrayed as a mosaic open air public space with many spatial layers embedded within the mise-en-scène, in a similar way to Hou's indoor space.

Although the whole generation of Taiwanese filmmakers shares the experience of the fusion of architectural styles, and the consequences of complex historical processes in postwar postcolonial Taiwan, Hou's camera explores space in multiple layers against the East Asian architectural background in a different way from his contemporaries. For example, Hou's contemporary Edward Yang, who was also exposed to the same spatial configurations and historical consequences, did not portray the dwelling in postwar Taiwan with multilayered mise-en-scène. In fact, Yang's *A Brighter Summer Day* (*Gu Ling Jie Shao Nian Sha Ren Shi Jian*, TW 1991) and Hou's *The Time to Live, The Time to Die* are both set in the 1960s and are both about the adolescence of the second generation immigrants from mainland China, the former being set in the urban north and the latter in the rural south. Yet Yang's framing of the Japanese-styled houses left by Japanese occupants and inhabited by the family of Xiao-Sir, a high school student in *A Brighter Summer Day*, creates a rather straightforward sense of space without accumulating layers. Xiao-Sir's family has migrated from Shanghai to Taiwan with the KMT Nationalists, after experiencing an eight-year war against Japan's invasion as well as a Civil War, and ends up living in their former enemy's Japanese house. While foregrounding the mise-en-scène of the Japanese house, the camera is often placed in the middle of the house and pans through a brown wooden door to the bathroom, a dining table where Xiao-Sir's siblings do their homework, a small corner with a radio which Xiao-Sir's father listens to every evening, and a bunk bed embedded in a closet-like space segmented by a paper screen door. With one pan, the spectator is fully aware of the spatial deployment of the house. Contrary to Hou's treatment of such space, Yang's camera does not occupy the 'half-outsider half-insider' seer position and therefore, in its panning, the straightforward screen space is not allowed to be layered and folded.

It is worth noting that Hou's multilayered mosaic space, which goes inwards in the mise-en-scène with great depth of field, is embedded with complicated issues of history and power relations. The more laden history is in the narrative, such as in *Flowers of Shanghai* and the first two sections in *Three Times*, the more layered screen space is through obstruction of vision. Coinciding with historical depth, space goes inward towards the back of the screen in the longitudinal sense instead of spreading towards the lateral margins. As *Flowers of Shanghai* is embedded in history, it is not surprising that the mise-en-scène is the most elaborately multilayered and fragmented into multiple sections through the partially obstructed vision. Set exclusively indoors in an elegant brothel in the late 19th century, the prostitutes, who are called Flower Girls, and their customers, both wearing delicately embroidered garments, develop complex interpersonal relationships within the layered mise-en-scène. Hou layers intricately decorated inner space and hints at space within space behind half closed wooden doors or window frames. The camera is almost always situated in such a way that the screen space is divided into many compartments by partial obstruction of doorframes and decorative furniture. Furthermore, the multilayered mise-en-scène is rendered apparent as the servants walk in and out between the room in the foreground and the room behind the doors in the background to serve food and drinks. In the scene where a young courtesan Golden Flower complains to the senior Flower Girl Emerald about being beaten up by the owner of the brothel, the camera is placed inside Emerald's room looking out. Emerald and Golden Flower sit around a table in the first spatial plane divided by engraved door frames; four corridors surrounding an inner patio compose the second layer. In the background, deep in the mise-en-scène, we can see another room behind the patio extending to the vantage point. Another example of Hou's deployment of mosaic space in the depth of screen space can be observed in the scene when the senior Pearl is waiting for the newly popular Flower Girl Jade to join her for dinner, in order to solve the conflicts between Jade and another young Flower Girl. The camera initially pans right and then left, between the dinner table and Pearl, in the beginning of the fragment. When Pearl sends a servant to fetch Jade, the camera stays in the same long take to explore the depth of the mise-en-scène. Within this frame we see a metal kettle in the foreground towards the centre, and Pearl sits on a black wooden armchair by a wall drinking tea. Above her head is a half-open window pane framed with delicately engraved wood and pasted with paper screen. Beside the window, we see a plant pot on the window frame, which partially blocks our view through the window. Through the crack the spectator can see in the furthest spatial plane a servant's vague and small image walking through a corridor leftwards towards the other corner of the patio, and afterwards Jade walking rightwards behind several spatial layers. It is within the multiple layers of the mise-en-scène that the interlaced interpersonal relationships unfold against the historically distant backdrop. In this simple fragment, with minimal action and characters, spatial configurations form a complex and multilayered mosaic, corresponding to the historical depth of the subject matter.

The multilayered space in correlation with the historical depth of the subject matter contrasts sharply with Hou's *Goodbye South, Goodbye* (*Nan Guo Zai Jian, Nao Guo*, TW / JP 1996) and *Millennium Mambo*, which lack temporal distance in their contemporary subject matter and, as a result, the spatial distance between camera and the filmed objects. When Hou's films do not go deep into history, his camera also loses its 'half-outsider half-insider' seer position, and his portrayal of space is deprived of rich layering and fragmentation of the mosaic space. Hou's construction of contemporary space is thus rather un-fragmented, un-layered, and flat, without going inwards towards the furthest spatial plane. In the absence of a multilayered mise-en-scène, these films rely a lot more on verbal expression, most of the time long arguments encompassed within a static frame, to push the narrative forward. For example, in the scene when Flathat, a young follower of the small gang leader Xiao Gao, jumps out of the window in order to avoid Xiao Gao's angry remarks in

Goodbye South, Goodbye, the screen space, captured by Hou's trademark long take and fixed frame, is not multilayered as it is in *Flowers of Shanghai*. The camera is situated inside the studio flat and hence does not occupy the 'half-outsider half-insider' seer position right outside the architectural threshold. Facing the half-open window from which Flathat jumps, the camera's vision, unobstructed by any piece of the mise-en-scène placed by the margins of the foreground, allows the spectator to approach the screen space in its whole. The non-ornate window, which simply faces a grey building wall, does not open up to more layers of space. Therefore, the screen space in the modernly furnished studio flat is rather shallow and does not form a mosaic of layers; there is not as much to be explored in these fixed frames as there is in Hou's films which are laden with historical resonances and associations. Brian Price remarks that Hou experiments with formal aspects such as colour, abstract shape, rotating camera, overlooking angle, and musical beats in the films with contemporary settings,[39] but these experiments actually stay on the surface plane of the screen without creating layers. In a roundtable discussion hosted by the literary journal *Chung Wai Literary Quarterly*, there are fierce debates between the participants about the lack of temporal distance in *Goodbye South, Goodbye*, as well as its problems. In the discussion, Li justly points out that watching *Goodbye South, Goodbye* is like seeing oneself in the mirror, and a deeper and a broader approach is missing from the viewing experience.[40] In fact, without temporal distance, although films with contemporary settings such as *Goodbye South, Goodbye* constantly refer to issues of a grand scheme such as globalisation and post-industrialisation in Taiwan, economic progress in China, and economic migration, they are largely presented at their face-value, accompanied by omnipresent images of Coca-Cola bottles. From the contrast between *Flowers of Shanghai* and *Goodbye South, Goodbye*, we can see that Hou's mosaic needs temporal distance in order to create spatial layers in the mise-en-scène.

39 Brian Price: Color, the Formless, and Cinematic Eros. In: Angela Dalle Vacche / Id. (eds): *Color: The Film Reader*. London: Routledge 2006, pp. 76–87, here p. 85.

40 Emilie Yueh-Yu Yeh / Xiaoyin Shen / Zhenya Li / Wenqi Lin: Roundtable: Goodbye South, Goodbye. In Liu Wei-Ran (ed.): *Chung Wai Literary Quarterly* 26,10 (1998), pp. 65–73, here p. 71.

In this section, I have demonstrated how Hou's mosaic is assembled by layers of the mise-en-scène through the 'half-outsider half-insider' seer position of the camera against the backdrop of East Asian architecture, corresponding to the historical depth of the subject matter. The multilayered mosaic will be exemplified further in the analyses of *Good Men, Good Women* and *Three Times.*

4. *Good Men, Good Women*

Following the international success of *A City of Sadness, Good Men, Good Women* brings transnational funding resources, filming locations, and cast together, which is made possible by Hou's travelling and the international circulation of his films. It is financed by the Japanese production company Shochiku and Hou's own 3-H Films, and filmed both in Taiwan and in Guangtong Province in mainland China. The travelling of the cast and the crew between Taiwan and Guangtong corresponds to the trajectory of the characters during the Second World War. The main actress, Annie Shizuka Inoh, appropriately fits in the transnational project, as she was born in Taiwan and grew up in Japan after her mother remarried a Japanese man. Correlating with the bringing-together of filmmaking resources from diverse geopolitical spaces, *Good Men, Good Women* interweaves narrative threads from two women, Liang Ching and Chiang Bi-yu (both played by Annie Shizuka Inoh), several decades apart, as well as their partners, Ah-Wei and Chong Hao-tong, played by Giong Lim. While blending uses of several language varieties, the mosaic demonstrates the complex assemblage of actual and virtual images, while wandering in and out of the film-within-the-film, and the past and present of Taiwan.

Like *In the Hands of a Puppetmaster, Good Men, Good Women* depicts a long period of modern Taiwanese history, spanning from the Sino-Japanese Resistance, through the White Terror, to 1995, the time of the filmmaking. The film begins with a group of young people in the clothing of the 1930s walking along a zigzagging path, which passes in front of a traditional Minnan house on the left margins of the frame. A mountain's silhouette is vaguely visible in the background. Accompanying the group singing, the song lyrics are typed on the right margins of the screen space, one Chinese character at a time (fig. 15), followed by a black screen with red calligraphy of the title "Good Men, Good Women". The title cuts to a shot starting from a close-up of an air-conditioner in the upper right margin of the frame, moving leftwards and downwards diagonally along pristine walls across Liang's modern flat until she is finally framed in pajamas, waking up from the ringing of a fax-phone. After Liang walks to the kitchen, the camera scans left and downwards diagonally to the TV set at the foot of her mattress, which is playing Yasujiro Ozu's *Late Spring* (*Banshun*, JP 1949). (Fig. 16) The camera tilts upwards to capture Liang taking a piece of paper from the fax machine, which is her old diary faxed back to her by an unidentifiable thief, while her voice-over reads it out loud. As Liang enters the bathroom and sings to herself, the static camera looks at the square pieces of translucent glass panes on the bathroom wall. The film then cuts to a close-up of a hand-dyed multicoloured T-shirt, from which the camera wanders downwards through some shapeless clothes hung by the window to capture Liang with her late boyfriend, Ah Wei, caressing each other in front of a mirror, which in fact comes from Liang's recollection-images of the past. The long take of the couple's passion jumps to stable shots of photo shooting sessions of Liang, along with other actors, dressed in 30s style clothing, facing the camera. A reflector is visible on screen from the left margins, and the photographers occasionally appear onscreen in the foreground. (Fig. 17) Following a fragment of Liang's rehearsal on stage looked at by several people whose silhouettes can be seen in the foreground, we see black-and-white images of Chiang's father smoking a pipe and Chiang sitting beside him. In Japanese, Chiang asks for her father's permission to join the war against Japan with Chong.

From the opening sequence, we can see that mosaic narrative in *Good Men, Good Women* interweaves images of different characters (the fictional diegetic character Liang and her enacted role of the actual person Chiang), temporalities (the contemporary period, a few years earlier before Ah Wei's death, the Second World War period), spatialities (colonised Taiwan, mainland China, postcolonial Taiwan, the contemporary urban space of Taipei City), virtualities (the diegetic images and the film-within-the-film), and colours (coloured images and black-and-white images). While it jumps back and forth between these different elements, the mosaic narrative brings together the storylines of two women, the fictional Liang and the real-life person Chiang, the former in the generation of the latter's grandchildren.

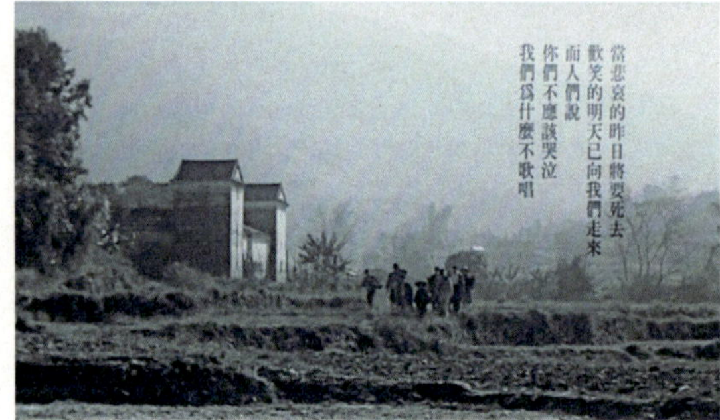

Fig. 15
A mountain's silhouette with the accompanying song's lyrics typed on the right margins of the screen space (*Good Men, Good Women*).

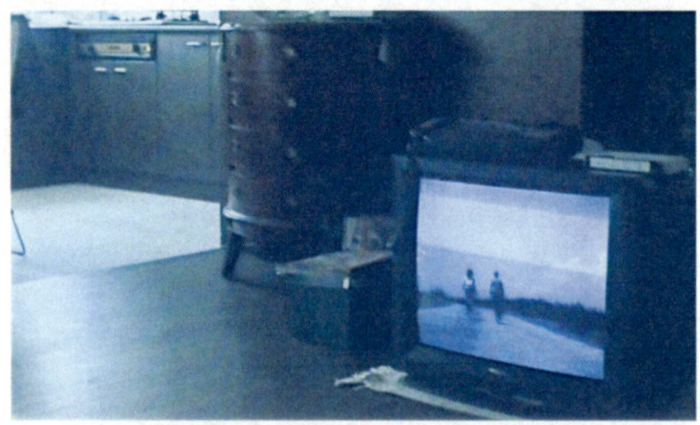

Fig. 16
The wandering gaze of the camera briefly stays with a television set on the floor projecting Yasujiro Ozu's *Late Spring* (*Good Men, Good Women*).

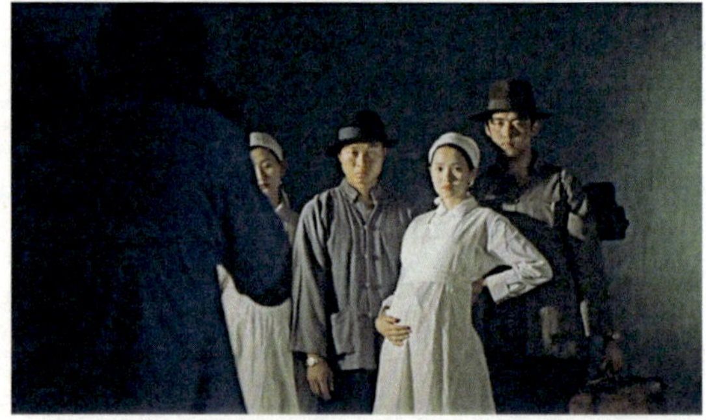

Fig. 17
During Liang's photo shooting for the film-within-the-film, a photographer's back blocks one third of the screen from the left margins (*Good Men, Good Women*).

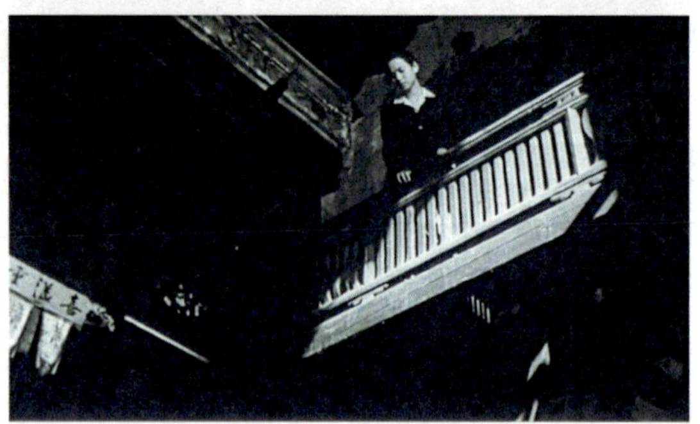

Fig. 18
Chiang as the seer in the postwar and postcolonial any-space-whatever in Taiwan within the multi-layered mise-en-scène (*Good Men, Good Women*).

Liang is a contemporary decadent actress whose gangster boyfriend Ah Wei died from a gunshot. Chiang's unusual life story, drifting from Taiwan to mainland China and back to Taiwan with her husband Chong, is a true story based on the biography of Chong, which is assembled by mosaic pieces written by the widow Chiang, Chong's friends, relatives, and fellow political victims. In fact, the life story of Chiang and Chong is a miniature version of contemporary Taiwanese history. As idealistic young intellectuals, they volunteered to join the guerilla army in mainland China during the Anti-Japan Resistance and were almost executed on suspicion of espionage because of their Taiwanese citizenship, a Japanese colony. After the Allies' victory in the end of the Second World War, they worked as a high school principal and a radio broadcaster in Taiwan, but were again imprisoned during the White Terror, because of their participation in the patriotic leftist movement. Later, Chong was executed by the KMT government. Chiang, judged as being a passive wife not actively involved in Chong's newspaper publications, was released. During her extraordinary trajectory, Chiang actually becomes the seer in the postwar and postcolonial any-space-whatever in Taiwan. (Fig. 18) Her displacement, different from Marks' postcolonial seers who migrate from the ex-colonies to the West, goes in two directions: from the colonised Taiwan to mainland China at war with Japan, and then back to the postwar postcolonial Taiwan flooded with politically dominant migratory populations. Having experienced the changes of political forces and being carried by the historical trajectory, she is fully aware of the violence committed in the intertwining past and present, and perceives the dominant culture, that is, the powerful Nationalists' culture, from both inside (as an ex-guerilla fighter within the Nationalist army) and outside (as a formerly colonised nativist), as the Third Eye. She sees the unfolding of personal and historical events, even the death of her husband, without reacting. Like Kuanmei in *A City of Sadness*, it is also thanks to her seer position that she survives to recount their life story.

By bringing together narrative threads along with the characters' diverse spaces embedded in specific time frames, mosaic narrative also assembles variegated language uses, which are subject to translation and mediation. This complex multilingual mosaic has been present since Hou's early commercial films. For example, the love triangle involving the photographer Shing-huei in *Cheerful Wind* is between her colleague Lo-Tzai from Hong Kong, speaking Mandarin with a stereotypical Cantonese accent, and a once blind doctor, speaking Southern Min and standard Mandarin. The struggle for love is also a struggle between ethnicities and dialects, which has been used for comic effect. The mosaic of language varieties in *A City of Sadness*, however, is devoid of comic elements and tainted with ethnic and political intolerance in the postwar era, when the use of dialects is an effective way to reinforce one's ethnic identity and distinguish oneself from other ethnic groups. For instance, the conflicts between the Lin family speaking Southern Min and the Shanghai gangsters speaking Suzhou dialect in *A City of Sadness* are not only socioeconomic and political, but also cultural and linguistic, which reflects the bigger struggle between the nativists and the mainlanders, whose dialects are mutually incomprehensible. In another sequence, Wenqing, the deaf-and-mute photographer played by Tony Leung, is almost attacked by a group of armed nativists because of his inability to answer the nativists' question in Japanese. Since a deaf-and-mute person's ethnicity cannot be evaluated according to spoken language use, the potential death of Wenqing for his deaf-muteness embodies the absurdity of categorising people according to ambiguous cultural manifestations. This mosaic of languages continues in *Good Men, Good Women*, especially in the striking translational triangles between Mandarin Chinese, Cantonese, and Southern Min, reminiscent of Jean-Luc Godard's translational triangle between German, English and French side by side with a love triangle in *Contempt* (*Le Mépris*, FR 1963), and between English and French in the beginning of *Pierrot le Fou* (FR 1965). The sequence happens when the guerilla fighters of the Nationalist army interrogate the Taiwan-born Chiang Bi-yu, Chong Hao-tong, and their friends, one after another, for suspicion of espionage. The same questions about their route and means of transportation are repetitively translated from the interrogator's Cantonese to the Taiwanese patriots' Southern Min, sometimes also through the use of Mandarin Chinese. Chiang, Chong, and their friends' answers are interpreted the other way round, recurrently. It is not coincidental that "motive" is the most repeated word in the interrogation. As the interpreter speaks Southern Min with a strong Cantonese accent, his enunciation of "motive" requires continuous repetition, sometimes up to five times of reiteration of the same word while struggling with the pronunciation. Indeed, since the Nationalists treat everyone from areas occupied by Japanese, including the East part of China and Taiwan, as a potential spy for the Japanese, they have difficulties believing the innocent and patriotic motives claimed by these young people. At the same time, Chiang and Chong are not only incapable of understanding the word "motive" that the interpreter pronounces with so much difficulty but are also unable to understand why the interrogator insists on the same question of motives. The more the interrogator doubts Chiang and Chong's motives of coming to the war zone in the mainland, the more the interpreter's pronunciation of "motive" sounds confusing and ambiguous to Chiang and Chong, and the more Chiang and Chong seem suspicious to the Nationalists. To reinforce the mechanical way in which languages are translated back and forth, Hou truncates the bodies of the interrogator and the interpreter who are seated on the right side of the frame. As their bodies are half cut off from the frame and their heads are off-screen, they become emotionless machine-like bodies which only carry incomprehensible voices.

The mosaic narrative of Liang and Chiang, the two women generations apart, is further complicated by the patchwork of different virtualities. Liang, who used to work as a bar hostess and dwell in a humid old shanty house with Ah Wei, takes up the role of Chiang, after Ah Wei's death, in a film about Chiang and Chong's unusual paths. The narrative line in *Good Men, Good Women* thus jumps back and forth between Liang's present as a film actress, her shady past, and indiscernible virtual images portraying the stories of Chiang and Chong. In the opening sequence, inserted between the actual images of Liang at the contemporary time, are the doubly-mediated sequences of the rehearsal scene, which is clearly framed as a rehearsal on stage by the blurry presence of the film professionals in the foreground, and the unframed doubly-mediated images of the black-and-white film-within-a-film. These two virtual images are signposted, because they foreground the presence of film professionals within the frame or use a different colour scheme. However, many subsequent doubly-mediated virtual images are simply inserted into the mosaic without being summoned or doubly framed. For example, in the second half of the film, following a close-up of the crown of a big Banyan tree, we see a long static shot of a meeting table around which a group of young people discuss the land policies in a study group. This sudden jump back into the virtual image, which depicts Chong and Chiang's postwar political activities after their return to Taiwan, is unmarked.

These images become indiscernible because we do not know if they are the recollection-images of the real-life Chiang or virtual reenactment of Liang on a film set within a diegesis (which is, the footage from the film-within-the-film *Good Men, Good Women* within the *Good Men, Good Women* that we are watching). Indiscernibility of images can also be seen in the opening sequence of the group singing and walking along the zigzagging path, which is repeated again in the very end of the film. It remains undetermined throughout the film whether this is a recollection-image of Chiang who recalls her marching towards the guerilla army, or a film-within-a-film, or an image simply conveying the atmosphere of the pre-postwar era without any narrative purpose. The spectator is rendered even more puzzled by the mosaic of the actual and the virtual when, near the end of the film, Inoh's voice-over tells us that Chiang has died two days before the release of *Good Men, Good Women*. It is indiscernible if she is talking about the release of the film that the spectator is watching or the film whose process of making is included in the diegesis. As a matter of fact, these images are produced in such a way that the recollection-image is not necessarily an image of the past, nor is it simply a virtual doubly-mediated image. Throughout the film, the indiscernible virtual images are juxtaposed with the actual images of Liang, and therefore they interweave into a mosaic in which images of different temporalities and virtualities chase one another, at the same time generating images which reflect a pre-existing reality and modifying it.[41] Within the mosaic, the indiscernible images approximate what Deleuze calls the "crystal-image". In *Cinema 2* he says, "This is Borges' reply to Leibniz: the straight line as force of time, as labyrinth of time, is also the line which forks and keeps on forking, passing through *incompossible presents*, returning to not-necessarily true pasts"[42]. And, according to Martin-Jones's reading of Deleuze's time-image and movement-image:

> Whether an image is a movement- or a time-image depends on the degree to which it de- or reterritorialises time. The closer it is to establishing a linear narrative, the more likely it is to be a movement-image. By contrast, the more visible the labyrinth, the closer to the time-image.[43]

41 Deleuze: *Cinema 2*, p. 123.

42 Ibid., p. 98.

43 Martin-Jones: *Deleuze, Cinema and National Identity*, p. 27.

Deleuze's crystal-image helps us see that the temporal line in *Good Men, Good Women* forks and keeps on forking, weaving together fragments of Liang Ching and Chiang Bi-yu in different layers of the past, some true and some not necessarily true, and the myriad splitting of the actual and the virtual. The deterritorialised time, with a labyrinth of different sheets of past which manifest in different layers of virtualities, carries a historical dimension in Hou's vertical mosaic. In fact, the indiscernible virtual images, in juxtaposition with the actual images, compose the historically informed spatial mosaic in *Good Men, Good Women*. As the representations of the past are embedded behind several layers of virtualities against the multilayered mise-en-scène, and are consequently deterritorialised and rendered ambiguous and indiscernible, Hou refuses to take up the task of directly representing historical events and providing single-minded readings of history. By forking into images with different qualities, Hou's portrayal of the unsettled and unsettling personal and collective trauma provides myriad ways of interpretation without being restraining and dogmatic. We can see that the mapping between the crystal of the actual and the virtual, and that of past and present, correlates with Hou's multiple identities, which embrace both his roles as a mainlander and as a nativist. Indeed, the strategy of using the virtual to deal with the impossibility of 'truthfully' representing the historical past in *Good Men, Good Women* resonates with Egoyan's vertical mosaic; in both cases, virtual distance is added to avoid direct confrontation with personal and collective trauma. However, whereas Egoyan always signposts and reterritorialises the virtuality of the doubly-mediated images, Hou simply leaves the actual and virtual to be juxtaposed in the labyrinth of the crystal-image.

The historical dimension of Hou's mosaic also corresponds to the camera's exploration of the celestial and the earthly space within the screen space. At the same time that *Good Men, Good Women* juxtaposes images with different temporalities and virtualities, the camera's wandering gaze places the earthly matters of here and now against the celestial space beyond the here and now. Instead of rushing to capture the centre of action, the camera tends to move freely upwards and downwards before capturing the object of observation. It is as if the camera were comparing the space on earth with the space above, and concluding that the suffering of people is trivial and unimportant compared to the vastness of nature. A bigger spatial perspective is thus provided on screen, and the spectator is allowed to jump away from the perspective of the here and now and access to wider and more tolerant readings of historical events. We see in the way Liang is introduced that the camera wanders down and left diagonally until it captures her presence. Similar camera movement is recurrent in portraying Chiang, Chong, and their friends walking towards the Nationalists' camp in order to join anti-Japanese resistance. With the ceiling or the sky as the beginning of these shots, it is as if the camera found the characters only accidentally during its journey towards the earthly world. Sometimes it is a well-grown old tree that initiates or ends camera movement; the camera takes its time fixing on a medium shot of its full shape, and wanders among its luxuriant foliage. Through the wandering gaze of the camera, Hou presents a sharp contrast between tumultuous earthly lower space, and the upper space beyond it as the space elsewhere. Furthermore, the wider spatial perspective generates wider historical perspective, which then works in combination with the multilayered mise-en-scène. Whereas the camera scans the screen vertically and contrasts celestial and earthly matters in *Good Men, Good Women*, the mise-en-scène is so multilayered and multifaceted on screen that the camera can explore the longitudinal space. For example, in the fragment of the rehearsal scene in the beginning, we see in the mid-ground the bodies of Chiang sitting on the wooden floor in front of a low wooden table and Chong standing on the right hand side. Some props are vaguely visible in the background, and the foreground is occupied by vague and truncated bodies of film professionals in front of a desk recording the progress of the rehearsal. Like the beginning fragment of *In the Hands of a Puppetmaster*, the screen space, corresponding to the historical depth of the subject matter, is layered by the presence of human bodies in the foreground. The moving bodies of film professionals create an extra layer of space in the mise-en-scène, further dividing the space between the camera and Liang and Chong in the mid-ground. This multilayered screen space is enabled by the 'half-outsider half-insider' camera position, which is placed right outside the edge of the stage, framing the characters in medium shots without zooming into close-ups. Hence, the historically informed mosaic in *Good Men, Good Women* is constructed in a myriad of ways. The indiscernible virtual images and the actual images are juxtaposed through mosaic narrative. The camera's wandering gaze explores the comparison between the celestial and earthly space vertically, to provide wider spatial perspectives, whereas screen space extends inwards longitudinally with the multilayered mise-en-scène.

In this section, I have demonstrated how Hou's historically informed mosaic space in *Good Men, Good Women* is constructed through mosaic narrative, which assembles languages, temporalities, spatialities and virtualities, the wandering gaze of the camera, and the exploration of the longitudinal space in the multilayered mise-en-scène. It is through the complex working of the mosaic that Hou's portrayal of historical events manifests its multiplying perspectives and forces. In the following section, I will continue to explore Hou's vertical mosaic with the analysis of *Three Times*, which structurally interweaves three time zones and three spaces.

5. *Three Times*

Three Times is Hou's second attempt at an overt structure of mosaic narrative by segmenting the whole film into three parts through montage, the first explicit mosaic narrative being *Flowers of Shanghai*. Approximating a miniature version of the Chinese folklore story *Romance Lasting Seven Lives*, in which the same couple in seven bodies of reincarnation suffers from their tragically everlasting and impossible love over seven eras, the three couples in three different eras, all played by the Taiwan-born stars Shu Qi and Zhang Zhen, also incarnate the characters caught in cycles by going back and forth in time. *Three Times* is co-produced by Hou's 3-H Productions, Sinomovie of Taiwan, and French production companies Orly Films and Paradis Films, with both the Taiwanese Huang Wen-Ying and the French Gilles Ciment as executive producers. It was nominated for Palme d'Or at Cannes Film Festival in 2005 and has also been widely distributed through international networks such as Filmmuseum Distributie in Netherlands, Bitters End in Japan, Océan Films in France, Palm Pictures and IFC Films in the USA, and Vértigo Films in Spain. *Three Times* thus combines production and distribution resources from France, Taiwan, and other locations, thanks to Hou's travelling and transnational filmmaking mode. Corresponding with the bringing-together of spaces in the extradiegetic filmmaking context through the travelling of Hou and his films, the three segments of the three couples are interwoven into a mosaic space, with multilayered mise-en-scène which corresponds to the film's movement back and forth in history. At the same time that images with different time frames are juxtaposed, the lingering gaze of the camera explores screen space vertically and horizontally, and facilitates the exploration of the longitudinal space in the mosaic of layered mise-en-scène, which corresponds to the depth of history.

Three Times' original Chinese title is *Best of Time*; the literal translations for each fragment's Chinese titles were "Dreams of Love", "Dreams of Freedom", and "Dreams of Youth", respectively, while the translations provided by the English subtitles are "A Time for Love", "A Time for Freedom", and "A Time for Youth", echoing the English title of Hou's earlier autobiographical film *The Time to Live, The Time to Die*. The original Chinese titles, similar to the original Chinese title "Drama, Dreams, Life" of *In the Hands of a Puppetmaster*, dwell on the portrayal of life as intertwining dreams in the course of history. The three couples' best time is their time together in places of entertainment: the pool-hall, brothel, and club, and they are evocative of three dreams, where small cycles merge into a bigger cycle. "A Time for Love" is the cycle of a romantic chase, beginning with a young man Chen in the 1960s, unsuccessfully attempting to gain the attention of Haruko, a pool girl. It continues with Chen's courting another girl, May, in a more persistent fashion. The natural cycle of life is the focus of "A Time for Freedom", set in the beginning of the 20th century, which ends with a little girl, who has just been sold to a brothel, learning to sing to the seven-stringed instrument. Ah Mei, the courtesan who is frequented by Mr. Chang, a revolutionary following the leadership of Sun Yat-sen, ages as the little girl is trained to be in her position. Jumping forward to the beginning of the 21st century in the third segment, "A Time for Youth", the cycle is composed of the pleasure-seeking young bisexual woman Jing having an affair with a young man Zhen behind the back of her girlfriend. By jumping back and forth in time and space, the film assembles mosaic pieces of the three stories from three distinct time frames and three locations. Temporally, it leaps between Japanese occupation, Sun Yat-sen's revolution against the Ching Dynasty government in the beginning of the 20th century, the 1960s, and the beginning of the 21st century. Spatially, it jumps between Kaohsiung port in the south of Taiwan, an old settlement in the north of Taiwan, and the urban cityscape of Taipei. Thematically, it explores obligatory military service, love of all kinds in different phases of life, the search for freedom of different natures, youth and age, and the contemporary and the bygone. As the spectator experiences three eras, three locations, and three atmospheres, language use shifts from Southern Min to written intertitles of Chinese characters, to Mandarin Chinese. The music changes from 1960s' songs such as *Rain and Tears* to the ancient tune of a zither-like seven-stringed instrument of 1911, which is replaced by the techno rock of 2005. The use of lamps evolves from a round yellowish light bulb, to an oil lamp, to the blue tone of a fluorescent lamp. It is also a film that opens up an intertextual mosaic space in Hou's oeuvre as a whole; it brings together the spaces from the port life in *Boys from Fengkui*, the pool table under a banyan tree in *The Time to Live, The Time to Die*, the claustrophobic silent imprisonment in *Flowers of Shanghai*, the turbulent modern couple's life in *Good Men, Good Women*, the road trip to the south in *Goodbye South, Goodbye*, and the neon lights and decadence in *Millennium Mambo*. Yet it departs from every single one of them in its time-travelling through montage. This is when Deleuze's theorisation of time-images, in which the present that passes and the past that is preserved chase after each other to indiscernibility, again becomes helpful.[44] As Deleuze writes:

> We constitute a continuum with fragments of different ages; we make use of transformations which take place between two sheets to constitute a sheet *of* transformation. [...] Perhaps, when we read a book, watch a show, or look at a painting, and especially when we are ourselves the author, an analogous process can be triggered: we constitute a sheet of transformation which invents a kind of transverse continuity of communication between several sheets, and weaves a network of non-localizable relations between them. In this way we extract non-chronological time. [...] All this is the territory of false recollections with which we trick ourselves or try to trick ourselves (*Muriel*). But it is possible for the work of art to succeed in inventing these paradoxical hypnotic and hallucinatory sheets whose property is to be at once a past and always to come.[45]

Seen in this light, the three fragments of different ages in *Three Times* are woven into a mosaic space with time frames connected by a non-localisable link. The non-linear and non-chronological time creates a zone "at once a past and always to come". We can see in *Three Times* that "The screen itself is the cerebral membrane where immediate and direct confrontations take place between the past and the future, the

44 Deleuze: *Cinema 2*, p. 119.
45 Ibid.

inside and the outside, at a distance impossible to determine, independent of any fixed point"[46]. As the film jumps from the 1960s back to the beginning of the 20th century and then forward to the 21st century, present, past, and future are no longer fixed notions lined up in a chronological order. The courtesan Ah Mei is not only the past life of May, but also the future. The body of Jing is not only May's next life, but also May's previous life. The stories of Ah Mei, May, and Jing are thus interconnected and essentially one story. At the same time that *Three Times* is a mosaic interwoven with the pre-industrial and post-industrial life, monarchy and democracy, imprisonment and mobility, innocent and decadent youth, traditional values, and modern thoughts projected on the screen, it is a mosaic of labyrinthine Deleuzian time, assembled by the images of the past, images of the present, and images to come. Meanwhile, it is also a mosaic of circular historical time, with interlaced historical periods unfolding against the backdrop of different architectural styles. As we are looking at the present from the past, and past from the present, *Three Times* portrays a historically informed mosaic, which allows us to step back to take a broader perspective and examine temporality beyond linearity. As discussed before, this is enabled by Hou's multiple identities as both the diasporic mainlander by birth and the adopted nativist by demeanor, and both insider and outsider.

This historical dimension of mosaic is also explored by the wandering gaze of the camera, as in *Good Men, Good Women*. In this mosaic space interwoven with past, present, and future, the camera's lingering gaze, juxtaposed with Hou's trademark long take and long shot, brings the earthly space of here and now and the celestial space of elsewhere together. Just as Hou introduces Liang, and contrasts the space far above and the earthly space in *Good Men, Good Women*, *Three Times* begins with a medium shot of a lamp hanging from the ceiling. The camera then tracks diagonally downwards to find May, before it moves leftwards to capture Chen. Its gaze lingers around the pool table, slowly shifting its attention to the movement of balls or characters. The brief moment of close but reserved interaction between the couple during the pool game is *in medias res* of the first fragment "A Time for Love". (Fig. 19) The narrative then jumps back in time to the backward tracking focusing on a close look at a rolling

46 Deleuze: *Cinema 2*, p. 125.

front bike wheel, followed by a close-up of Chen riding joyfully on a bike. These two fragments in the beginning pool scene and in the scene of bike-riding are also indiscernible images, because although we gradually get to know the character Chen, we cannot determine until the end of the film exactly when they take place in terms of the time line of the narrative.

Through this lingering gaze, mobility and immobility alternate under "the form of the trip/ballad"[47] in the mosaic space. The camera follows the protagonists, but also allows protagonists to leave the frame at due course. In "A Time for Love", a romantic hide-and-seek game becomes a road-trip around Southern Taiwan. Because of its geographical proximity to the sea, the ferryboat is the essential means of transportation to take Chen and May leftwards to leave and rightwards to enter Kaohsiung. In the second sequence of Chen's ferryboat journey, the camera traces Chen's boat left until another boat going in the opposite direction enters the frame. The camera then abandons Chen and turns its attention to the second boat, full of standing or seated women facing the shore. It pans across it and lingers on it, content with the absence of the main protagonist. The same lingering gaze of the camera, which scans the space from a means of transportation, can also be observed in "A Time for Youth". The camera is positioned on a vehicle driving in a lane parallel to that designated for motorbikes. It tracks the flank of Fu-ho Bridge, which connects Taipei city and Yung-ho County, even when the motorbike of Jing and Zhen falls behind and leaves the frame eventually.

The lingering gaze of the camera, which explores screen space vertically and horizontally, facilitates the exploration of the longitudinal space in the mosaic of layered mise-en-scène with great depth of field, which corresponds to the depth of history. Echoing the spatial fluidity and flexibility of architectural styles in Taiwan, in "A Time for Love", with a certain amount of temporal distance, the layering of screen space also rearranges spatial configurations. By shooting May, who works as a pool girl, as she routinely opens and closes the doors of the pool room in repetition, Hou constructs and reconstructs the space and unfolds its adjustability. Every morning, May pulls open two layers of sliding doors, and every evening, she closes them. The

47 Ibid., p. 3.

outer layer is made with a glass pane and the inner layer is made of wood as a safeguard. The glass door creates a feeling of openness even when it is closed, because it lets light in and keeps the indoor space visible while blocking wind, rain, and dust at the same time. In the various instances of long take in the pool room, the camera is placed right between the pool room and the inner room facing the two layers of front doors, in a 'half-insider half-outsider' seer position. On the left hand side of the frame there is a fragment of an undetermined wooden object, which is possibly a flexible screen or a piece of furniture. The screen space is thus sliced into three layers of space: the foreground, which is half obstructed by the wooden object, the mid-ground of the pool room, and the background of the outdoor space beyond the two layers of door. The same mosaic space can be observed in May's home and her neighbour's house, both examples of common postwar Minnan architecture, which Chen visits in search of May. Both houses are filmed with the camera from Chen's perspective in front of the front door, which is connected to the back door with a straight corridor. The camera position right outside the front door, in combination with the structure of the Minnan architecture, foregrounds the long and narrow household space, similar to the exploration of the cinema space in Hou's *The Electric Princess House* in the compilation film *Chacun son cinéma*. In the foreground, the screen door is closed to stop mosquitoes from flying in. The wooden doorframe partially blocks the foreground and creates an extra layer of space, but still allows the camera's vision to penetrate the inner layers of the house and reach the brightly lit space outside the back door right in the depth of the background. The outdoor space beyond the back door, vaguely visible in the remote end, forms an extra layer of space. In some other cases, the foreground is half-obstructed not by door frames or objects, but by human bodies, in a similar way to the beginning dining room long take of *In the Hands of a Puppetmaster*. For example, near the end of "A Time for Love", when May and Chen finally reunite, they have a conversation, May smiling and Chen smoking in the mid-ground. Instead of a door frame which partially obstructs our vision, an anonymous back of a pool-hall customer constantly comes into the foreground and blocks our view of the couple. The presence of the unknown human body thus creates an extra layer of space by the pool table immediately close to the camera.

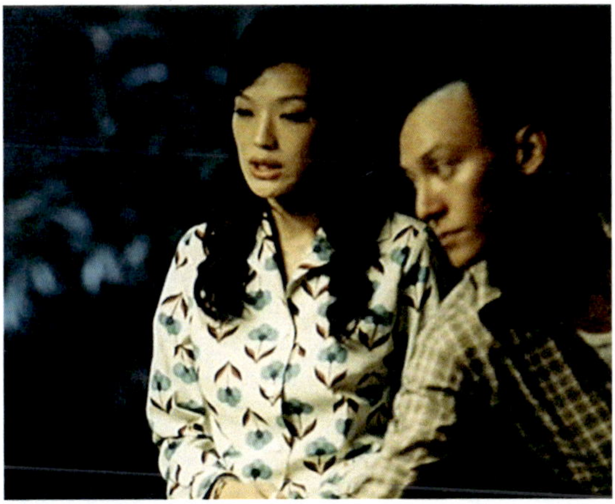

Fig. 19
The brief moment of togetherness on screen between the couple during the pool game (*Three Times*).

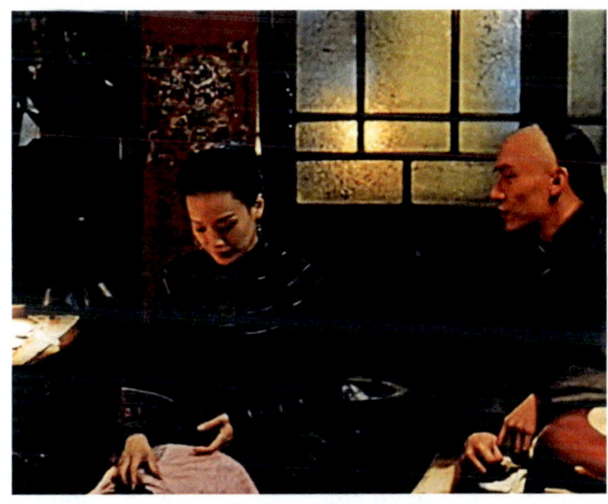

Fig. 20
The inner silent space multilayered with engravings and ornaments (*Three Times*).

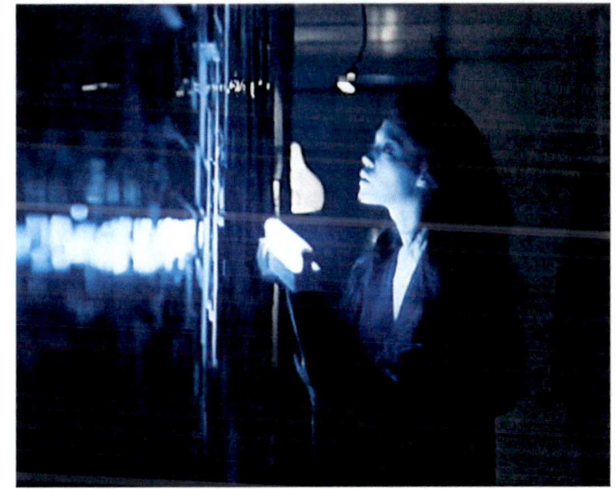

Fig. 21
Jing looks at Zhen's photographic portraits with fluorescent lighting from a lamp (*Three Times*).

The second segment, "A Time for Freedom", set the farthest from the present, is the segment most laden with history, and also the most layered in terms of mise-en-scène. Set in Taiwan under Japanese occupation in 1911, the Japanese government was still at the stage where they focused on exploiting the material resources of the island before systematically Japanising Taiwanese people in terms of hairstyle, clothing, housing, and urban planning. Taiwan was thus a Japanese colony with remnant late Qing Dynasty appearances. During this period, Japan approved of subversive activities against their Chinese enemy for their own benefits, and, therefore, Taiwan became a convenient geographical base against the monarchy in the mainland. At the same time that Taiwan is a transit space for the revolutionary Mr. Chang during his trips between Japan and mainland China, the courtesan Ah Mei's room is a transit space within the transitory space of Taiwan. The transit time frames and spaces compose a mosaic of layered mise-en-scène, corresponding to the folded historical background. Also starting with a shot of a lamp, the first shot of this fragment is a medium shot of the corridor leading to the bright outdoor space, framed in a way similar to the sequence in May's family home. In the mid-ground, a servant standing on a stool lights the oil lamp and covers it with a glass lampshade. In the background, we see a fragment of the outdoor space, which is blurry but visible through the half open sliding door behind layers of space. This space behind space, with great depth of field, lets light shine in and brings another spatial layer into the frame. It is also the only hint of outdoor space, since "A Time for Freedom" is completely set indoors. In addition, sound is banished from the still space and time, as it is shot in a silent film style with intertitles inserted between conversations. "A Time for Freedom" is thus like a luxurious cage, enclosed in an inner silent space, in which the mise-en-scène is multilayered with elaborately decorated engravings and ornaments on the furniture and screens. (Fig. 20) For example, in the scene of the negotiation between the owner of the brothel and Mr. Su's family about the marriage between Mr. Su and a courtesan, the camera, positioned in the corner right next to the door of the room, captures the complex triangular space defined by two wooden screens with delicately embossed patterns on each side, looking at the people in the room through the gap between the two screens. The plant pot is situated on the left side of the foreground, and a male servant on the right. A round table is situated in the mid-ground and, further in the background, we see the upper body of Mr. Su. As the camera occupies the 'half-insider half-outsider' position right outside the threshold, and never zooms in to study the negotiators' emotions, it allows the spectator to explore the complex, ornate, segmented, and layered mosaic space in the mise-en-scène.

As the female protagonist Jing's self-description on the internet says, "no past, no future, just a hungry present", the space in "A Time for Youth" is a contemporary urban space with very few traces of history, and thus fewer layers of space compared to the first two fragments. After time-travelling into postwar Taiwan and colonised Taiwan, we come back to the era of digital communication and neon lights. Jing, a rock singer, cheats on her girlfriend by having an affair with Zhen. Through a speedy physical and emotional journey in the urban world, as the opening tracking shot of the segment shows, it is a time of mobility devoid of complicated layering. As we can see from the dwelling of the protagonists Jing and Zhen, the space is white, thin and devoid of ornate decoration; neatly divided into sections of space according to practicality. In contrast to the light bulb and oil lamp hung from the ceiling earlier, the fluorescent lamp is casually put on the floor in the corridor connected to the entrance door. The lamp, instead of being fixed on the ceiling, is mobile; Jing picks it up to use its blue light to illuminate Zhen's collection of photographic portraits pasted on the walls of the corridor. (Fig. 21) The camera also tends to stay very close to the characters' faces, instead of occupying the 'half-outsider half-insider' seer position, so no extra layer of space is allowed to unfold in the mise-en-scène. For example, in the beginning of the segment right before the first intimacy between Jing and Zhen onscreen in Zhen's flat, we see Jing checking her mobile phone against a large windowpane, through which, if watching Hou's films laden with historical depth, we would expect to see the layering of the mise-en-scène with great depth of field. Yet in this scene, dark blue curtains cover most of the window, and the crack in front of which Jing stands leads to a foggy urban background covered in complete white, which does not open up to more layers. Subsequently the intertwining bodies of Jing and Zhen in the corner between a wall and a wardrobe, portrayed in close-ups, occupy most of the screen space and hence, no further layers behind the wall are added in the mise-en-scène. The same kind of space without multilayered mise-en-scène can also be seen in filming the flat shared by Jing and her girlfriend.

The camera stays closely with the protagonists, framing their faces in close-ups, in which faces occupy most of the frame in focus, and the small chunk of space behind them is blurry and invisible. Even in medium shots, the camera is positioned within the room, looking at a curtained window or a wall in the mid-ground, which stops the gaze from going deeper towards the background. Sometimes the screen space is even completely filled with unframed virtual images from communication devices, such as the screen of mobile phones, which show text messages, and the screen of computers, on which the protagonists type and edit music or photos. As there is no ornate screen door or embossed windows in the foreground, and the distance between the camera and the subject matter is shortened, the vision to the background is unobstructed. The screen space is thus shallow, instead of being layered in the longitudinal sense in the mise-en-scène. As the era of neon lights, digital communication, and massive visual production with the aid of photographic means is spatially rid of ornaments and minimalistic, the screen space is transient, amorphous, minimalistic, and less of a mosaic of multilayered mise-en-scène.

Corresponding to Hou's multiple heritage and transnational filmmaking networks in Taiwan, mainland China, Japan, and France, Hou's mosaic of multilayered mise-en-scène in the East Asian context goes vertically into the historical dimension. This kind of mosaic space is facilitated by the 'half-outsider half-insider' seer position of the camera placed right outside the architectural threshold, which explores the flexible space of Minnan and Japanese architecture. The more screen space is laden with marks of history, the more the gaze of the camera is obstructed through multilayered reframing and the more the screen space is layered with multiple segments building depth of the field. Therefore, the deeper the sense of history is, the deeper and richer the mosaic space is in Hou's films. In the following chapter, I will demonstrate how Haneke's three-dimensional fluid mosaic integrates both the horizontal dimension of socioeconomic and geopolitical mosaic and the vertical dimension of history.

Part III

Three-dimensional Mosaic: Horizontal and Vertical

Chapter 4
Michael Haneke: Fluid Mosaic, Crossing and Recrossing Boundaries

1. Introduction

Michael Haneke's mosaic, going both horizontally across spaces and vertically towards the depth of history, interweaves a three-dimensional mosaic of geopolitics. In this form of mosaic, there is an interplay between the underdeveloped and developed, under-privileged and privileged, and colonial and postcolonial worlds. It manifests through the fluid exchanges between the smooth and the striated, the actual and the virtual, and places and non-places at the horizontal level; at the same time, it forms the vertical mosaic which brings together fragments from different time frames. As mosaic narrative weaves narrative threads of the bodies of multiple Georges, Annes, Bennys, and Eves, the prototypical bourgeois family members in Haneke's films, with those of other characters, not only are socioeconomic and geopolitical spaces assembled, but the historical consequences of post-Berlin wall and a postcolonial reality are also brought into the same spatial plane. The bringing-together of spaces in Haneke's film works correlates with the assemblage of global flows of money, cast, crew, settings, and distribution networks in the film-making process, thanks to his border-crossing as a mosaic director. As Haneke travels between the bourgeois societies of the West, Austria, Germany, France, the USA, and establishes his unique transnational filmmaking milieu, he gathers filmmaking resources from different geopolitical spaces and is able to combine the best deal, such as the cheapest location with the best cast, within his film production context. I will first analyse Haneke's status as a mosaic auteur, and then analyse his construction of three-dimensional mosaic space, which correlates with the transnational filmmaking mode. This will be followed by the detailed analyses of the mosaic in *Code Unknown* and *Caché*.

2. Michael Haneke: The Mosaic Auteur in the West European Context

Haneke's mosaic space correlates with his assemblage of filmmaking resources, mainly from a variety of nations in Europe, through travelling. Roy Grundmann has pointed out the complicated multiple identities of Haneke, being "un-French", and not fully German or Austrian. He says that in Haneke's works, "artistic identification with(in) specific national contexts was hampered by a lack of membership in any of the groups that constitute national cinema as a historical and sociocultural formation"[1]. This lack of membership in fact implies multiple belongings and multiple identities. Born in Bavaria, Germany to German parents, Haneke was raised in Wiener Neustadt in Austria and educated in Vienna. In the beginning of his career, he was based in the German-speaking milieu while making TV films such as *Lemminge* (AU 1979, D: Michael Haneke et al.), *Three Paths to the Lake* (*Drei Wege zum See*, AU 1976), and *Wer war Edgar Allan?* (AU 1985) for the Austrian TV station ORF (Österreichischer Rundfunkt) and Schönbrunn-Film, as well as German TV station SWF (Südwestfunk), ZDF, and Sender Freies Berlin. His debut feature films *The Seventh Continent*, *Benny's Video*, and *71 Fragments* are all mainly set in urban Austria and funded by Wega Film in Vienna, which works in Thomas Elsaesser's "post-Fordist" model of European cinema production[2] by being based in a nation but looking for transnational investors such as European Union funding. Since *The Seventh Continent* was screened at Cannes and won awards at the Flanders International Film Festival and the Locarno International Film Festival, Haneke started to receive attention from a wider art cinema circuit. *Funny Games*, which follows the debut trilogy, was funded by Wega Film, ORF, and Austrian Film Institute, and filmed in the Viennese studio Rosenhügel. *Funny Games* was nominated for Palme d'Or at Cannes, which opened up more distribution routes for Haneke. His

1 Roy Grundmann: Haneke's Anachronism. In: Id. (ed.): *A Companion to Michael Haneke*. Malden, MA: Wiley-Blackwell 2010, pp. 1–50, here p. 9.

2 Elsaesser: *European Cinema*, p. 69.

first four feature films are based in Austria mainly with Austrian funding, but the cast comes from different places in the Germanophone world, such as Birgit Doll, Dieter Berner, Arno Frisch, and Otto Grünmandl from Austria; Udo Samel, Ulrich Mühe, Angela Winkler, and Susanne Lothar from Germany; and Anne Bennent from Switzerland. Crossing national borders and continuing his career in Paris after *Funny Games*, he directed French-speaking films *Code Unknown*, *The Piano Teacher* (*La pianiste*, AT / FR / DE 2001), *Time of the Wolf* (*Le temps du loup*, FR / AT / DE 2003), and *Caché* with French casts, including renowned actors such as Juliette Binoche, Isabelle Huppert, Daniel Auteuil, Benoît Magimel, and Béatrice Dalle, as well as German supporting casts, including Susanne Lothar and Udo Samel. *Code Unknown* and *Caché* are set in Paris, *The Piano Teacher* in Vienna, and *Time of the Wolf* in the countryside south of Vienna. The funding comes from diverse geopolitical spaces such as France (Canal+, MK2), Germany (Bavaria Film), Austria (Wega Film, ORF), and transnational European production (Arte). The crew is also international, with Austrian cinematographer Christian Berger, German cinematographer Jürgen Jürges, and French editor Nadine Muse. *Code Unknown* and *Caché*'s distribution routes will be discussed in the end of the chapter. *Time of the Wolf*, although not having attracted much attention at important international film festivals, has been widely distributed in Europe (through Artificial Eye in the UK, Atlanta Filmes in Portugal, and Ventura Film in Germany for example), Russia (through Intercinema Art Agency), and Australia (Madman Entertainment). *The Piano Teacher* has secured broad international distribution after winning best actor, best actress, and the grand prize from the jury at Cannes. In 2007, Haneke crossed over to the other side of the Atlantic by remaking his original *Funny Games* into *Funny Games U.S.*, in which he plants the global issues of violence and image consumption within the more localised and rooted context of the USA. In *Funny Games U.S.*, the European funding from the French Celluloid Dreams, British Halcyon, and Tartan Films is juxtaposed with the US setting of the film. It has been widely distributed through global networks such as CP Classics in Russia, Shaw Organisation in Singapore, Bir Film in Turkey, California Filmes in Brazil, and Nordisk Film in Finland. Haneke's latest films, *The White Ribbon* (*Das Weiße Band*, DE / AT / FR / IT 2009) and *Amour* (FR / DE / AT 2012), return to his familiar European context and is produced by Haneke's long-term collaborators, such as Wega Film, ORF, and Canal+, Les Films du Losange, and Bayerischer Rundfunk. As they were circulated within film festival circuits, such as San Sebastian, and both crowned with Palme d'Or at Cannes, its distribution route is truly global, ranging from Europe (including Serbia through MegaCom Film and Poland through Monolith), Latin America (including Mexico through Canana Films, Brazil through Imvision, and Argentina through Zeta Films), North America (Canada and USA through Sony Pictures), and Asia (including Hong Kong through First Distributors). With the established transnational filmmaking milieu, Haneke is now fully grounded in the international industry of art cinema, regularly funded by both national and international organisations, and his films are widely circulated within international film festivals and arthouse circuits.

As Haneke is a European citizen and an established auteur, he has the privilege to move freely within Europe and beyond Europe, and enjoys multiple identities as a Germany-born Austrian who works in France, Germany, Austria, and the US without being forced to choose one single belonging. Unlike the exilic or diasporic auteurs in Hamid Naficy's framework of accented cinema, Haneke's travelling is unimpeded and without any visa issues. In his French career, he is both an outsider-observer and an insider-observer, simultaneously being European (at the centre) but non-French (at the periphery) in the contemporary French society of the postcolonial era. In the Germanophone film world, on the other hand, he is both an insider because of cultural affiliations with Germany and Austria, and an outsider because he is equipped with filmmaking experiences in France and the USA.

3. Fluid Mosaic, Crossing and Recrossing Boundaries

Correlating to Haneke's transnational filmmaking mode and his complex identities, facilitated by his travelling, his films also bring cinematic and representational spaces together into a fluid mosaic. In the introduction I have illustrated that Haneke's *71 Fragments* interweaves fragmented storylines of Marian, Mrs. Brunner, Tomek, Hans and Max from diverse socioeconomic and geopolitical spaces through mosaic narrative. Instead of focusing on the trajectory of a certain character, *71 Fragments* jumps from one character's routine, trouble and partial perspective to another. Although the cause and effect of the chain of events are deliberately ambiguous, especially compared with the works of Iñárritu and Egoyan, the narrative gradually proceeds as the events unravel the characters' relationships and their impact on one another's lives. In fact, mosaic narrative brings not only fragments from different protagonists' points of view, but also a diverse range of spatial configurations, into a bigger picture. Different temporal and spatial planes are juxtaposed in the globalised local space, where disjunctive flows of all kinds cut space into fragmented pieces demarcated by lines. The different planes of space, here and elsewhere, the proximal and the faraway, the rural and the urban, and the public and the private, traversed by voluntarily or involuntarily wandering figures, coexist in Haneke's films. For example, the space of Romania is carried by Marian in *71 Fragments* and by Maria in *Code Unknown* to Vienna and Paris, respectively. The space of countryside is juxtaposed to urban life through the travelling of Jean in *Code Unknown*, Georges in *Caché*, and the unnamed girl who is later killed by Benny in *Benny's Video*. The colonised and later decolonised space is summoned to the postcolonial Paris by the family of Amadou in *Code Unknown* and that of Majid in *Caché*. In addition, Georges in *Code Unknown* brings the space of Kosovo back to Paris through his photos. While they encounter one another by chance, their spatial planes of race, gender, nationality, and social class cross over in the mosaic of Western bourgeois society, and sometimes result in conflicts of different degrees.

Haneke's bourgeois white characters usually carry perfectly white spaces with them, in opposition to the more frequent use of bright colours in the dwelling of the underprivileged and/or diasporic characters. These two colour schemes in the mise-en-scène, which connote social and cultural milieus, are assembled together into Haneke's mosaic. The use of white approximates what Gilles Deleuze describes as "cell-like and clinical white" with "a terrifying, monstrous character" in Robert Bresson's films.[3] For example, in the Viennese flats in *The Seventh Continent* and *Benny's Video*, the Parisian flats in *Code Unknown* and *Caché*, and in the countryside house in *Funny Games* and *Funny Games U.S.*, the minimalist walls and sofas of the flats of Anne and Georges are whitewashed, well-lit, and pristine, in

3 Deleuze: *Cinema 1*, p. 117.

combination with wooden furniture in dark tones, much to the taste of the bourgeoisie. In Richard Dyer's extended discussion in *White* of the notion of white in terms of hue, skin colour, symbol, and representation, he points out that white connotes the systematically privileged racial group in the Western society with socioeconomic dominance and advantages,[4] "cleanliness [...] the absence of dirt, spirituality the absence of flesh, virtue the absence of sin, chastity the absence of sex"[5], embodying Christianity[6] and morality[7]. In Haneke's films, however, the colour white often connotes the reverse of this tradition because it conveys the coldness and hypocrisy of a bourgeois dwelling. *Funny Games* goes even further and uses the white colour to imply horror and oppression, which, instead of protecting the bourgeoisie, menaces and destroys them. The spacious holiday home of Georg, Anna, and Schorschi in *Funny Games* is predominantly white everywhere: the main gate, walls, doors, cupboards, and banisters. Paul and Peter, the two aggressors, completely covered in white with white long sleeves, shorts, and gloves, first appear innocent and harmless because their white clothing has the connotation of purity, joy, and angelic presence. Their clean and unthreatening colour of clothing makes them melt perfectly into the mise-en-scène of the leisured class and creates the effects of camouflage for them. Paul and Peter's completely white gear, in combination with good manners and good hygiene, thus disguise them as adherents of bourgeois values and virtues so that their physical and psychological violence to the bourgeois family becomes even more unexpectedly shocking and unbearable to the audience.

On the other hand, the dazzling whiteness of the bourgeois world in Haneke's films is sharply contrasted with the multicoloured mise-en-scène in the dwelling of the working class. As we can see from the fragment which portrays the morning routine of the working class Hans' family in *71 Fragments*, a stable shot shows Hans waking up in a bedroom pasted with wallpapers in square and diamond patterns. It cuts to another stable shot, which reveals a corridor in the midground, decorated with faded and dusty wallpapers of geometrical

4 Richard Dyer: *White*. London / New York: Routledge 1997, p. 9.

5 Ibid., p. 75.

6 Ibid., pp. 15–17.

7 Ibid., p. 59.

patterns; the corridor is stuffed with many unorganised objects, which are piled on a washing machine. In the background, the kitchen tiles have complicated brown flowery patterns. Although the door and walls in the mise-en-scène are painted in white, their whiteness has a grey and filthy tone and is not as shining and impeccable as in the bourgeois household in *Funny Games*. In *Caché*, the colourful mise-en-scène indicates the dwelling of the second generation diasporic population from ex-colonies of France, in contrast to the white bourgeois households of the West European former colonisers. Majid, the son of Algerian immigrants in the colonial era, lives in a small studio flat, where the main door is painted blue and the kitchen door is bright yellow. When Georges is ushered in by Majid, the camera frames a plastic closet with black diagonal lines on the left margins and shows the wallpapers printed with patterns of green trees in the background. When Majid sits down on the light blue kitchen chair, the wallpaper behind him has the pattern of big and small green dots assembled into the shape of a cross. Not only far from being untainted white, all the wallpapers are covered in dirt and greasy filth and have faded from their original colours. From a stable shot framing Georges interrogating Majid, we can see in the mise-en-scène that Majid's personal objects, on a green cupboard behind Georges, are piled up to the ceiling. We can also see from Majid's shapeless red cushion and duvet on the green sofa that, unlike the bourgeoisie, he does not opt for white and is not afraid of vivid colours. By bringing the thread of Majid into the narrative, *Caché* also brings a space full of colours and patterns, which would not be seen in the mise-en-scène of a bourgeois space, as well as the space of the postcolonial character into the spatial plane. More will be said about the seer in postwar postcolonial any-space-whatever later, but it is important to point out here that Majid's colourful space brings in the historical/vertical dimension of postcolonialism. This vertical dimension, in combination with the horizontal dimension of socioeconomic and geopolitical divides, makes Haneke's mosaic three-dimensional.

The mosaic pieces in different colour schemes work in conjunction with an assemblage of disembodied close-ups dissociated from their immediate visual contexts, as we have seen in the example of *71 Fragments*. The framing of truncated body and object parts through the use of close-ups in fact starts from Haneke's first feature film *The Seventh Continent*. In this film, he explores the fictional beforehand of the actual inexplicable collective self-destruction of a bourgeois family of three, which happened in Linz, Austria. The very first shot of *The Seventh Continent* shows a close-up of a registration number being sprayed with foam, followed by close-ups of a car wheel, a frontal light, and a windowshield, which are dissociated from the rest of the car and their visual contexts. The close-ups of car parts are followed by a long take, in which the camera is situated in the middle of the backseat inside the car looking at the shadowy contours of two adults sitting in the front. Placed on two margins of the frame in darkness, the two human figures motionlessly face the car front. We later realise that they are Anne and Georg, the mother and the father of the bourgeois family, and the camera very likely occupies the position of their daughter Evi. In front of them is the windowshield being sprayed with foam and water and rubbed by big automatic white and blue brushes as the car goes through the car wash. The car wash sequence is captured by static camera for more than three minutes, while the credits are typed on screen in white. At the end of the car wash session, the film cuts to the reverse shot, showing the car front from the outside, driving out of the machine. The camera then pans right and fixates on a close-up of a poster with holey rocks in the foreground, sands in the mid-ground, and sea and mountain in the background, entitled "Australia". Immediately after, we are shown a chain of close-ups focusing on objects or truncated body parts: a clock-radio, feet slipping into bright red slippers, the lower part of a body getting out of a duvet, curtains being drawn open, a hand holding a toothbrush and squeezing toothpaste, binding shoe laces, operating the coffee machine, and spooning out milk and cereals. In these shots, bodies appear truncated and faceless because they are framed from the back, the crown of their head, or in segments. Occasionally, we see Georg's full body from the front in long shots when the camera follows his daily routine in the laboratory, but his face is barely discernible against the white and cold costumes and settings. It is 13 minutes into the film when we see the first close-up of a human face, when Evi feigns blindness at school. As the whole sequence of the waking-up ritual in close-ups is also repeated in the beginning of the second and the third part of the film, the use of close-ups and repetition work side by side to express the machine-like movement of the bourgeois family who only enacts their functional roles and loses their agency. In the seesaw-like, and repetitive, movement of numb and object-like human bodies manipulating objects, the family seems to live an inanimate and disembodied existence. With their torsos on screen and faces offscreen, their bodies are deterritorialised, depersonalised, nullified, and unidentifiable, and blended into the artificial space of their creation. They are mobile physically, but expressionless as objects, for trunks alone are incapable of voicing out or delimiting new territories.

Haneke's comment on *Au Hasard Balthazar* (FR 1966, D: Robert Bresson) can be seen as a comment on his own use of framing:

> Left out is the pretence of any kind of wholeness, even in the depiction of people. Torso and limbs come together for only scant moments, are separated, are treated like and at the mercy of objects, the face is one part among many, an immobile, expressionless icon of melancholy at the loss of identity.[8]

Haneke's close-ups, which deprive human bodies of agency, are edited together in a chain to compose a mosaic without revealing a complete and coherent whole. This marks the difference between Haneke's mosaic pieces of close-ups, and those of Egoyan, who always ties loose ends together after showing disembodied close-ups. Whereas Egoyan, in *The Adjuster,* separates the male protagonist's hand from its immediate visual context through framing and then zooms out to reterritorialise the image back to screen space, the fragments of close-ups in Haneke's mosaic are inserted as such and never reterritorialised into their visual contexts.

In Haneke's mosaic, the space of the setting and that of the cast (as well as their language use in the film) are sometimes disjoined to interweave a variety of geopolitical spaces together. Contrary to the consistent correspondence between the shooting location and where the setting is supposed to be in the diegesis, in Iñárritu's and Egoyan's mosaic, the 'real' location is sometimes ambiguous in Haneke's films as space becomes a mosaic where diverse spatial markers intermingle and the artificiality of film space is foregrounded. The discrepancy between spaces is especially poignant in the production of *The Piano Teacher* and *Time of the Wolf,* which casts French actors and actresses for the main roles (important figures in French cinema such

8 Michael Haneke: Terror and Utopia of Form, Addicted to Truth, A Film Story about Robert Bresson's *Au Hasard Balthazar.* In: James Quandt (ed.): *Robert Bresson*, trans. from French by Robert Gray. Toronto: Cinematheque Ontario 1998, pp. 551–559, here p. 559.

as Isabelle Huppert, Annie Girardot, and Benoît Magimal in *The Piano Teacher*; Isabelle Huppert, Béatrice Dalle, and Patrice Chéreau in *Time of the Wolf*) against Austrian settings (Vienna in *The Piano Teacher* and Ebenfurth and Frankenau-Unterpullendorf, south of Vienna, in *Time of the Wolf*) throughout the entire films. In both instances the diegetic world in Austria is juxtaposed with the space brought by French cast and crew. Staying faithful to the eponymous novel by Austrian writer Elfriede Jelinek, awarded The Nobel Prize in Literature in 2004, *The Piano Teacher* is set in Vienna. The distinctively Viennese settings, including the representational Viennese Konzerthaus in the ending sequence in front of which Erika (Isabelle Huppert) stabs her shoulder with a knife, is occupied by the body of the iconic French actress Isabelle Huppert with her French dialogues. The French cast pronounces all the original German names *à la française*; when Erika's mother watches TV in darkness while waiting for Erika's return at night, the TV programme is in French too. On the other hand, the German-speaking supporting actors and actresses, such as Susanne Lothar and Udo Samel, are dubbed into French. Their unsynchronised lips on screen clearly indicate that they are strangers in their own language zone, as they lose their voices. Rosalind Galt has attributed the mismatch of language use and location to *The Piano Teacher*'s overtly spoken coproduction mode.[9] Indeed, the jarring spaces carried by the cast and the setting correspond to its multinational funding resources from France (Canal+, MK2), Austria (Filmfonds Wien, Wega Film, ORF), and Germany (Bavaria Film International and Bayerischer Rundfunk), and the cultivation of audiences in the three nations, who are familiar with Germanophone literary works and/or French cinema. In the case of *Time of the Wolf*, although it also juxtaposes the spaces of French cast and an international crew (French editor Nadine Muse, Austrian editor Monika Willi, and German cinematographer Jürgen Jürges) to the setting of an unrecognisable Austrian countryside, the spatial disjointedness is hidden from the spectator. Since the diegetic setting of the unnamed post-apocalyptic countryside is deprived of national characteristics in *Time of the Wolf*, it can be anywhere in the

9 Rosalind Galt: The Functionary of Mankind: Haneke and Europe. In: Brian Price/John David Rhodes (eds): *On Michael Haneke*. Detroit: Wayne State UP 2010, pp. 221–244, here pp. 235–236.

world, including France. As a result, the actors and actresses' French dialogue creates a similar jarring feeling as *The Piano Teacher* only when the spectator becomes aware of the extradiegetic information of the shooting location. Though implicit in *Time of the Wolf* and explicit in *The Piano Teacher*, different geopolitical spaces in Europe are brought together into a mosaic through the incongruity between the cast and the setting; extra-diegetic elements thus bring a different layer of space to the diegetic world. This mode of spatial juxtaposition is possible only thanks to Haneke's transnational filmmaking milieu, which enables him to make the best strategic decision from a pool of talents and locales across national borders.

As Haneke's mosaic brings spaces together, the boundaries between spatial configurations such as the centre and the periphery, the smooth and the striated, and places and non-places are blurred and fluid through the characters' crossing and recrossing. As we can see in the first diegetic fragment of *71 Fragments*, Marian travels from the smooth rural space of the countryside to the striated urban metropolis full of non-places when he reaches the other side of the river. Haneke brings Marian's nomadic space into the hustle and bustle of the city of Vienna and opens up a dialogue between the privileged bourgeois West Europeans and the wandering orphan from the postcommunist Eastern Europe. Through travelling, the characters' position in relation to the centre and the periphery of a certain space is shown to fluctuate, because they shift between insiders and outsiders, and between residents and immigrants. This is also how mosaic space in Haneke's films is fluid and constantly under redefinition, with shifting and interchanging boundaries. In *Time of the Wolf*, for example, the white Parisian upper middle class family of Anne, Eve, and Benny, who supposed to be at the centre in terms of the dominance of their race, ethnic, and socioeconomic background, is marginalised to the position of underprivileged immigrants, like Marian in *71 Fragments*, Maria in *Code Unknown*, and Majid's family in *Caché*, once they leave Paris and enter their countryside house. Instead of being the dominant class with the usual privileges and socioeconomic prestige, they are helpless and hungry, like everyone else in the cold post-apocalyptic world, and are ruled by an ambiguous authority. Their accusation of murder against the couple who kill the father of the family in front of their very eyes loses credibility, contrary to the favoured position of Anne and Jean over the second generation Malian Amadou in front of the policemen on Boulevard Saint-Germain in *Code Unknown*. The status of cities, too, shifts between central and peripheral positions. The two glamorous capitals, Vienna and Paris, populated by the dominant white West European population and still shining with the glory of the vanished empires, usually occupy a 'central' position in terms of their economic, national, and cultural power, especially compared to locations such as Kosovo, Romania, Algeria, or Mali. However, Haneke's films deliberately reject their centrality by inserting fragments from different geopolitical spatial planes, including images from 'peripheral' locations, into the settings of Paris and Vienna, which disrupts their occupation of the screen space. In *71 Fragments*, we see that the spaces of Somalia, Haiti, and Kosovo in war are constantly brought into the diegesis set in Vienna through the unbidden news reportage. In *Code Unknown,* between two Parisian fragments of Anne dubbing for a film and being intimidated in a metro, we see a fragment of Amadou's father driving down a slope from a boat through a crowded market in Mali. The static camera, placed between two front seats, captures the images of the local Malians in colourful robes and selling piles of bananas by the road, jumping away from Paris and Vienna to other spaces within a couple of minutes. Thus, the characters' and the cities' positions at the centre and at the periphery are fluid and fluctuate, instead of being absolute and categorical.

We can also see the fluidity of boundaries in the exchange between places and non-places of Marc Augé. In fact, non-places proliferate in Haneke's mosaic, as we can see from the sequence before Erika enters a sex shop at a mall in *The Piano Teacher.* Twenty minutes into the film, we see a stable medium shot of a modern lift with silver metal structures and large glass pane windows, in front of which a truncated male body in a beige coat walks in the foreground before Erika walks out of the lift. The camera follows her walking rightwards and then leftwards as she walks around a corner. She passes an escalator, towards which two unknown men walk in the background. As she walks past a busy café, she almost bumps into a couple and is pushed abruptly by a man in black leather jacket absorbed in a phone conversation. When she turns her head back from staring at the man, she walks by a gaming parlour with car race machines and slot machines. After passing a small bakery, Erika enters a sex shop. This sequence demonstrates that 'travellers' (or people in transit) of different kinds, such as Erika, pass through transient spaces such as escalator, lift, café, gaming parlour and façades of different shops, and brush past strangers whom they are not going to meet again. These non-places, which proliferate sameness, are blank, standardised, and lacking identities and sustainable relations. They are the locations which can be easily transplanted to other films and other countries because they are bereft of characteristics of their own. Yet the status of these non-places is actually a lot more fluid in Haneke's mosaic than what Augé suggests. Although Augé recognises the interconnectivity between places and non-places, his notions of places and non-places seem to remain mutually exclusive concepts opposing each other. He writes,

> In the concrete reality of today's world, places and spaces, places and non-places intertwine and tangle together. The possibility of non-place is never absent from any place. Place becomes a refuge to the habitué of non-places (who may dream, for example, of owning a second home rooted in the depths of the countryside). Places and non-places are opposed (or attracted) like the words and notions that enable us to describe them.[10]

To think about Augé's distinction between places and non-places through the lens of Deleuze and Guattari's framework, it would be fundamentally "a formalizing, linear, hierarchized, centralized arborescent model"[11]. Seen in this light, the model of non-places provides useful but oversimplified binaries, which divide 'terrains' into categories and subcategories and establish linear relations from one centre to another. Haneke's spatial configurations portrayed in his film world, on the contrary, clearly demonstrate that places and non-places are not fixed, divided, and opposed concepts, but rather, they flow into each other. The supposed residing places are represented as contractual and unaffectionate, whereas the supposed non-places of chance encounter are where the hasty passers-by are forced to stay and establish a relationship of some kind because of chance encounter and the resultant conflicts. Haneke's films are thus the mosaic space in which places and non-places work in the process of change and negotiation without being restricted in a fixed or stable notion. While crossing one another's path, a supposedly transitional space becomes a dwelling; when the sustainable relationship is lost, a place stops being a dwelling with relationships and identities. We have

10 Augé: *Non-Places*, p. 107.

11 Deleuze / Guattari: *A Thousand Plateaus*, p. 361.

seen how non-places cease being transitional and start to acquire a sustainable relationship in the example of *71 Fragments*. Mrs. Brunner, Hans, Max, and Tomek come to the bank area for specific reasons but they fail to simply pass by because of Max's shooting. This transformation goes hand in hand with the portrayal of the residing places becoming dysfunctional and purely pragmatic. The supposedly relational 'places', which are people's refuge after a whole day passing by transit non-places, seem to lack their identity and generate a merely contractual bond. For example, family, which is supposed to contain the most intimate interpersonal relationship, becomes such a non-place for the Austrian bourgeois family in *The Seventh Continent* that they are ready to abandon it at all costs. Anne, Georg, and Evi in *The Seventh Continent* physically observe the codes of interaction but psychologically simply pass by their home as though they were passing by petrol stations and cinemas. Instead of sustainable bonds and relational connections, only functional relationships are established because the characters experience a communication breakdown. Interacting at home, according to mutually agreed functional convention, the characters go through the quotidian family life in a chain of ritual interaction assembled by greeting, exchanging small talk and having meals together.

The fluctuating nature of boundaries and the shifting positions in Haneke's mosaic can also be seen in terms of Deleuze and Guattari's notions of the smooth and the striated, which correspond to the urban and the rural. The urban space, such as Vienna in *71 Fragments* and *Benny's Video* and Paris in *Code Unknown* and *Caché*, is often portrayed as the striated space: signposted, demarcated, and confined. The rural outdoor space, such as the setting in *Time of the Wolf* and *Funny Games*, on the other hand, is often the smooth space which is open and infinite, and possesses a stronger power of deterritorialisation. Ewa Mazierska and Laura Rascaroli point out that the hearing-impaired children's futile guesses ("alone", "hiding place", "bad conscience", "sad", "imprisoned") to a girl's mimed gesture in the opening sequence of *Code Unknown* serve as a guide to the whole film.[12] They propose that the expressions "alone", "sad", and "bad conscience" describe the experiences of communication breakdown

12 Ewa Mazierska / Laura Rascaroli: *Crossing New Europe: Postmodern Travel and the European Road Movie*. London: Wallflower 2006, pp. 142–143.

between Anne and Georges, Anne and her neighbours, and Jean and his father, which are common in Western society, whereas "hiding place" and "imprisoned" are related to the postcommunist diaspora and the new migratory movement.[13] Here, I argue that these expressions approximate the characters' struggle with the level of striation in their surroundings. As I have demonstrated in the analysis of Iñárritu's *Babel* in chapter 1, there seems to be a required amount of striation without which or exceeding which people feel uncomfortable and have the task to adopt themselves to the surrounding space. Striation renders their bodies numb and automatic, and too much striation implies imprisonment and suffocation. Too much smoothness, however, implies danger and uncertainty. On the one hand, Haneke's characters in the Western bourgeois society are bound in their assigned position and space without having an exit which could possibly open up to the smooth. They are used to striation and move within spaces well demarcated by walls, but striation also connotes confinement and repetitiveness. For example, Evi in *The Seventh Continent*, Erika in *The Piano Teacher*, and Max in *71 Fragments* are always placed within four walls, shuttling between school, home, and limited choices of other locations. Even the sportive activities are performed indoors, such as Evi's vaulting horse in *The Seventh Continent*, Max's table tennis in *71 Fragments*, and Anne's and Pierrot's indoor swimming in *Code Unknown* and *Caché*. Their confinement within enclosed spaces is emphasised through Haneke's portrayal of these activities in repetition and long duration. The fragment of Max repetitively waving a table tennis racket back and forth to hit the balls automatically thrown from the offscreen table tennis robot lasts for almost three minutes on screen in *71 Fragments*. In the fragment of vaulting horse in *The Seventh Continent*, we see the offscreen instructor's two hands repetitively helping children jump over the vaulting horse placed in the lower centre of the frame. In the striated space, bodies are confined and become a machine part moving autonomously and repetitively instead of spontaneously. When the level of striation becomes extreme, as will be illustrated in the analysis of *Code Unknown*, the well-demarcated space stops being a safely guarded fortress for the bourgeois and becomes horrifying. However, when a space is completely devoid of striation in complete smoothness,

13 Ibid., p. 143.

such as the rural settings in *Funny Games* and *Time of the Wolf* in which outdoor sport is practiced, it exposes the protagonists, who are accustomed to a certain level of striation, to danger, threat, and uncertainty. In these smooth spaces, which cannot be regulated, the protection of well-regulated indoor space is broken down. Golfing, boating, and horse-riding substitute for table tennis, vaulting horse, and indoor swimming, but these practices in the smooth wilderness are haunting and ominous rather than liberating. Instead of being repetitive and confining activities for one's well being, like the sport in striation, they are a tool for violence and reinforcement of lawful regulations. In *Funny Games*, the golf club is used to attack both the father of the family Georg and the dog. The boating facilities by the lake are used to kill Anna by dropping her in the water with bound hands and feet, and to take the killers Peter and Paul to the next victim. In *Time of the Wolf*, horse-riding indicates power, freedom, and more access to information and goods because the self-appointed enforcers of rules come on horseback.

The shifting positions of different but interchangeable places and non-places and the delicate balance between the smooth and the striated in Haneke's mosaic space resonate with what Mazierska and Rascaroli term the alternation between travel and home. They argue that *Code Unknown* portrays the forming of a new society because of post-Berlin wall migratory movements, "in which the old Western bastions of national and personal identity have been undermined and replaced by a void, a fragmentation of experience and a diffuse awareness of the increasing ambiguity of the real and of the lack of codes to interpret it"[14]. It is in this context that "sedentariness and rootedness have lost their meaning and have been replaced by movement, which is often senseless and inconclusive"[15]. Here, I relate this space of redefined frontier and territory to the contextualised any-space-whatever 40 years after the Second World War. In fact, Europe in Haneke's films is not the same postwar deserted shantytown that Deleuze considers in *Cinema 2*, since the cityscapes have been reconstructed and rebuilt. It becomes the new kind of postwar and postcolonial any-space-whatever, within which the dwellers come from a

14 Mazierska / Rascaroli: *Crossing New Europe*, p. 145.

15 Ibid., pp. 145–146.

spectrum of geopolitical and socioeconomic backgrounds resulting from historical causes. Some characters are the empowered bourgeois at the centre, such as the family of Georg, Anne, and Evi in *The Seventh Continent* and Walter Klemmer in *The Piano Teacher*. Some come from relatively underprivileged areas in the developed West, such as Hans in *71 Fragments*. Some migrate from developing post-communist East European countries, such as Marian in *71 Fragments* and Maria in *Code Unknown*, and others from ex-colonies of Western European countries, such as Amadou in *Code Unknown* and Majid in *Caché*. Especially salient in the French part of Haneke's career, the variegated characters' paths cross in any-space-whatevers and bring postwar, postcolonial, and postcommunist spaces together. Although the lines between the protagonists are carefully drawn on the basis of social class, ethnicity, gender, and migratory status in Haneke's films, the presence of diversity, brought along in the postcolonial globalised world, clearly indicates a society overcoded with boundaries, which fail to define it. In fact, the original symbols and frontiers lose their anchorage in Haneke's films, because of the multiplicity of signs and spaces carried by the characters into the mosaic.

Haneke's any-space-whatevers manifest themselves in the way that city spaces are portrayed as deglamourised and disjointed duplicates of one another. Unlike Haneke's early emphasis on the travelling camera along Venice's signature canals and alleys in his TV film *Wer war Edgar Allan?*, his feature films refuse any portrayal of cities' singularity and uniqueness. The cities' atmospheres are preserved at a minimum level and their trademarks are not explicitly portrayed. Usually the camera observes cities from the height of an average person, and does not view them like Icarus flying over rivers and valleys with the bird's-eye view. Instead of overviews and establishing shots, the disengaged camera frames the façades of the buildings stably, or tracks them as well as the people walking beside them. The spectator is not shown any grandiose architecture, but only some façades in front of which the chance encounters between people from different backgrounds happen. In fact, the landmarks of Eiffel Tower and Cathédrale Notre-Dame de Paris in Paris, and Ring Boulevard or Stephansdom in Vienna, are deliberately avoided by Haneke's choice of settings. By eschewing landmarks and focusing on the mise-en-scènes of anonymous façades, Linz, Vienna, and Paris seem shockingly similar, all overwhelmed by non-places. They are stripped of glamour and made banal. The peep-show shop in which Erika satisfies her sexual desire in *The Piano Teacher* and the video shop Benny frequents in *Benny's Video* could easily be situated in Paris instead of in Vienna. Meanwhile, in *Caché*, the cinema where Georges takes shelter after witnessing Majid's suicide and the gas station with vending machines where Georges takes a deep breath before venturing into the tower block shown in an anonymous videotape could be Vienna instead of Paris.

As there is no fixed rootedness anymore, this mosaic any-space-whatever of the postcolonial globalised Western Europe becomes mixed and disjoined with all its fluid boundaries, and the dwellers become the seers who don't know how to react to the space which they reside in. The bodies of Georges, Anne, and their children, portrayed by different actors and actresses, become the multiplication of seers who try to make sense of the emerging new space in which various spatial configurations juxtapose. For example, in *The Seventh Continent*, the bourgeois family of Georg, Anna, and Evi does not know how to react to the surroundings when their striated space is juxtaposed with the smooth virtual space of Australia, which is carried into the actual spatial plane through a poster. Filmed almost exclusively indoors in complete striation, they are completely immersed in their automated space with all the repetitive gestures and machine-like movements. Apart from the transitional space between a car and a building, the only moments when the family is exposed to an open space are before leaving their grandparents' place and while Georg sells their car. Even in these two sequences, they are not immersed in the open smooth space and remain confined in striation. In the first instance, we see a chain of images showing their truncated body parts putting luggage in the car boot, opening and closing car doors, and a hand twisting a key in the ignition. Whereas the grandparents' faces, captured in frontal close-ups against the background of a wall embedded with wooden fragments, are clearly visible, Georg, Anna, and Evi are framed between chest and thigh in this sequence. Even at the moment that they are outdoors in the smooth, they are about to return to striation already, and are portrayed as faceless disembodied fragments interacting with metal parts of the vehicle. In the latter sequence, Evi wanders between rows of second-hand cars resembling a deserted land taken over by machines. Although the garage is in an open space, the presence of discarded cars, which have also been a symbol of striation in the end of Iñárritu's *Amores Perros*, further segment space. At the same time that the family of Anna, Georg, and Evi is rooted in their assigned striated position in Western Europe and becomes truncated bodies who do not know how to react to the actual space, the dreamy images of the faraway Australia constantly intrude in their space and question their fixed status. Australia signifies the imaginary ideal smooth space in the imagination of the leisure class family who loses actual connection with their striated life. It is first represented in a tourist poster with the slogan "Welcome to Australia" glued at the exit of the carwash machine frequented by the family. The contrast between brown pitted rocks, brown sand and the blue sea is so striking that the colours seem artificial and virtual. The dreamlike smooth outdoor space on the beach of Australia, situated in the opposite hemisphere to Austria, is a sharp contrast to the gridded indoor space of Linz. At a later point in the film, the still image of the poster is transformed into a moving image without being summoned. This fragment, inserted between the diegetic moments of the family, shows the tides batting the shore, accompanied by diegetic sound of the seaside. Whereas the frozen image on the poster comes alive in the moving pictures, the family, on the pretext of immigration to Australia, gradually refuses the status of being alive. To a certain extent, the image of the dreamy Australia unroots, detaches and disconnects Georg, Anna, and Evi from their space in Austria, by bringing in the smooth space, providing the vision of an alternative space to their dwelling of any-space-whatever, and hence rendering the boundaries fluid and difficult to react to.

Furthermore, this postcolonial globalised any-space-whatever is saturated with doubly-mediated virtual images. Continuing the example of *The Seventh Continent*, the TV set dominates the household. In the scene right after a medium shot of Anna receiving a phone call from the school teacher telling her that Evi feigns blindness, we see a close-up of the TV set, which occupies most of the screen. The TV screen is further reframed into several layers. Within the frame of the TV, on the left hand side, we see a square screen of a computer game on which a car goes through gridded streets, and a small square showing the programme presenter in front of a computer in the right corner. Later on, after Anna's brother has a nervous breakdown at the dinner table, we see a medium shot which focuses on the TV set embedded within a wooden bookshelf. In darkness, the TV screen, which plays the Eurovision Song Contest, is the only place which emits light. In *71 Fragments*, when Tomek talks to his alienated daughter on the phone, we see truncated TV images in front of him projecting close-ups of children, birds in the sky, water flowing, black and white images of military marches and riots on the street with a tank. These omnipresent, multiply-reframed virtual images in Haneke's films sometimes overwhelm the dwellers in the West European any-space-whatever and put them in the seer position; they see their surrounding spaces like a spectator in front of a screen onto which their life is projected without being empowered to react. Benny in *Benny's Video*, for example, is this kind of seer who loses connection with the actual space and always perceives the world through the virtual recording behind the camera. He spends all his time indoors, shuttling between home, the video rental shop, school, fast food restaurants, and a club where his friends hang out. Instead of looking out of the window to see the outside space directly, he records the street view from a camera situated by the window and projects the images on a TV screen in his dark room in which the long thick curtains are always drawn. He also repetitively pauses, rewinds, and replays the recorded image on the TV screen, especially the images of a pig being shot by a syringe gun in his parents' farm. Not only is Benny always seeing the actual space through doubly-mediated virtual layers, he is also represented as doubly framed by home camcorder at the only occasion of being outdoors in the smooth space of Egypt with his mother. Against the backdrop of sand hills in the desert, instead of reacting to the actual space, Benny remains locked behind doubly-mediated virtual images. He is thus caught in the image-saturated any-space-whatevers within double reframings and between mosaic pieces with different virtualities with fluid boundaries. Even the shocking scene when he kills a runaway girl from the countryside, whom he met in front of a video rental shop, is portrayed behind several layers of mediation on screen. After Benny pulls the trigger of the syringe gun at her for the first time, it is only from the monitor within the screen space, which projects the image filmed from behind her back, that we see the girl's body falling to the floor. Subsequently the camera stays at the close-up of the TV monitor, which continues to film from the same angle. From this reframed virtual image, we see the girl climbing on the floor, Benny dragging her to the space beyond both the diegetic screen, and the screen within the screen, appearing on the doubly-mediated screen again to refill the bullet in a hurry and rushing offscreen. This is accompanied by the continuous sound of the girl's shouting, which stops after we hear a second firing of the syringe gun. These examples show that it is in the virtual that Benny sees and is seen, and his existence in the virtual keeps on intruding into the actual. In his refusal to see the actual unmediated world, Benny is the seer who hides behind the virtualised images reframed by the camera and projected on a screen; we thus see a mosaic space of the *mise-en-abyme* of images within images.

In this section, I have discussed how Haneke's mosaic is fluid through the characters' crossing and recrossing between the boundaries. In the following analyses of *Code Unknown* and *Caché* I will illustrate in more detail how the horizontal plane of socioeconomic divides and geopolitical differences, between non-places and places and the smooth and the striated, is juxtaposed with the vertical plane of historical consequences through the bringing-together of the spaces between formerly-colonised people and their former-colonisers.

4. *Code Unknown*

Code Unknown demonstrates Haneke's three-dimensional mosaic, in which both the horizontal mosaic of diverse socioeconomic and geopolitical spaces, and the vertical mosaic of historical cause and effect manifest themselves in the constantly shifting positions of places and non-places, as well as the changing positions of the characters in relation to the surroundings and the screen space. All the dynamism thus composes a fluid mosaic on screen.

Code Unknown draws funding from France (Canal+, MK2), Germany (Bavaria Film, ZDF), Romania (Filmex, Romanian Culture Ministry), and transnational European productions (Arte). The cast comes from a wide geopolitical range including Juliette Binoche and Thierry Neuvic from France, Josef Bierbichler from Germany, Luminiţa Gheorghiu from Romania, the Lebanon-born Armenian-Canadian Arsinée Khanjian, and Maimouna Hélène Diarra from Mali, who has also acted in *Mooladé* (SN 2004, D: Ousmane Sembene) and *Bamako* (ML 2006, D: Abderrahmane Sissako). The crew is the usual international team of Haneke, with the German Jürgen Jürges as cinematographer, and French Nadine Muse and Austrian Andreas Prochaska as editors. It has been awarded a minor Prize of the Ecumenical Jury at Cannes without causing a stir within international film festival circuits, and although not widely distributed at the time of its release, it has been circulated through the Western European networks such as MK2 in France, Artificial Eye in the UK, and Vértigo in Spain.

As the full title, *Code Unknown: Incomplete Tales of Several Journeys* suggests, the film explicitly foregrounds mosaic narrative like *71 Fragments*, by interweaving narrative threads from a variety of characters and hence bringing a diverse range of spaces together. This corresponds to the juxtaposition between spaces from diverse geopolitical backgrounds in the transnational filmmaking mode, which is enabled by Haneke's travelling. The film begins with a long shot of a girl stepping sideways towards the pristine wall behind her, while shrinking her body with a confused and frightened look. It is followed by a series of close-ups of children's faces gesturing with sign language to guess the meaning of the previous performance. These close-ups alternate with close-ups of the girl shaking her head. Then the film jumps to a tracking shot, which will be discussed in detail later on, in which the teenager Jean, the runaway younger brother of the war photographer Georges who lives with the actress Anne, asks Anne for shelter in their flat. After Jean throws a wrinkled paper bag on the lap of Maria, a begging Romanian woman in front of a bakery, Amadou, the descendent of a Malian diasporic family, starts a fight with him and policemen intervene. This jumps to a series of still photos of dead bodies, a burning house, distressed human faces, and civilians and soldiers dragging wounded people, accompanied by Georges' voice-over reading aloud a letter to Anne recounting his experiences in war-ridden Serbia. The scene cuts to a stable camera by the side window of a taxi, framing the profile of a driver speaking in an African dialect on the phone and politely leaving a passenger by a taxi stop after the phone conversation. What follows is a fragment in which the camera closely fixates on the face of Anne, who acts the role of a frightened woman being captured and imprisoned by a psychopath according to the offscreen director's instruction, on an unframed stage. (Fig. 22) The cameraman slightly shakes the camera in response to the director's call, and the director's voice stands in for the psycho-killer's role. The fragment afterwards is filmed from inside the countryside house of Jean's father, who serves Jean beetroot upon his arrival and is revealed as emotionally tormented by Jean's alienation when the father is in the bathroom alone.

From these fragments we can see that the film's mosaic narrative continuously jumps between narrative threads of characters who are involved in the conflict, which takes place in the very centre of Paris on Boulevard Saint-Germain in the opening tracking shot. With the interweaving narrative, characters with diverse socioeconomic and geopolitical backgrounds encounter and bring their respective spaces together. Jean is a teenager who rebels against the prospect of working at his father's farm in the countryside; Georges, Jean's brother, is a war journalist, coming back to Paris only between missions in war-ridden zones such as Kosovo and Somalia; Anne (played by Juliette Binoche), the partner of Georges, is an established actress who is working in both film and theatre projects. Amadou teaches the deaf and mute children drum-playing; his father later abandons the family and goes back to Africa for an unknown reason. Maria smuggles herself to Paris in order to build houses for her children in Romania. We are first introduced to them through the tracking which brings them together, and we later follow their respective journeys to visit their separate spaces. This is how their spaces are brought together into the same spatial plane. Therefore, through the bringing-together of these characters, Haneke's mosaic explores the horizontal dimension of space, contrasting the urban space of Anne with the rural space of Jean, the developed Western Europe of wealthy Anne and Georges with the underprivileged postcommunist Eastern Europe of Maria, countries in Europe with the African country Mali, and countries in peace, such as France and Romania, with countries at war, such as Kosovo. These diverse spaces are brought together into the same spatial plane as the narrative threads of Anne, Georges, Jean, Maria, and Amadou are interwoven. Consequently, the boundaries between smooth spaces of the developing areas such as Jean's countryside, Maria's Romania, and Amadou's Mali, and striated spaces of the prosperous Paris of Anne[16], are blurred, as they are juxtaposed, intertwined, and plaited. Furthermore, at the same time that this mosaic narrative assembles geopolitical and socioeconomic spaces, it also brings in the vertical dimension of historical concerns. The character Maria, who emigrates from a rural village of Romania to the very centre of Paris, evokes the dimension of the post-Berlin wall diasporic

16 The war space of Serbia and Kosovo, on the other hand, is the becoming-striated of smooth space.

population, which migrates from the postcommunist Eastern European countries in search of a better material life for their families. As in the post-wall era, the Western Europeans encounter the migrants from Eastern Europe and have the task of redefining pre-established territories and borders; Maria's presence indicates Western Europe's highly industrialised society's dilemma between the wish of obtaining a massive flexible labour supply and that of maintaining their national cultural integrity. The migratory need and force represented by Maria challenges the concept of citizenship, based on the sedentariness and rootedness in striated space, and "the role of the frontier in the post-communist diaspora"[17]. Whereas we follow Maria going back to the developing postcommunist space of the East and becoming the resultant economic migration of labour to Western Europe, we see France's colonial past in the South from the Malian-French Amadou's space in Paris and his father's drive back to Mali. The dwelling of Amadou's family in postcolonial Paris is colourful, in contrast to the clinically white walls behind the deaf-mute girl's performance at the lexical charade and the indoor film set, in which Anne wears a perfectly white dress with a white windbreaker to act as a polished upper class lady inspecting a spacious house. Amadou's living room wall is painted in dark blue, like the kitchen cupboard and window frames; the wall beside the dining table is pasted with yellow wallpaper. Although there is no explicit discussion about Amadou's Malian family and France's past as a coloniser, the postcolonial space in cosmopolitan Paris is hinted at by the problems that Amadou's family goes through. For example, after Amadou starts a fight with Jean and is arrested by the policemen, Amadou's mother resorts to the help of a witch doctor. In the fragment, we can see that the camera frames Amadou's mother in a close-up in a corner in front of yellow handmade wall decoration. In tears, she complains about the policemen's unfair treatment of Amadou to the witch doctor, whose out-of-focus back of the head can be seen on the left margin of the frame. The witch doctor's response is that "we must not forget where we come from and who we are. We are not sons of slaves". He also says that in order to avoid misfortune, Amadou should stop seeing so many whites and should return to the land of the ancestors. At a later point, when Amadou explains to his deaf-and-mute younger sister Salimata

17 Mazierska / Rascaroli: *Crossing New Europe*, p. 141.

that their father goes back home to Africa in sign language, the fragment ends with Samalita gesturing back "Where is Africa?". Through the constant reference to the presence of Africa, African identity, and the colonial past in Amadou's family life, Amadou's space provides a historical dimension. In fact, the fight between Amadou and Jean in the tracking sequence is not only a fight about how one should treat a beggar on the street, but also a struggle between the descendants of the colonisers and of the colonised people, the privileged and the underprivileged, the white and the black, and the space of pristine white and the space of colours. Through the multiple interlacing spatial planes involved in the chance encounter and conflicts, *Code Unknown* brings together not only the horizontal spaces of socio-economic and geopolitical divides in our contemporary time, but also the vertical dimension which reminds us that the meeting of these characters in metropolitan Paris is the result of the aftermath of colonialism and communism.

From the beginning of the film, we can also see that, apart from interweaving narrative threads of characters across age, class, social, and ethnic groups carrying different historical backgrounds, images of different natures, such as moving images and still images, and the actual images and the doubly-mediated virtual images are also juxtaposed into a mosaic. The unframed series of still photos taken by Georges from the war zone occupy the whole of the screen space, and bring the virtual doubly-mediated space into the actual diegetic world, between the fragment of the fight between Amadou and Jean, and of Amadou's father driving a taxi. Near the end of the film, another series of black-and-white photos shows close-ups of faces of people from different age groups, genders, ethnic origins, social classes, and with different emotions against the backdrop of Parisian metro. These virtual images against the black screen are again accompanied by the voice-over of Georges, this time recounting his experience as a captive. Whereas the insertion of Georges' photography knits together the spaces between different war zones and the urban Paris (Fig. 23), the moving images and still images, as well as the actual diegetic space and the static virtual image-within-image, Anne's performance on stage and onscreen as an actress juxtaposes the spaces between the actual diegetic space and the film-within-a-film and theatre-within-a-film space. In fact, if we look at the four fragments of Anne's presence as an actress as a whole, they seem to be woven into another story about Anne's characters' incomplete journeys within the diegesis. The four fragments, which go deeper and deeper into indiscernibility, are chronically ordered in reverse and recount an upper-class lady, fearing for the safety of her child on the 20th floor, embarking upon a flat-hunting journey during which she falls into the trap of a psycho-killer. The two fragments in the middle are well situated as performance within the film, whereas the first and last fragments initially create a distinct but indiscernible virtual-actual relationship. Anne's first appearance on stage, in which she acts the role of a frightened victim of a psychopath, has been illustrated earlier on. In the second sequence of Anne's performance, the spectator first hears sounds penetrating into the dark room, whose dim light shines from outside the door. A sound operator with a boom, a steadicam operator, and a script supervisor then enter the frame by walking backwards, before Anne and the actor who plays her estate agent enter the frame. (Fig. 24) Later they restart shooting an earlier part of the scene. The third appearance is in a long shot which includes the whole stage in the background, seats in the auditorium, and two staff in front of a monitor amidst the seats close to the camera. The stage is the only illuminated space and the two staff in the foreground are indiscernible shadows immersed in complete darkness. Anne, laughing hysterically on stage, is merely a white and vague figure. (Fig. 25) At the end of her acting Anne says "is there anyone?", and jumps out of her role on stage. The fourth appearance is qualitatively different from the rest of them. The suspense of the image's origins is kept longer than the rest. The spectators are led to believe in the diegetic nature of the unframed image when a fragment begins with shots and reverse shots of Anne swimming, flirting with a man who has not been introduced in diegesis before, and rushing to stop their child from falling from the 20th floor. This image is later paused, rewinded and zoomed out to reveal its origin as the projected doubly-mediated images on the big screen for Anne and the actor to dub. Anne's screen presence in the four fragments thus juxtaposes her diegetic presence as a Parisian actress and her roles as a character-within-a-character. The mosaic between the actual and the virtual can be summed up in the poster image of *Code Unknown*, a close-up of Anne taking a breath while swimming, which is supposed to be taken from the film footage within the film of the fourth fragment. Instead of taking an image from the diegetic world, *Code Unknown*'s

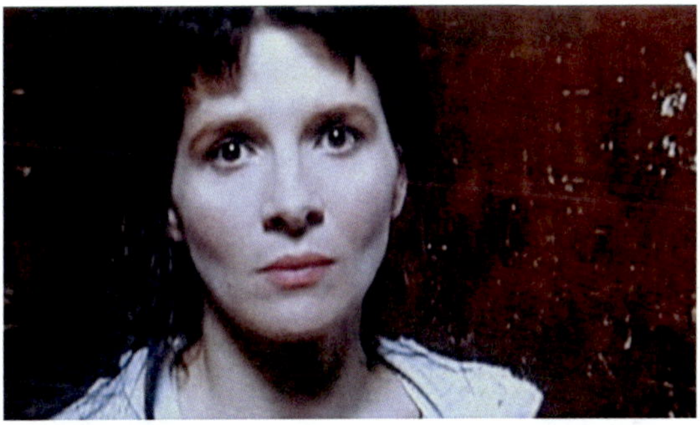

Fig. 22
Close-up of Anne's frightened face on an unframed stage (*Code Unknown*).

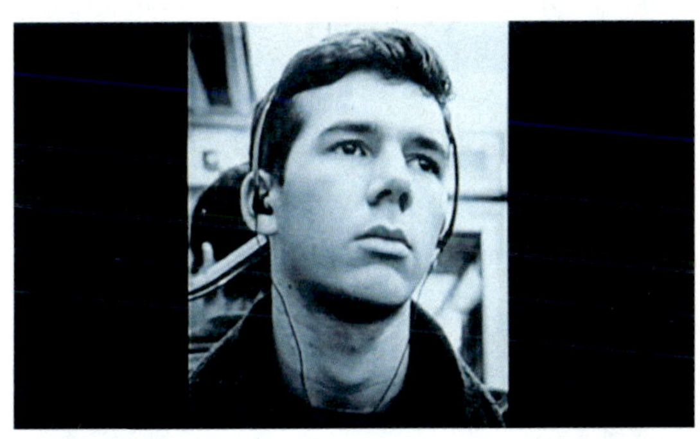

Fig. 23
Georges' portrait of a passenger in the Parisian metro (*Code Unknown*).

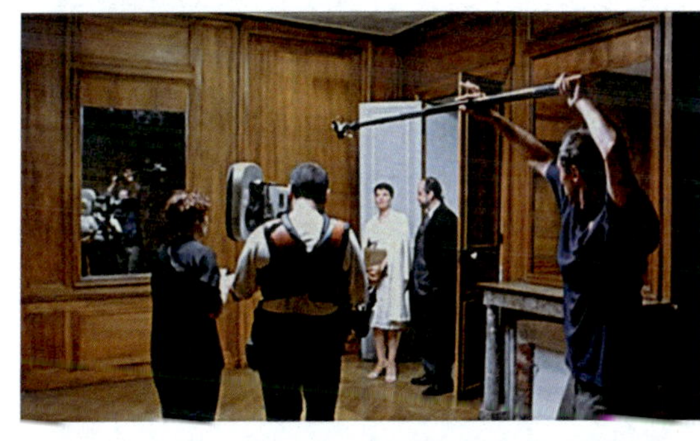

Fig. 24
A sound operator with a boom, a steadicam operator, and a script supervisor are visible on screen in the film-within-the-film (*Code Unknown*).

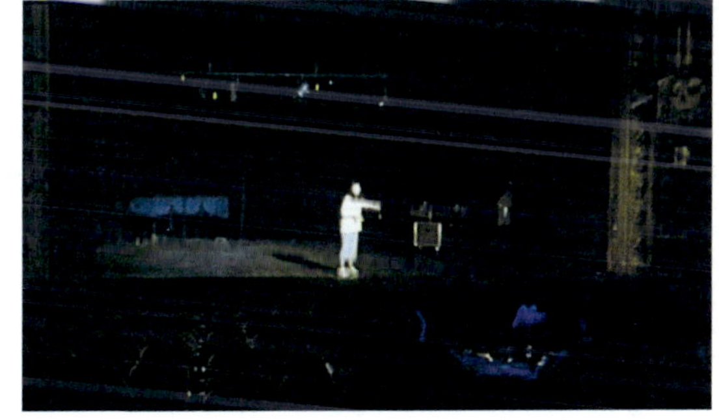

Fig. 25
The vague figure of Anne is illuminated in the background whereas two stage staff in the foreground are indiscernible shadows immersed in complete darkness (*Code Unknown*).

poster implies the *mise-en-abyme* of the film-within-a-film, the virtual within the actual. Actually, as this virtual space is actualised to be the actual poster representing the film, the whole film is an assemblage of the falsifying images whose actual space is in fact the virtual space and vice versa. The virtual, being amorphous at present, and the actual, which is virtually crystallisable, are in constant exchange and multiply in the myriad of layers. In *Code Unknown*, the virtual always exists immanent to the actual, and the boundaries between actual and virtual are rendered fluid. This corresponds to the immanent existence of the smooth spaces of the developing underprivileged parts of the world within the striated spaces of the developed world, and the fluid boundaries between the two. With the insertion of snapshots of spaces from different geopolitical backgrounds with different levels of smoothness and different virtualities, the film is composed of mosaic pieces with fluid boundaries through which the bodies of the characters traverse.

Furthermore, instead of constructing a rooted home in contrast to the act of mobility, the mosaic of *Code Unknown* explores the dynamism between travel and home, and non-places and places, which are in constant oscillation and exchange. Resonating with Mazierska and Rascaroli's claim that the concept of home in *Code Unknown* "no longer exists in the sense of a permanent hub"[18] because of the post-Berlin wall era, here I will demonstrate the becoming-place of non-places and the becoming-non-place of places. For example, in the opening tracking shot, the non-place of Boulevard Saint-Germain, which the passers-by want to go through swiftly, becomes a place where they have to stay. Instead of being one-directional, the tracking, following the movement of characters in non-places, is a constant right and left movement, at the end of which Anne, Jean, Amadou, Maria, a middle-aged bourgeois travel agent, French policemen, and unnamed onlookers gather in the same frame. It starts with a medium shot of Jean, not knowing the new entrance code, waiting outside a flat and catching Anne who leaves in a hurry. The camera follows them both left to right and briefly loses Anne when she goes into a bakery shop. Then Anne returns to the frame to join Jean for a short while before she leaves the frame again from the right. The camera continues tracking Jean in the opposite direction as he walks back nonchalantly,

18 Mazierska / Rascaroli: *Crossing New Europe*, p. 142.

eating a piece of pastry wrapped in a paper bag. It stops briefly when Jean stops to listen to the singing of a street artist. After it captures Jean tossing the wrinkled food wrapper unthinkingly into the lap of Maria begging against a wall, it intends to continue with the right-to-left tracking. However, the camera movement is halted when Amadou grabs Jean's arm demanding an apology to Maria. Whereas the tracking scans through various non-places on Boulevard Saint-Germain, such as a real estate agency, a florist's, and a bakery, the camera imitates the movement of passers-by in non-places by glancing right and then left, without staying. However, at the moment that the conflict between Jean and Amadou starts, non-place stops being a non-place and passers-by are forced to stay. Meanwhile, the camera also has to stop tracking. The characters thus enter or exit from the almost immobile frame, such as the travel agent entering with his scolding and Anne's return to intervene, without being followed by the camera. Stopping the passers-by as well as the camera, the brief moment of chance encounter between these people who rarely have anything in common is a microcosm of a mosaic society, which is haunted by the past of France as the coloniser, the inter-racial and social tension, the uneven development inside Europe, globalisation, and dubious representatives of public justice. As Georgina Evans points out, it is only in moments of violent conflicts that "society is shattered into autonomous splinters that come into contact"[19]. Supporting Augé's observations of non-places in supermodernity, in the chance conflict, which transforms a non-place into a place and assembles diverse spaces into a mosaic, the identities of individuals are only recognised with the presentation of valid printed papers and only in cases of authoritative intervention. We can see this in the intervention of the policemen who request to see everyone's papers in the first instance, without listening to Amadou's flesh and blood explanation, and stop Maria from walking away; the inanimate ID paper is apparently more convincing than a living human being. This is also an interesting sequence when we consider it through the lens of Michel de Certeau's work. Jean's wandering, closely followed by the camera, is his means of rebellion against the patriarchal authority, which praises physical

19 Georgina Evans: Social Sense: Krzysztof Kieslowski and Michael Haneke. In: Steven Woodward (ed.): *After Kieslowski: The Legacy of Krzysztof Kieslowski*. Detroit: Wayne State UP 2009 pp. 99–112, here p. 105.

stability and digital mobility. On the contrary, Maria is immobile both in terms of her posture and her lack of access to data. She is not only unable to subvert the established structure through "walking acts", but also incapable of using "speech acts" in the language of her space. Among all the characters it is in fact the policemen who have the most mobility. Once the policemen, the representatives of institutionalised power, interfere, they immediately occupy the central space of the frame. Their authority shows in their physical mobility and their power to impose immobility on others. It is also couched in their priority in speech acts and their power to decide who is allowed to speak. Maria's attempted escape and Amadou's struggle are in vain because the panoptic power is far stronger than individuals. By the policemen's occupation of the centre of the screen space, the camera stops wandering and becomes static, except for the moment when it follows one policeman who grabs hold of Maria, as if the camera were also confined in the limited space along with the protagonists under the command of the policemen.

Lacking agency and speech acts at the margins of the centre of West Europe, Maria is not followed by the camera and is constantly elided from the frame. As she is always quite far from the camera in medium or long shots, her face is barely discernible. Even when the camera does centrally place her in medium to long shots, and follows her back and forth along Boulevard Saint-Germain in the ending tracking shot, she is still deprived of speech acts. The parallel ending tracking shot starts when Maria, while walking, sees a young woman with an infant sitting in her original niche. The camera stops when Maria stops in front of the florist, worriedly looking around for a potential spot, and starts tracking right when Maria turns back. However, we do not hear Maria talking at all, even in the scene where two men chase Maria away from her newly found corner after uttering some seemingly menacing words. With the diegetic sounds completely muted, we only hear non-diegetic drumplaying, possibly performed by the deaf-mute children Amadou teaches. There is thus a parallel between biological deaf-mute and cultural linguistic deaf-mute. Although the voices of the deaf-mute children cannot be heard, their drumplaying is foregrounded many times in *Code Unknown*. Maria's voice, however, is completely absent from the Parisian fragments, and can only be heard in Romania. In fact, when she returns to her Romanian village, she not only recovers her voice but is also situated at the centre of the screen space. In Romania, she often faces the camera, which captures her in close-ups; this is when the spectator can finally take a closer look at her face. In a fragment of the neighbourhood's wedding celebration, the camera follows Maria's dance, first in the outer circle and then inside the circle with her husband, always being positioned in the centre of the frame. As we closely see her face carved with wrinkles and expressive of emotions, in Romania, she finally becomes an individual who has the verbal and gestural power of expression in front of the camera.

Georges' presence on screen goes in the opposite direction from Maria, as he comes from the elite class in the privileged Western Europe. When he is in Kosovo, he does not even have agency of his survival of the day. Being marginal and disempowered in that particular context, he is only an audial presence, without any physical presence onscreen. What we see is a series of still photos projected on screen one after another, against which his voice-over recounts his stay. The first moment that we see his face onscreen is in Anne's flat in Paris. Georges' return to the part of Europe in a time of peace is also a return to the centre. He was framed in medium shot in the midground, and then he comes to the foreground and faces the camera while calling his office. From such a close distance to the camera, he occupies the centre and most of the frame, with even his finest hair visible onscreen.

Code Unknown thus portrays the fluid mosaic in which the characters drift from the centre to the periphery, and from the periphery to the centre. When the characters have agency in a certain place, they have a strong cinematic presence onscreen and determine camera movement to a certain extent. When they are where they have no agency, however, they lose their presence onscreen or become truncated bodies. In the case of Amadou, when he regains screen presence in the restaurant fragment in which he dines with his white girlfriend, he is also taking the position of an oppressor. Whereas the policemen's dominance of the screen space and discriminative attitude towards Amadou in the tracking at the start of the film remind us of the role of France as the former coloniser, Amadou's behaviour and screen presence in the restaurant actually mirror the policemen. The fragment starts with Anne, Georges, and their friends having dinner around a table. When they stand up to greet two other friends, the camera moves slightly upwards. At the moment that Amadou's face enters the foreground very close to the camera, the camera abandons filming the white intellectual and artist group of Anne and Georges and follows Amadou leftwards. When Amadou and his white girlfriend settle down at the table, the camera also lowers down in order to keep them in the centre of the frame. Dominating the screen space and leading the movement of the camera, Amadou becomes the patronising and oppressing figure in this fragment, contrary to the tracking shot in which he is forced to obey the white authoritative people's words. He first complains to the waiter for not getting the reserved window table in a patronising tone, despite coming three quarters of an hour later than the reserved time. He is also the authoritative person who decides if his girlfriend keeps or abandons her watch. When he tells the girl that he finds her watch "comme ça", she takes the watch from her wrist immediately and throws it into an ashtray. In return she wins a kiss on the newly exposed wrist from Amadou. This fragment is read by Evans as a positive connection between these two bodies through touch in "a rather nervous occasion infused with tentative promise"[20], but we can also see it as a reversal of the inter-racial power relationship compared to the opening tracking. Here Amadou is at the centre of the frame, whereas the white waiter and girlfriend become subordinate figures. In relation to Amadou's central position, the waiter even becomes a truncated and faceless body that can only be seen waist-down handing out menus and serving drinks.

Whereas non-places become places in the opening tracking shot, the supposed place of home is portrayed as a transit station lacking permanence in *Code Unknown*; a non-place where Georges passes by between his trips to war zones, and where Jean wanders back occasionally between his flight from the countryside. This is also why home, the place, becomes "code unknown" to both Georges and Jean. We can see the cinematic portrayal of the becoming-non-place of places in Jean's relationship with the mise-en-scène. At the same time that Jean's home with his father on the farm stops providing him with identities, he is portrayed as melting into the surrounding background and becomes a piece of furniture in the dwelling space. In the fragment where we see Jean returning to his father's farm after

20 Evans: Social Sense, p. 110.

briefly taking shelter in Anne's flat in Paris, he wears the same light green jacket on top of a dark blue shirt in squared patterns as in the opening tracking shot. The green shade makes him seem like a piece of decoration in the non-relational home, whose wall and window frames are painted in light green and the curtains have a different shade of green. From a medium shot of Jean eating beetroot in silence, he melts in the background and does not seem to have any identity of his own, as if Jean were devoured by the green shade of the non-place home altogether. A few fragments later, we see the camera following Jean's father pushing the motorbike in bright red and black chunks of colours out of his white van and walking left towards the barn. After the father vanishes in the barn door, the static camera sees Jean coming out of the barn, exiting the frame and a few seconds later riding away with the bike. At this moment he wears an unbuttoned bright reddish orange shirt, which makes him stand out from the green and brown tone of the surroundings. The striking colour contrast between Jean's clothing and the mise-en-scène indicates his dissociation from the surroundings, as well as imminent fugue from the home which is turned into a non-place.

At the same time that the boundaries between places and non-places are blurred, the characters struggle to reach a balanced state of striation within the mosaic. The theatrical and cinematic performances of Anne, the actress, in *Code Unknown* illustrate the paradoxical feeling of the city-dwellers, torn between the desire of staying indoors between walls within the safe boundaries of striation, and that of being free to leave the indoor space and enter the smooth at their will. For example, in the film footage when Anne plays an upper class lady visiting a flat whose windows are stuffed with cement, the real estate agent tells her that "the trees and hedges ensure total privacy" as the selling point. Privacy, in this case, implies complete striation, which secludes the bourgeois family from danger and threat from the outside world, and at the same time fresh air and smoothness. Private properties are the most rigidly segmented and thus the most "secure" place, because they have been gridded and overcoded. However, the horrific elements come from the smooth sphere outside the safe boundaries of striation, as well as from too much striation without exit. In the film footage sequence within the film diegesis, from which the poster of *Code Unknown* showing Anne swimming comes, the possibility of falling outside the boundaries of striation becomes the thrilling moment. When the wealthy couple's young child climbs on the narrow chest-high walls of the balcony on the 20th floor in an attempt to reach a balloon, he is at the brink of stumbling out of the striated space into the smooth outside the building, and hence losing his life. This shows how the realm outside the borders of striation is meant to be dangerous, and how the bourgeois rely on the boundaries of striation to protect themselves. When too much striation impedes the bourgeois characters from free access to the space outside the striation, it stops being protective and also becomes horror. In Anne's first appearance on stage, facing the camera, she stands in a small room with mottled brown walls and brown-white checkerboard floor. Her facial expression becomes more and more frightened as she is told that she will never be allowed to leave the locked room. The fragment ends with her tearful and confused face. Therefore, we can see that the delicate balance of striation is difficult to achieve in a mosaic. All these virtual fragments of film-within-a-film, or theatre-play-within-a-film, illustrate the desire of city-dwellers to demarcate their borders between spaces and their vulnerability when they are exposed to unpossessed space or space outside borders. The borders have to be well regulated and controlled in order to achieve an illusion of being free, because their sense of security comes from being willingly imprisoned in the striated space by themselves behind the protective walls they build. They try to striate the space to suit the degree of striation that they want, which is enough striation for protection, but too much can be suffocating.

By playing with journeys of various directions, and revising relative positions of each character according to the surrounding space, *Code Unknown* is a mosaic space in which it is difficult to determine a fixed centre. As the characters cross and recross the blurry boundaries between spatial configurations, the "centre" can no longer be firmly stated as such, and neither can "places" and categories of all kinds. The presence of centre flows into the margins and vice versa. It is thus a fluid three-dimensional mosaic interwoven by interchanging places and non-places, actual and virtual images, and the characters' central and peripheral positions on screen in relation to power struggles between races, class, and ethnic groups. At the same time that horizontally different cultural, socioeconomic, and geopolitical spaces are juxtaposed in the mosaic, Maria's space and Amadou's space bring in the vertical dimension of postcommunism and postcolonialism, which is rendered more explicit in Haneke's *Caché*, illustrated in the next section.

5. *Caché*

In *Caché*, Haneke continues the intersection between the horizontal mosaic, which juxtaposes spatial configurations carried by the characters from different ethnic, socioeconomic, and geopolitical backgrounds, and the vertical mosaic, which brings in the spatial planes carrying a historical dimension in the context of Western European bourgeois society. In this section, I will demonstrate how the positions of seer and *actant*, and the smooth and the striated, interchange and interact in this mosaic, how the boundaries between the actual and the virtual are rendered indiscernible while bringing in the haunting past, and how the casting of Juliette Binoche and Daniel Auteuil brings intertextual spaces to the mosaic.

Caché is funded by Les Films du Losange (France), Wega Film (Austria), and Bavaria Film (Germany), among others. The film won Haneke the award of best director at Cannes, and many European Film Awards, thereby securing a wide international distribution, reaching the Czech Republic with Intersonic, Hong Kong with First Distributors, Australia and New Zealand with Madman Entertainment, and Venezuela with Amazonia Films. It brings French stars Juliette Binoche, Daniel Auteuil, Algeria-born Maurice Bénichou, and Senegal-born Aïssa Maïga, together. The transnational filmmaking mode of *Caché* corresponds to the bringing-together of spaces in the film. Although *Caché* does not have an explicit mosaic narrative like *71 Fragments* or *Code Unknown*, which weave together narrative threads by editing back and forth between a diverse range of characters, it nevertheless cuts between not only fragments of different socioeconomic and geopolitical spaces, but also different virtualities and extradiegetic intertextual spaces, which are assembled into a mosaic. The film starts with a static shot lasting almost three minutes, on an ordinary street early in the morning, fixating on a house whose front door is mostly covered by green bushes. At the end of the three minutes, we hear a dialogue between a man and a woman who ponder the origin of the rolling image. By the time that the voice-over appears, we realise that the images we are seeing are the unframed doubly-mediated images projected on a screen within the film diegesis, which we watch accompanied by the diegetic characters. The static shot then cuts into a closer look at the house from which Georges (played by Daniel Auteuil), walks out, followed by a vague silhouette of his wife Anne (played by Juliette Binoche), who stays beside the bushes. This actual image is a lot darker than the previous one, indicating a later point of the day. The film then returns to the original unframed doubly-mediated static shot, which is fast-forwarded, rewound, and paused, again accompanied by the voice-over of Georges and Anne. (Fig. 26) Afterwards, the film cuts back to the actual image, in which Georges and Anne extensively discuss the purpose and creator of the videotape in the kitchen and at the dinner table in medium shots, joined by their son Pierrot a bit later. This cuts to a new space, filmed with a tilting up and down of the camera to capture several boys, including Pierrot, swimming back and forth within a lane of a swimming pool, accompanied by the instructor's voice-over in the background. The next fragment goes back to the initial static shot at the house with the same camera placement, but this time in sombre darkness at night. This is then cut to a close-up of Georges smiling straight at the camera to end a TV programme, which discusses books, from which the camera zooms out to reveal a wall full of model books behind Georges and four participants around a black table.

From the beginning of the film, we can see that although the main characters remain Georges and Anne, the film cuts back and forth between the same framing of the same house at different times of the day, between inside and outside of the house, between images with different virtualities (the actual images of the diegesis, and the framed or unframed doubly-mediated virtual images within the film), and between images from different locations (a household, a swimming pool, and a studio set for the TV programme). The assemblage of horizontal spaces is further complicated by the vertical space of the postcolonial reality brought by the character Majid. Without any warning to the spectator, Majid is introduced at the mid-point of the film. After rewinding and pausing the images of one of the anonymous videotapes which indicate the route to a flat within a block building, Georges follows the trajectory and meets Majid for the first time since childhood. This is also the first time the spectator meets the character Majid. It is gradually revealed that Georges' parents wanted to adopt Majid after the disappearance of his parents, who worked on Georges' parents' farm, during the massacre of Algerian demonstrators in 1961. However, Majid was sent to an orphanage because of Georges' lies. Therefore, upon the encounter between Georges and Majid, *Caché* also assembles the spaces between the white French

Fig. 26
Anne and Georges rewinding and fast-forwarding the video footage of their house façade (*Caché*).

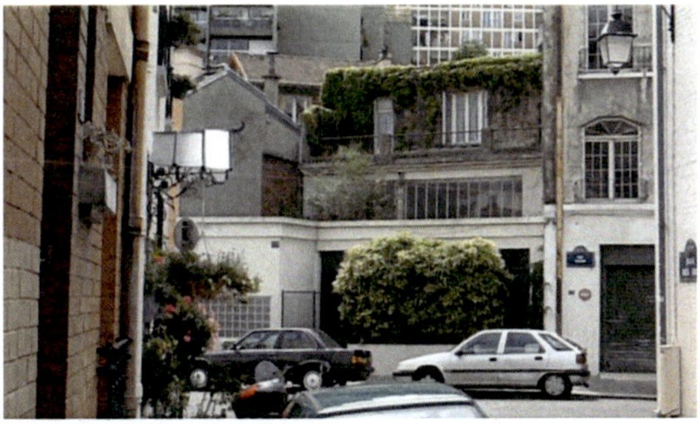

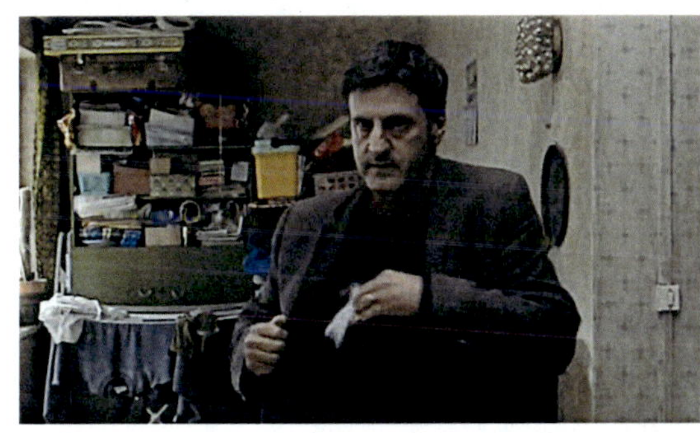

Fig. 27
Georges in Majid's flat which is piled with objects and full of colours (*Caché*).

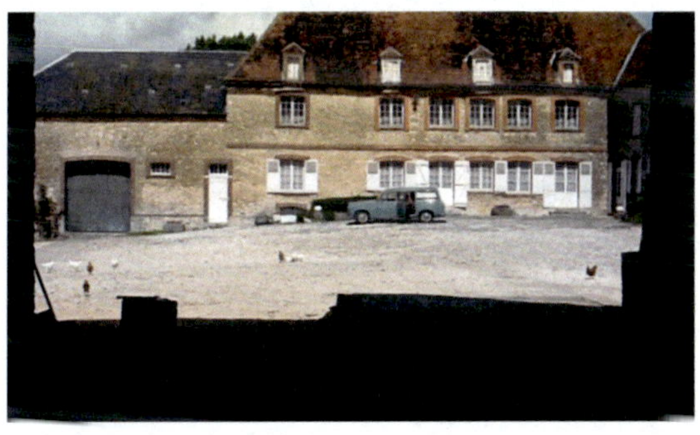

Fig. 28
Georges' family house shot from inside a shaded barn, with the car in the background waiting to take Majid away (*Caché*).

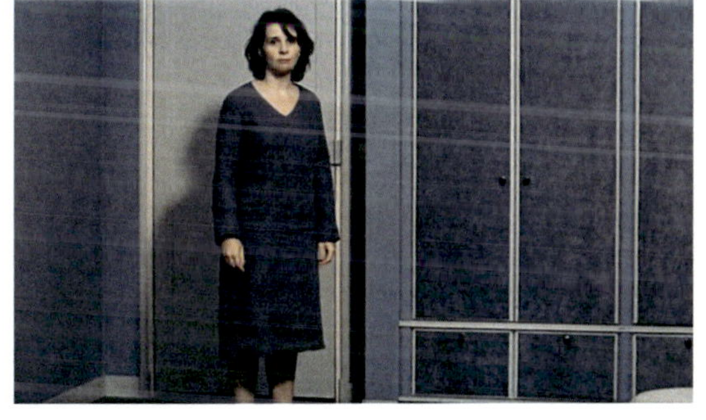

Fig. 29
Anne's greyish blue baggy dress makes her blend into the background with wallpaper of the same colour (*Caché*).

bourgeois intellectual space of Georges and Anne, and the working-class Algerian-French space of Majid and his son in postcolonial Paris. As pointed out earlier in the chapter, the former dwells in a space with pristine white walls and minimalist dark brown wooden furniture, whereas the space of the latter is piled with objects and full of colours. (Fig. 27) It is through the bringing-together of their respective spaces that *Caché* goes beyond the assemblage of socioeconomic and geopolitical spaces and explores the vertical dimension of historical events and consequences. At the same time that the space of Majid evokes the space of postcolonial France, in which the former colonisers and colonised people live together in the same space, it brings together different historical periods of France. As Majid's parents came from the colonised Algeria to work in France, disappeared in 1961, and his son was born in the contemporary France by the end of the 20th Century, Majid's narrative thread traverses France's role as coloniser, oppressor of the Algerian demonstration, and host country of the descendents of these colonised, oppressed, and even massacred Algerians. Contrary to the attempt of the oppressive authorities to regard time as linear and separable entities from which they can cut off one section of the unwanted past like cutting any material, the colonial past, which the authorities strive to repress and eradicate, remains, its haunting presence evident in the convergence between familial and collective histories. For example, in the fragment right before the ending static shot in front of a school, and right after a medium shot of Georges sleeping in the dark bedroom shielded by curtains, we see a static image in which the camera shoots from inside a shaded barn towards a courtyard and Georges' family house behind it. (Fig. 28) The long shot shows a boy being taken from the house, running away towards the right margins of the frame, and then being brought back into a car by force. This unframed virtual image is presumably Georges' recollection-image or dream-image of the moment that Majid was taken to the orphanage. Although Georges strives to suppress the evocation of the past by refusing to talk about it with Anne and resorting to deep slumbers of oblivion, the haunting images of the past, that are not necessarily true, still return without being summoned, to be inserted within the mosaic of myriad spaces, time frames, and virtualities.

Majid's evocation of postcolonial France can be understood in relation to Marks' postcolonial seer in the any-space-whatever of the metropolitan West. Like Marks' postcolonial seer, Majid in *Caché* also enters Western metropolis from a non-Western formerly repressed culture after the dismantlement of colonial power, and brings the space of the ex-colonies with him to Paris. Being at the same time a descendant of Algerians and a French citizen, Majid sees the violent colonial history and the 1961 massacre in Paris, which the westerners such as Georges and Anne ignore and the authority denies, from both inside and outside. He sees the double displacement: his parents' exile for economic reasons, and his own displacement because of the child Georges' jealous slander, as well as the continuation of violence, injustice, and discrimination exercised by the French policemen against his son and himself. His surrounding space thus becomes an any-space-whatever for him, because it is a space dominated by a culture which repressed the culture of his ancestors' land and possibly also killed his own parents; he sees and does not react to the unfolding of events in the any-space-whatever. The only moment that he takes an action as an *actant* is when he slits his own throat with a folding knife in front of Georges and thus imposes the position of the seer upon Georges. Whereas Majid faces the camera throughout this fragment, even after falling down on the floor, we can only see the back of Georges in a beige raincoat most of the time. After Majid's blood dramatically splashes on the wall, quite to the surprise of Georges and the spectator, Georges stares at Majid's body along with a long trace of blood on the wall for one whole minute without reacting. This is also the only moment when Georges, instead of running around and always trying to 'do' something and to 'react' to the anonymous videotapes, starts becoming the 'seer', which is what the videotapes have continuously tried to force him to be. Right after the one-minute-long take of Georges' 'seeing' in the reversal of seer-*actant* position, we see a static shot for twenty seconds, which puts a cinema with its six film posters above its front door, including Pedro Almodóvar's *Bad Education* (*La mala educación*, ES 2004) and Christophe Barratier's *The Chorus* (*Les choristes*, FR 2004), in the background and the busy traffic from both directions in the foreground. Then we see Georges walking out of the cinema, supposedly after having sought comfort through the role of a cinematic seer. After Majid's suicide, the former *actant* Georges can no longer react and goes from one seer position to another.

The post-colonial any-space-whatever in Paris is a mosaic interwoven with fluid boundaries between the spaces of the former colonisers and the formerly colonised people, and of the seers and the *actants*, but the bourgeois couple, Georges and Anne, is totally unaware of the fluid mosaic which surrounds them, and insists on having a very clear-cut and unambiguous sense of boundaries throughout the film. Like the bourgeois Mrs. Brunner in *71 Fragments*, they live in complete striation, which approximates what Elizabeth Ezra and Jane Sillars call a fortress[21], always looking for points and demarcations, and do not know how to open up to the smooth. Their spaces, where lines have been drawn to indicate segments, are "overcoded and gridded by surveying"[22] according to Deleuze and Guattari. Content in the enclosed and limited bourgeois space, Georges draws the line between Majid and himself on the grounds of individuality, class, strength, age, race, education, and culture, like animals marking their territories with smell. When the anonymous videotapes and letters arrive at Georges and Anne's doorstep, these images challenge their safe fortress of striation and force them to open up to the smooth. The videos and letters, trying to make Georges and Anne 'see' and blur the striation, bring in the spatial plane of Georges and Anne's flat seen from the perspective of a voyeur, that of Georges' past, and of Majid's working-class life. Yet, instead of embracing the smooth, Georges and Anne cling to striation and strive to create even more demarcation through the practice of map-reading. As Ezra and Sillars point out, Georges and Anne are very good at reading maps. Their initial focus of their investigation is the geographical point of origin of the anonymous tape more than anything else.[23]

Instead of opening up to the smooth to understand the anonymous videotapes, Georges and Anne are stuck in the practice of striating the surrounding spaces into gridded segments and separating themselves from the space of others such as Majid, and hence become a part of the striating lines. By melting into their surroundings, they become an inseparable piece from the striated environment. Ezra and Sillars suggest that by the use of costume and setting, Georges and

21 Elisabeth Ezra / Jane Sillars: *Hidden* in Plain Sight: Bringing Terror Home. In: *Screen* 48,2 (2007), pp. 215–221, here p. 215.

22 Deleuze / Guattari: *A Thousand Plateaus*, pp. 233–234.

23 Ezra / Sillars: *Hidden* in Plain Sight, p. 215.

Anne are depicted as "prisoners of their own making or at least of their own circumstances"[24], living in their grey and shapeless clothes behind a gated fortress. They continue, "When the outside world intrudes upon their carcereal existence, they attempt to banish it"[25]. I would argue that we can also see the mise-en-scène and costume of *Caché* as indistinction between the characters' bodies and their surrounding space, almost like animal mimicry. Whereas in *The Seventh Continent*, human bodies are truncated and disembodied like pieces of objects through framing, the bodies in *Caché* are nullified through the merging between the setting and the costume. As we can see from the very beginning of the film, the mise-en-scène in the dwelling of Georges and Anne is dominated by pale and bleak tones with perfectly white walls, corresponding to the minimalist style of the bourgeois households in all of Haneke's films. The sofa and cushions are white, in contrast with dark brown shelves and the black frame of the TV screen; bright colours are almost completely absent from their space. Georges and Anne's costumes reflect the same colour scheme. In most scenes, Georges wears an oversized beige pullover whereas Anne is in a black shapeless dress. On the night of Pierrot's mysterious disappearance, Georges and Anne both wear black tops, and Anne's windbreaker and skirt are beige. Their clothing and dwelling space are both dyed with only single neutral and unobtrusive colours; dark blue, black, or beige, which create camouflage for their bodies. The most striking indistinction between their bodies and the setting can be seen in the very end of the film, after Georges witnesses Majid's suicide. When Anne enters the dark bedroom where Georges sits, she intuitively switches on the light. Before Georges tells Anne to switch the light off, we can see a medium shot which frames her beside the big wardrobe. As the walls are painted in a lighter blue, wardrobe doors in a darker blue, and the door in grey, Anne's greyish blue baggy dress makes her body indistinguishable from the background. She almost becomes a piece of the wallpaper of the same colour, and therefore, a piece of the striated space that they strive to maintain. (Fig. 29)

At the same time that the bodies of Georges and Anne become indistinguishable from the surrounding space, the bodies of the actor

24 Ibid., p. 216.

25 Ibid.

and actress who portray the characters bring extradiegetic cinematic spaces beyond the 110 minute duration of the film into the mosaic. In fact, the casting of the two stars in French cinema, Binoche and Auteuil, whose screen images travel across films, allows *Caché* to weave a bigger mosaic through intertextuality. For example, the fluid watery screen image that Binoche embodies carries the film spaces of Krzysztof Kieślowski, among others, into *Caché*. Evans has remarked that Binoche is bathed in the melancholy tone of watery blue colour in *Three Colors: Blue* (*Trois couleurs: Bleu,* FR 1993, D: Krzysztof Kieślowski), "in a shimmering turquoise swimming pool that recalls one of the leitmotifs of *Blue*"[26], and in the end of Kieślowski's trilogy *Three Colors: Red* (*Trois couleurs: Rouge*, FR 1994, D: Krzysztof Kieślowski), she is rescued from a shipwreck along with the protagonists from *Three Colours: White* (*Trois couleurs: Blanc*, FR 1994, D: Krzysztof Kieślowski) and *Red*. In addition, in *Chocolat* (UK 2000, D: Lasse Hallström), the life of Binoche's character Vianne Rocher is interconnected with the life of the head of river drifters played by Johnny Depp, whereas in the end of *The Lovers on the Bridge* (*Les amants du Pont-Neuf,* FR 1991, D: Leos Carax), Michèle, played by Binoche, is dragged into the Seine by her lover. As for Auteuil, his screen images as someone with hidden secrets are also brought into *Caché*. He acts the role of the malign Ugolin, who is pushed by his greedy uncle Cesar Soubeyran to block the water source in *Jean de Florette* (FR 1986, D: Claude Berri), and the good cop with a hidden past in *36th Precinct* (*36 Quai des Orfèvres*, FR 2004, D: Olivier Marchal). In combination, the couple formed by Binoche and Auteuil in *Caché* can be seen as a cynical duplicate of the ideal couple of Jean and Madame La in *The Widow of Saint-Pierre* (*La veuve de Saint-Pierre*, FR 2000, D: Patrice Leconte). In the latter, Binoche and Auteuil's stardom has been fully used to emphasise the aestheticised image of the romantic drama genre, as we can see in the poster, on which Jean kisses the naked back of the glamourous Madame La in soft focus. Jean and Madame La are the kind-hearted couple of the French elite class in the colonial era, who are prepared to sacrifice everything for the good cause, in contrast to the contemporary bourgeois couple Georges and Anne in *Caché*, who are ready to accuse the underprivileged Majid's family at the first

26 Evans: Social Sense, p. 100.

instance without any evidence. Instead of the portrayal of romantic unfading love in *La veuve de Saint-Pierre*, the marriage of Georges and Anne seems to be established on quotidian practical matters; even fidelity in their relationship is in doubt, as we see a fragment of Pierre affectionately caressing the tearful Anne and kissing her hand. Hence, Binoche's and Auteuil's previous screen personae have been intentionally deconstructed in *Caché* to help demonstrate that there is an extra layer of the mosaic beyond the diegetic textual film space of *Caché*, which encompasses intertextual screen spaces, and that the mosaic is not a closed-circuit system, but rather an open-ended and fluid mosaic modifiable according to the spectator's knowledge of film repertoires.

From the beginning assemblage of images, we can also see that *Caché* pieces together mosaic segments of actual images and virtual images, which bring together the horizontal dimension of socioeconomic and geopolitical spaces and vertical dimension of the space from the past. They become indiscernible three-dimensional crystals, which go in and out of the actual and the virtual, and present and past, which are divided by fluid boundaries. From the moment the film opens with the virtual doubly-mediated image of Georges and Anne's front door, it jumps back and forth between the unframed doubly-mediated images to the actual diegetic images several times. When the same framing of the façade of Georges and Anne's flat in the darkness appears, we do not know if the image is a doubly-mediated image, like the opening long take, from another anonymous videotape, or if it is the actual image in the diegetic film world. Since the images' virtuality is not signposted, the line between the actual diegetic space and doubly-mediated virtual space is often blurred. This creates a trans-spatial system, which opens up the range of the out-of field. In light of Deleuze's works, it seems that in *Caché*, the out-of-field does not merely suggest the existence of elsewhere but implies more clearly "a more disturbing presence, one which cannot even be said to exist, but rather to 'insist' or 'subsist', a more radical Elsewhere, outside homogeneous space and time"[27]. Through the indiscernible virtual images, which bring a bigger offscreen space to the mosaic, the on-screen space and the doubly-on-screen space, such as the space presented in videotapes, open up to circuits of indiscernibility instead

27 Deleuze: *Cinema 1*, p. 19.

of being confined in a closed system. As Marks puts it, "the original point at which actual and virtual image reflect each other produces, in turn, a widening circuit of actual and virtual images like a hall of mirrors"[28]. Furthermore, the out-of-field existence of elsewhere is a disturbing presence, which unexpectedly brings the haunting past into the space of the actual images of the present, as the past is preserved in the doubly-mediated virtual as recollection-images, dream-images, or recorded doubly-mediated images. We see the past, which is not necessarily true, coming into the mosaic in the form of the virtual, in the anonymous video images observing Georges and Anne's flat, the video images showing the drive to Georges' childhood house in the countryside, the images of the child Majid stained with blood after killing a rooster, and the images of the child Majid being sent to the orphanage. These circuits of the seen and the unseen, the real and the imaginary, the actual and the virtual, the present and the past, the well-situated and contextualised images, and the indiscernible images with ambiguous origins and natures, are all interwoven into a mosaic, which defies 'completion' and 'truth' in cinema. This is how *Caché* reaches the Deleuzian "powers of the false"[29] of crystalline images, whose truthfulness is constantly in doubt and where there is no definite representation of the past. Images of the past, preserved in the virtual, become falsifying, labyrinthine, and indiscernible. Unlike Egoyan's mosaic, the virtual and the imaginary in Haneke's mosaic are not reterritorialised into a singular continuum in the actual and the real, and maintain the myriad of layers with "the coexistence of not-necessarily true pasts"[30] until the end of the film. The haunting past being not only personal but also collective, we also see the intermingling between colonial and postcolonial histories and developing and developed worlds in the jumping back and forth between the actual and the virtual. Therefore, at the same time that the actual brings in the horizontal dimension of the geopolitical and socioeconomic planes, the virtual carries the vertical dimension of the haunting past. The juxtaposition between the virtual and the actual, which chase each other into a forking labyrinth, is at the same time the assemblage between the horizontal and the vertical.

28 Marks: *The Skin of the Film*, p. 65.

29 Deleuze: *Cinema 2*, p. 122.

30 Ibid., p. 127.

In correlation with Haneke's personal travelling and his transnational funding resources and distribution channels, his films construct a fluid mosaic with the possibility of crossing and recrossing the boundaries and exchanges between the characters' relative positions. It is at the same time horizontal spaces, which spread across spatial configurations of our contemporary time, and vertical spaces, which go deep into the consequences of historical causes. This three-dimensional mosaic space, integrating the different trajectories of the mosaics examined in Parts I and II, is filled with multiplicities of borderlines, temporalities, spatialities, and virtualities.

Conclusion

The book answers the research question of how we can understand films with multi-character narratives in contemporary auteur cinema from around the world, and proposes a spatial reading of the phenomenon. In this model, instead of being restricted to the consideration of interweaving of narrative threads, the mosaic finds itself at the intersection between the transnational filmmaking context, spatial aesthetics, and assemblage of spatial configurations. As I observe that the mosaic spatial aesthetics corresponds to the travelling and the bringing-together of spaces in some mosaic auteurs' filmmaking contexts, I form a link between the spatial aesthetics of the films and their specific transnational modes. In these auteurs' films with multi-character narrative, we can observe a correlation between the bringing-together of the narrative threads and screen spaces, and the bringing-together of filmmaking milieus and resources from a variety of geopolitical contexts. At the same time that the auteur assembles filmmaking resources across borders and distributes the film products to different corners of the world, screen space is mosaic in terms of both formal cinematic aspects, with the combined use of narrative, framing, and mise-en-scène, among others, and in terms of the compilation of diverse spatial configurations, such as underdeveloped and developed, underprivileged and privileged, the global and the local, colonial and postcolonial, places and non-places, the smooth and the striated, and the actual and the virtual. From chapter 1 to chapter 3, I moved from the horizontal mosaic of contemporary mosaics of socioeconomic and geopolitical spaces in Iñárritu's films, to the vertical mosaic embedded with historical concerns, including Egoyan's diasporic and cinematic mosaic of deterritorialisation/reterritorialisation and actualisation/virtualisation and Hou's historical mosaic of the multilayered mise-en-scène. I then demonstrated a three-dimensional mosaic which incorporates both the horizontal (spaces at the same time frame) and the vertical (spaces across time frames) with Haneke's fluid mosaic of crossing and recrossing of the boundaries. The mosaic model is thus gradually built up from the space of the same period of time to the space which is marked by different periods of time, and subsequently, to the combination of the two. Furthermore, the context of any-space-whatever moved from Egoyan's post-displacement and/or post-trauma any-space-whatever in Canada and Armenia, to Hou's postwar postcolonial any-space-whatever in Taiwan, and finally, to Haneke's image-saturated postcolonial any-space-whatever in Western Europe. With a balanced, coherent, and non-Eurocentric model in mind, the four auteurs I have chosen thus illustrate very different forms of mosaic in three continents, America (Iñárritu), Asia (Hou), Europe (Haneke), as well as in Egoyan's intercontinental context between Canada and Armenia, corresponding to their divergent transnational filmmaking networks through travelling.

Whereas aesthetically mosaic can be achieved through jump cuts, match cuts, visual and audial juxtaposition, close-ups, tracking shots, wandering gaze of the camera, reframed mise-en-scène, and film-within-a-film, thematically it can be understood as a chance encounter between people, time, space, and narratives – like the dramatic chance encounter through a car accident in *Amores Perros*, the unanticipated evocation of the past in *Calendar*, the encounter of reincarnated couples across history in *Three Times*, and a street fight encounter in *Code Unknown*. Mosaic can be the very brief and almost indiscernible chance encounter through violence at individual and collective levels in *A Touch of Sin* (*Tian Zhu Din*, CN 2013, D: Zhangke Jia), in which the killer Dahai in the first segment brushes against the second killer Zhou San next to a turned truck a few minutes into the film, who in turn takes the same bus to Yichang with the lover of the third killer. And then, the young man who jumps from his factory dormitory in the fourth segment is loosely connected with the experiences of migrant workers from Zhou San's village – the connection between horizontal spaces of Shanxi, Chongqing, Hubei, and Guangdong is only casually and loosely formed through chance encounter. Mosaic can also be a more long-term encounter, such as in Hou Hsiao-hsien's *The Assassin* and in Michael Haneke's *White Ribbon*. In the latter film, for example, the feudal community with a social spectrum composed of landlord, priest, doctor, village teacher, school kids, and farm workers prompts constant encounter and perpetual co-existence between the mentally-challenged, socially-challenged, the rebellious, the conservative, the repressor, the repressed, the dogmatic, and the disciplined,

Or, mosaic can be mystic like in *Kaili Blues* (*Lu Bian Ye Can*, CN 2015, D: Gan Bi). In its labyrinth we wander within static shots of objects such as a dissembled ventilator next to a pile of books, a bucket collecting rain water, and close-ups of skin turned purple because of being sucked up by cupping therapy, between the perspectives of the village doctor Yongzhong Chen, various characters in the village, and an unspecified gaze, as well as between the present and the past, and the actual and the virtual. Mosaic is thus immersed in the indiscernibility between "incompossible presents" and "not-necessarily-true pasts"[1]. It is also in the 'impossible', incongruent, and puzzling juxtaposition of images of a continuously running train accompanied by machine noises on the shabby interiors of Yongzhong Chen's house, as well as in repetition and reiteration of folk stories about mountain savages.

Instead of being confined in the film medium, mosaic has found a bigger playground in the prosperous scene of TV drama production nowadays. A prominent example is *Game of Thrones* (US 2011–2018, HBO, Creators: D.B. Weiss / David Benioff), in which mosaic enables maintenance of suspense throughout eight seasons by shifting attention from one location to another and from one main character to another, gradually pushing the narrative forward. With all its multifacetedness, it is a mosaic that moves, transforms, and reshapes along the course of time.

1 Deleuze: *Cinema 2*, p. 127.

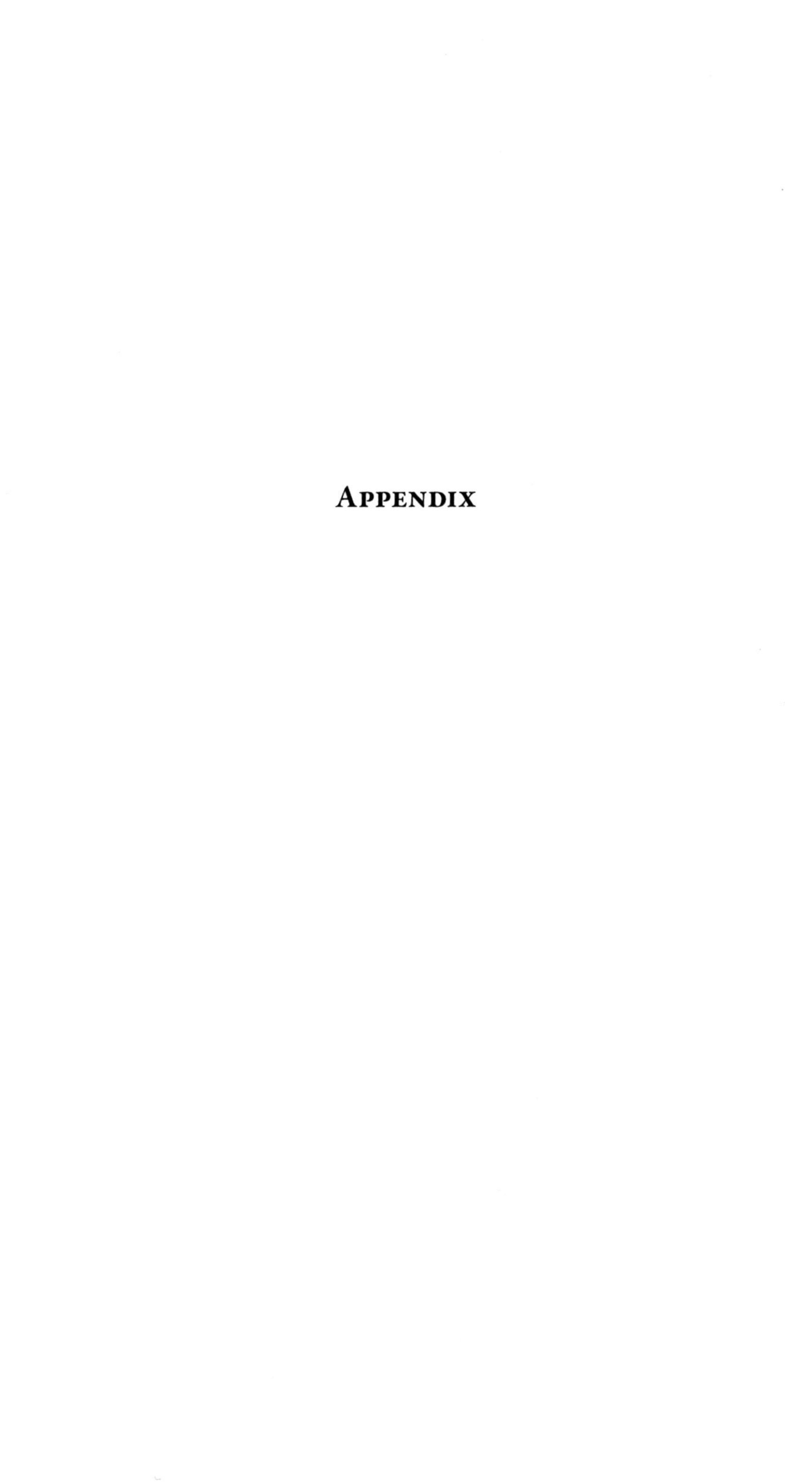

Appendix

Bibliography

Theoretical Works

Appadurai, Arjun: *Modernity at Large: Cultural Dimensions of Globalization*. Minneapolis: University of Minnesota Press 1996.

Augé, Marc: *Non-places. Introduction to an Anthropology of Supermodernity*, trans. from French by John Howe. London: Verso 1995.

—: Paris and the Ethnography of the Contemporary World. In: Michael Sheringham (ed.): *Parisian Fields*. London: Reaktion 1996, pp. 175–179.

—: *Non-Places: An Introduction to Supermodernity*, trans. from French by John Howe. Second Edition. London: Verso 2009.

Barthes, Roland: The Death of the Author. In: Stephen Heath (ed.): *Image/Music/Text*, trans. from French by Stephen Heath. New York: Hill & Wang 1977, pp. 142–148.

Bergson, Henri: *Matter and Memory*, trans. from French by Nancy Margaret Paul / W. Scott Palmer. Mineola, NY: Dover 2004.

Boyd, Andrew: *Chinese Architecture and Town Planning 1500 B. C.–A. D. 1911*. London: Tiranti 1962.

Buchanan, Ian: Space in the Age of Non-Place. In: Ian Buchanan / Gregg Lambert (eds): *Deleuze and Space*. Edinburgh: Edinburgh UP 2005, pp. 16–35.

Buchanan, Ian / Gregg Lambert: Introduction. In: Ibid., pp. 1–15.

Cameron, Ian: Films, Directors and Critics. In: Barry Keith Grant (ed.): *Auteurs and Authorship: A Film Reader*. Oxford: Blackwell 2008, pp. 29–34.

Canclini, Néstor García: From National Capital to Global Capital: Urban Change in Mexico City. In: Arjun Appadurai (ed.): *Globalization*, trans. from Spanish by Paul Liffman. Durham: Duke UP 2001, pp. 253–259.

Caughie, John: Introduction. In: Id. (ed.): *Theories of Authorship: A Reader*. London: Routledge & Kegan Paul 1981, pp. 9–16.

Conley, Tom: Space. In: Adrian Parr (ed.): *The Deleuze Dictionary*. Edinburgh: Edinburgh UP 2005, pp. 257–259.

De Certeau, Michel: *The Practice of Everyday Life*, trans. from French by Steven Rendall. Berkeley / Los Angeles: University of California Press 1984.

—: *The Certeau Reader*, ed. by Graham Ward. Oxford: Blackwell 2000.

Deleuze, Gilles: *Cinema 1: The Movement-Image*, trans. from French by Hugh Tomlinson / Barbara Habberjam. London: Continuum 1986.

—: *Cinema 2: The Time-Image*, trans. from French by Hugh Tomlinson / Robert Galeta. London: Continuum 1989.

—: *The Fold: Leibniz and the Baroque*, trans. from French by Tom Conley. London: Continuum 1993.

—: *Dialogue II*, trans. from French by Hugh Tomlinson / Barbara Habberjam / Eliot Ross Albert. London: Continuum 2006.

Deleuze, Gilles / Félix Guattari: *Anti-Oedipus: Capitalism and Schizophrenia*, trans. from French by Robert Hurley / Mark Seem / Helen R. Lane. Minneapolis: University of Minnesota Press 1983.

—: *Kafka: Toward a Minor Literature*, trans. from French by Dada Polan. Minneapolis: University of Minnesota Press 1986.

—: *A Thousand Plateaus: Capitalism and Schizophrenia*, trans. from French by Brian Massumi. London: Continuum 2004.

—: *What is Philosophy?*, trans. from French by Graham Birchill / Hugh Tomlinson. London: Verso 1994.

Ehrlich, Linda C. / David Desser (eds): *Cinematic Landscapes: Observations on the Visual Arts and Cinema of China and Japan*. Texas: University of Texas Press 1994.

Featherstone, Mike: Localism, Globalism, and Cultural Identity. In: Rob Wilson / Wimal Dissanayake (eds): *Global/Local: Cultural Production and the Transnational Imaginary*. Durham: Duke UP 1996, pp. 46–77.

Foucault, Michel: What is an Author? In: Vassilis Lambropoulos / David Neal Miller (eds): *Twentieth-Century Literary Theory*. Albany: State UP of New York 1987, pp. 124–142.

Genosko, Gary / Adam Bryx: After Informatic Striation: The Resignification of Disc Numbers in Contemporary Inuit Popular Culture. In: Ian Buchanan / Gregg Lambert (eds): *Deleuze and Space*. Edinburgh: Edinburgh UP 2006, pp. 109–125.

Grant, Barry Keith (ed.): *Auteurs and Authorship: A Film Reader*. Oxford: Blackwell 2008.

Hamilton, Roberta: *Gendering the Vertical Mosaic: Feminist Perspectives on Canadian Society*. Mississauga: Copp Clark 1996.

Hardt, Michael / Antonio Negri: *Empire*. Cambridge, MA: Harvard UP 2000.

Harvey, David: *The Condition of Postmodernity: An Enquiry into the Origins of Cultural Change*. Oxford: Basil Blackwell 1989.

Hjort, Mette: On the Plurality of Cinematic Transnationalism. In: Nataša Ďurovičová / Kathleen Newman (eds): *World Cinemas, Transnational Perspectives*. London: Routledge 2010, pp. 12–33.

Jameson, Fredric: *The Geopolitical Aesthetic: Cinema and Space in the World System*. London: British Film Institute 1995.

Julien, Isaac / Kobena Mercer: De Margin and De Center. In: Houston A. Baker, Jr. / Manthia Diawara / Ruth H. Lindeborg (eds): *Black British Cultural Studies*. Chicago: The University of Chicago Press 1996, pp. 194–209.

Kael, Pauline: Circles and Squares. In: Barry Keith Grant (eds.): *Auteurs and Authorship: A Film Reader*. Oxford: Blackwell 2008, pp. 46–54.

Kaplan, Caren: Deterritorializations: The Rewriting of Home and Exile in Western Feminist Discourse. In: *Cultural Critique* 6 (1987), pp. 187–198.

Lefebvre, Henri: The Social Text. In: Id.: *Key Writings*, eds. by Stuart Elden / Elizabeth Lebas / Eleonore Kofman. London: Continuum 2003, pp. 88–92.

Li, Chenlang: *20 Speeches on the Appreciation of Ancient Taiwan Architecture*. Taipei: Artist Publishing 2005.

Liu, Laurence G.: *Chinese Architecture*. London: Academy Editions 1989.

Marks, Laura U.: *The Skin of the Film: Intercultural Cinema, Embodiment, and the Senses*. Durham: Duke UP 2000.

Martin-Jones, David: *Deleuze, Cinema and National Identity: Narrative Time in National Contexts*. Edinburgh: Edinburgh UP 2006.

—: *Deleuze and World Cinemas*. London: Continuum 2011.

Morley, David: *Home Territories: Media, Mobility and Identity*. London: Routledge 2000.

Naficy, Hamid: The Accented Style of the Independent Transnational Cinema: A Conversation with Atom Egoyan. In: George E. Marcus (ed.): *Cultural Producers in Perilous States: Editing Events, Documenting Change*. Chicago: University of Chicago Press 1997, pp. 179–232.

—: *An Accented Cinema: Exilic and Diasporic Filmmaking*. Princeton: Princeton UP 2001.

—: Phobic Spaces and Liminal Panics: Independent Transnational Film Genre. In: Ella Shohat / Robert Stam (eds): *Multiculturalism, Postcoloniality, and Transnational Media*. New Brunswick: Rutgers UP 2003, pp. 202–226.

Neale, Steve: Art Cinema as Institution. In: *Screen* 22,1 (1981), pp. 11–39.

Nishi, Kazuo / Kazuo Hozumi: *What is Japanese Architecture?*, trans. from Japanese by H. Mack Horton. Tokyo: Kodansha International 1985.

Nute, Keven: *Place, Time and Being in Japanese Architecture*. London: Routledge 2004.

Parnreiter, Christof: Mexico: The Making of a Global City. In: Saskia Sassen (ed.): *Global Networks, Linked Cities*. London: Routledge 2002, pp. 145–182.

Parr, Adrian: Deterrotiralisation/Reterritorialisation. In: Id. (ed.): *The Deleuze Dictionary*. Edinburgh: Edinburgh UP 2005, pp. 66–69.

Sarris, Andrew: Notes on the 'Auteur' Theory in 1963. In: *Film Quarterly* 59 (2007), pp. 6–17.

Sassen, Saskia: Spatialities and Temporalities of the Global: Elements for a Theorization. In: Arjun Appadurai (ed.): *Globalization*. Durham: Duke UP 2001, pp. 260–278.

—: *Territory. Authority. Rights. From Medieval to Global Assemblages*. Princeton: Princeton UP 2006.

Shapiro, Michael J.: *Cinematic Geopolitics*. London: Routledge 2009.

Staiger, Janet: Authorship Approaches. In: David A. Gerstner / Janet Staiger (eds): *Authorship and Film*. London: Routledge 2003, pp. 27–57.

Stoddart, Helen: Auteurism and Film Authorship Theory. In: Joanne Hollows / Mark Jancovich (eds): *Approaches to Popular Film*. Manchester: Manchester UP 1995, pp. 37–57.

Sutton, Damian / David Martin-Jones: *Deleuze Reframed: A Guide for the Arts Student*. London: Tauris 2008.

Wexman, Virginia Wright: Introduction. In: Ead. (ed.): *Film and Authorship*. New Brunswick: Rutgers UP 2003, pp. 1–18.

Wood, Robin: Ideology, Genre, Auteur. In: Barry Keith Grant (ed.): *Auteurs and Authorship: A Film Reader*. Oxford: Blackwell 2008, pp. 84–92.

Young, David / Michiko Young: *Introduction to Japanese Architecture*. Hong Kong: Periplus 2004.

Works on Films

Allon, Yoram / Del Cullen / Hannah Patterson: *Contemporary North American Film Directors: A Wallflower Critical Guide*. London: Wallflower 2002.

Armour, Robert A.: *Fritz Lang*. Boston: Twayne 1977.

Baronian, Marie-Aude: History and Memory, Repetition and Epistolarity. In: Monique Tschofen / Jennifer Burwell (eds.): *Image and Territory: Essays on Atom Egoyan*. Waterloo, ON: Wilfrid Laurier UP 2007, pp. 157–176.

Beard, William: *Exotica*: Atom Egoyan, 1994. In: Jerry White (ed.): *The Cinema of Canada*. London: Wallflower 2006, pp. 195–203.

Beugnet, Martine: *Claire Denis*. Manchester / New York: Manchester UP 2004.

Bianco, Jamie Skye: Techno-Cinema. In: *Comparative Literature Studies* 41,3 (2004), pp. 377–403.

Bogue, Ronald: *Deleuze on Cinema*. London: Routledge 2003.

Bordwell, David: Film Futures. In: *SubStance* 31,1 (2002), pp. 88–104.

—: Transcultural Spaces: Toward a Poetics of Chinese Film. In: Sheldon H. Lu / Emilie Yueh-Yu Yeh (eds.): *Chinese-language Film: Historiography, Poetics, Politics*. Honolulu: University of Hawai'i Press 2005, pp. 141–162.

—: *The Way Hollywood Tells It*. Berkeley / Los Angeles: University of California Press 2006.

—: *Poetics of Cinema*. New York: Routledge 2008.

Branigan, Edward: Nearly True: Forking Plots, Forking Interpretations: A Response to David Bordwell's 'Film Futures.' In: *SubStance* 31,1 (2002), pp. 105–114.

Browne, Nick: Hou Hsiao Hsien's *The Puppetmaster*: The Poetics of Landscape. In: Chris Berry / Feii Lu (eds): *Island on the Edge: Taiwan New Cinema and After*. Hong Kong: Hong Kong UP 2005, pp. 79–88.

Brunette, Peter: *Michael Haneke*. Urbana / Chicago: University of Illinois Press 2010.

Buckland, Warren: Introduction: Puzzle Plots. In: Id. (ed.): *Puzzle Films: Complex Storytelling in Contemporary Cinema*. Chichester: Wiley-Blackwell 2009, pp. 1–12.

Cameron, Allan: Contingency, Order, and the Modular Narrative: *21 Grams* and *Irreversible*. In: *The Velvet Light Trap* 58,1 (2006), pp. 65–78.

Chen, Kuan-Hsing: Taiwan New Cinema, or a Global Nativism? In: Valentina Vitali / Paul Willemen (eds.): *Theorising National Cinema*. London: British Film Institute 2006, pp. 138–147.

Chen, Kuan-Hsing / Paul Willemen / Ti Wei: Editorial Introduction. In: *Inter Asia Cultural Studies* 9,2 (2008), pp. 169–172.

Chow, Rey: *Primitive Passions: Visuality, Sexuality, Ethnography, and Contemporary Chinese Cinema*. New York: Columbia UP 1995.

Corrigan, Timothy: *A Cinema Without Walls: Movies and Culture after Vietnam*. New Brunswick: Rutgers UP 1991.

D'Lugo, Marvin: *Amores Perros / Love's a Bitch*. In: Alberto Elena / Marina Díaz López (eds): *The Cinema of Latin America*. London: Wallflower 2003, pp. 221–230.

De Valck, Marijke: *Film Festivals: From European Geopolitics to Global Cinephilia*. Amsterdam: Amsterdam UP 2007.

Desbarats, Carole: Conquering What They Tell Us Is 'Natural.' In: Ead. / Jacinto Lageira / Daniele Riviere / Paul Virilio: *Atom Egoyan*, trans. from French by Brian Holmes. Paris: Dis Voir 1993, pp. 9–32.

Dazheng, Hao: Chinese Visual Representation: Painting and Cinema. In: Linda C. Ehrlich / David Desser (eds): *Cinematic Landscapes: Observations on the Visual Arts and Cinema of China and Japan*. Texas: University of Texas Press 1994, pp. 45–62.

Driedger, Leo: Introduction: Ethnic Identity in the Canadian Mosaic. In: Id. (ed.): *The Canadian Ethnic Mosaic: A Quest for Identity*. Toronto: McClelland & Stewart 1978, pp. 9–22.

Dyer, Richard: *White*. London / New York: Routledge 1997.

Egoyan, Atom: Preface. In: Jerry White (ed.): *The Cinema of Canada*. London: Wallflower 2006, pp. xii–xv.

Egoyan, Atom / Paul Virilio: Video Letter. In: Carole Desbarats / Jacinto Lageira / Daniele Riviere / Paul Virilio: *Atom Egoyan*, trans. from French by Brian Holmes. Paris: Dis Voir 1993, pp. 105–117.

Eisner, Lotte H.: *Fritz Lang*. London: Secker & Warburg 1976.

Elsaesser, Thomas: *European Cinema: Face to Face with Hollywood*. Amsterdam: Amsterdam UP 2005.

—: The Mind-Game Film. In: Warren Buckland (ed.): *Puzzle Films: Complex Storytelling in Contemporary Cinema*. Chichester: Wiley-Blackwell 2009, pp. 13–41.

Estudio Mexico Plans US Distribution Operation. Staff Reporters in Berlin. In: *Screen International*, 11.03.2002.

Evans, Georgina: Social Sense: Krzysztof Kieslowski and Michael Haneke. In: Steven Woodward (ed.): *After Kieslowski: The Legacy of Krzysztof Kieslowski*. Detroit: Wayne State UP 2009, pp. 99–112.

Everett, Wendy: Fractal Films and the Architecture of Complexity. In: *Studies in European Cinema* 2 (2005), pp. 159–171.

Ezra, Elisabeth / Jane Sillars: *Hidden* in Plain Sight: Bringing Terror Home. In: *Screen* 48,2 (2007), pp. 215–221.

Focus Takes the World on Inarritu's *21 Grams*. Staff Reporters in Los Angeles. In: *Screen International*, 16.07.2002.

Frodon, Jean-Michel (ed.): *Hou Hsiao-hsien*. Paris: Cahiers du Cinéma 1999.

Galt, Rosalind: The Functionary of Mankind: Haneke and Europe. In: Brian Price / John David Rhodes (eds): *On Michael Haneke*. Detroit: Wayne State UP 2010, pp. 221–244.

Gerstner, David A / Janet Staiger (eds): *Authorship and Film*. London: Routledge 2003.

Glassman, Marc / Wyndham Wise: Ontario's New Wave. In: *Take One* (Summer 1996).

Goodridge, Mike: Mike Goodridge in Cannes. In: *Screen International*, 11.05.2005.

Grant, Catherine: www.auteur.com? In: *Screen* 41,1 (2000), pp. 101–108.

Grundmann, Roy: Haneke's Anachronism: Introduction. In: Id. (ed.): *A Companion to Michael Haneke*. Malden, MA: Wiley-Blackwell 2010, pp. 1–50.

Haddon, Rosemary : Hou Hsiao Hsien's *City of Sadness*: History and the Dialogic Female Voice. In: Chris Berry / Feii Lu (eds): *Island on the Edge: Taiwan New Cinema and after*. Hong Kong: Hong Kong UP 2005, pp. 55–65.

Hagerman, Maria Eladia (ed.): *Babel: A Film by Alejandro Gonzalez Inarritu*. Photographs by Mary Ellen Mark / Patrick Bard / Graciela Iturbide / Miguel Rio Branco. Hong Kong: Taschen 2006.

Haneke, Michael: Terror and Utopia of Form, Addicted to Truth, A Film Story about Robert Bresson's *Au Hasard Balthazar*. In: James Quandt (ed.): *Robert Bresson*, trans. from French by Robert Gray. Toronto: Cinematheque Ontario 1998, pp. 551–559.

Hillman, Roger: Transnationalism in the Films of Fatih Akin. In: *Europe and Its Others: Essays on Interperception and Identity*. Bern: Lang 2010, pp. 263–276.

Hsu, Hsuan L.: Racial Privacy, The L. A. Ensemble Film, and Paul Haggis's *Crash*. In: *Film Criticism* 31,1–2 (2006), pp. 132–156.

Hunter, Alan: Alan Hunter in Cannes. In: *Screen International*, 28.05.2006.

Jensen, Paul M.: *The Cinema of Fritz Lang*. New York: Barnes 1969.

Kerr, Paul: *Babel*'s Network Narrative: Packaging a Globalized Art Cinema. In: *Transnational Cinemas* 1,1 (2010), pp. 37–51.

Kickasola, Joseph G.: *The Films of Krzysztof Kieslowski: The Liminal Image*. New York: Continuum 2004.

Konstantarakos, Myrto: What Mapping of the City? *La Haine* (Kassovitz, 1995) and the *Cinéma de Banlieue*. In: Phil Powrie (ed.): *French Cinema in the 1990s: Continuity and Difference*. Oxford: Oxford UP 1999, pp. 160–171.

Lageira, Jacinto: The Recollection of Scattered Parts. In: Id. / Carole Desbarats / Daniele Riviere / Paul Virilio: *Atom Egoyan*, trans. from French by Brian Holmes. Paris: Dis Voir 1993, pp. 33–82.

Lavoie, André: I've Heard the Mermaids Singing: Patricia Rozema, 1987. In: Jerry White (ed.): *The Cinema of Canada*. London: Wallflower 2006, pp. 195–203.

Leach, Jim: *Film in Canada*. Oxford: Oxford UP 2006.

Li, Zhenya: Historical Space/Spatial History: On Memory and the Construction of Geographical Space in *A Time to Live, A Time to Die*. In: *Chung Wai Literary Quarterly* 26,10 (1998), pp. 48–63.

Lin, Wenqi: Realist Style and Narrative in Hou Hsiao-hsien's Early Films. In: Id. / Xiaoyin Shen / Zhenya Li (eds): *Passionate Detachment: Films of Hou Hsiao-hsien*. Taipei: Rye Field 2000, pp. 93–111

Maciel, David R. Cinema and the State in Contemporary Mexico, 1970–1999. In: Id. / Joanne Hershfield / (eds): *Mexico's Cinema: A Century of Film and Filmmakers*. Oxford: SR 1999, pp. 197–232.

Magder, Ted: *Canada's Hollywood: The Canadian State and Feature Films*. Toronto: University of Toronto Press 1993. Marshall, Bill: *Quebec National Cinema*. Montreal: McGill-Queen's UP 2000

Mazierska, Ewa / Laura Rascaroli: *Crossing New Europe: Postmodern Travel and the European Road Movie*. London: Wallflower 2006.

McGowan, Todd: The Contingency of Connection: The Path to Politicization in *Babel*. In: *Discourse* 30,3 (2008), pp. 401–418.

Menne, Jeff: A Mexican Nouvelle Vague: The Logic of New Waves under Globalization. In: *Cinema Journal* 47,1 (2007), pp. 70–92.

Mi, Tzo / Liang Shinhua (eds): *The Death of New Cinema: From* Everything for Tomorrow *to* A City of Sadness. Taipei: Tangshen 1991.

Mishra, Vijay: *Bollywood Cinema: Temples of Desire*. London: Routledge 2002.

Mittel, Jason: Narrative Complexity in Contemporary American Television. In: *Velvet Light Trap* 58,1 (2006), pp. 29–40.

Montoliú, Maria del Mar Azcona: A Time to Love and a Time to Die: Desire and Narrative Structure in *21 Grams*. In: *Journal of the Spanish Association of Anglo-American Studies* 31,2 (2009), pp. 111–123.

—: *The Multi-protagonist Film*. West Sussex: Wiley-Blackwell 2010.

Needham, Gary: Ozu and the Colonial Encounter in Hou Hsiao-Hsien. In: Id. / Dimitris Eleftheriotis (eds.): *Asian Cinemas: A Reader & Guide*. Edinburgh: Edinburgh UP 2006, pp. 369–383.

Neri, Corrado: *A Time to Live, a Time to Die*: A Time to Grow. In: Chris Berry (ed.): *Chinese Films in Focus: 25 New Takes*. London: British Film Institute 2003, pp. 160–166.

Ni, Zhen: Classical Chinese Painting and Cinematographic Signification. In: Linda C. Ehrlich / David Desser (eds): *Cinematic Landscapes: Observations on the Visual Arts and Cinema of China and Japan*. Texas: University of Texas Press 1994, pp. 63–80.

Orr, John: *Contemporary Cinema*. Edinburgh: Edinburgh UP 1998.

Pevere, Geoff: *Exotica*, co-written with Atom Egoyan. Toronto: Coach House 1995, pp. 9–42.

Pisters, Patricia: The Mosaic Film – An Affaire of Everyone: Becoming-Minoritarian in Transnational Media Culture. In: Second Encountro Murcia-Amsterdam on Migratory Aesthetics, 19–21.09.2007. http://home.medewerker.uva.nl/m.g.bal/bestanden/Pisters%20Patricia%20Encuentro%20Migratory%20Politics%20READER%20OPMAAK.pdf (accessed 21.07.2011).

Podalsky, Laura: Affecting Legacies: Historical Memory and Contemporary Structures of Feeling in *Madagascar* and *Amores Perros*. In: Catherine Grant / Annette Kuhn (eds): *Screening World Cinema: A Screen Reader*. London: Routledge 2006, pp. 198–215.

Price, Brian: Color, the Formless, and Cinematic Eros. In: Id. / Angela Dalle Vacche (eds): *Color: The Film Reader*. London: Routledge 2006, pp. 76–87.

Rio, Elena del: Fetish and Aura: Modes of Technological Engagement in *Family Viewing*. In: Monique Tschofen / Jennifer Burwell (eds): *Image and Territory: Essays on Atom Egoyan*. Waterloo, ON: Wilfrid Laurier UP 2007, pp. 29–52.

Riviere, Daniele: The Place of the Spectator. In: Ead. / Carole Desbarats / Jacinto Lageira / Paul Virilio (eds): *Atom Egoyan*, trans. from French by Brian Holmes. Paris: Dis Voir 1993, pp. 83–104.

Romney, Jonathan: *Atom Egoyan*. London: British Film Institute 2003.

Shen, Cong-Wen: *Shen Cong-Wen Autobiography*. Taipei: Lianhe Wenxue 1987.

Shen, Xiaoyin: Meant to be Watched Several Times: Film Aesthetics and Hou Hsiao-hsien [Benlai jiu yingai duo kan liangbian: Dianying meixue yu Hou Xiaoxien]. In: Wenqi Lin / Xiaoyin Shen / Zhenya Li (eds): *Performance that Loves Life: Researching the Cinema of Hou Hsiao-hsien [Xilian Rensheng: Hou Hsiao-hsien Dianying Yanjiu]*. Taipei: Maitian 2000, pp. 61–92.

Siraganian, Lisa: Telling a Horror Story, Conscientiously: Representing the Armenian Genocide from *Open House* to *Ararat*. In: Monique Tschofen / Jennifer Burwell (eds): *Image and Territory: Essays on Atom Egoyan*. Waterloo, ON: Wilfrid Laurier UP 2006, pp. 133–156.

Smith, Paul Julian: Heaven's Mouth. In: *Sight and Sound* 12,4 (April 2002), pp. 16–19.

—: *Amore Perros*. London: British Film Institute 2003.

Stewart, Michael: Irresistible Death: *21 Grams* as Melodrama. In: *Cinema Journal* 47,1 (2007), pp. 49–69.

Stock, Ann Marie: Authentically Mexican? *Mi Querido Tom Mix* and *Chronos* Reframe Critical Questions. In: Joanne Hershfield / David R. Maciel (eds): *Mexico's Cinema: A Century of Film and Filmmakers*. Lanham: SR 1999, pp. 269–283

Stolar, Batia Boe: The Double's Choice: The Immigrant Experience in Atom Egoyan's *Next of Kin*. In: Monique Tschofen / Jennifer Burwell (eds): *Image and Territory: Essays on Atom Egoyan*. Waterloo, ON: Wilfrid Laurier UP 2007, pp. 177–192.

Taylor, Jeremy E.: From Transnationalism to Nativism? The Rise, Decline and Reinvention of a Regional Hokkien Entertainment Industry. In: *Inter-Asia Cultural Studies* 9,1 (2008), pp. 62–81.

Turrent, Tomás Pérez: Crises and Renovations (1965–91). In: Paulo Antonio Paranaguá (ed.): *Mexican Cinema*. London: British Film Institute 1995, pp. 94–115.

Tweedie, James: Morning in the New Metropolis: Taipei and the Globalization of the City Film. In: Darrell William Davis / Ru-Shou Robert Chen (eds): *Cinema Taiwan: Politics, Popularity and State of the Arts*. London: Routledge 2007, pp. 116–145.

Udden, James: *No Man an Island: The Cinema of Hou Hsiao-hsien*. Hong Kong: Hong Kong UP 2009.

Vincendeau, Ginette: Binoche: The Erotic Face. In: *Sight and Sound* 10,6 (June 2000), pp. 14–16.

Wheatley, Catherine: *Michael Haneke's Cinema: The Ethic of the Image*. New York / London: Berghahn 2009.

White, Jerry: Introduction. In: Id. (ed.): *The Cinema of Canada*. London: Wallflower 2006, pp. 1–10.

Williams, Linda Ruth: Songs for Swinging Lovers. In: *Sight and Sound* 15,12 (December 2005), pp. 32–35.

Wilson, Emma: *Memory and Survival: The French Cinema of Krzysztof Kieslowski*. London: Modern Humanities Research Association / Maney 2000.

—: *Atom Egoyan*. Urbana / Chicago: University of Illinois Press 2009.

Wollen, Peter: *Paris Hollywood: Writings on Film*. London: Verso 2002.

—: The Auteur Theory: Michael Curtiz, and *Casablanca*. In: David A. Gerstner / Janet Staiger (eds): *Authorship and Film*. London: Routledge 2003, pp. 61–76.

Wood, Jason: *The Faber Book of Mexican Cinema*. London: Faber & Faber 2006.

Woodward, Steven: Introduction. In: Id. (ed.): *After Kieslowski: The Legacy of Krzysztof Kieslowski*. Detroit: Wayne State UP 2009, pp. 1–16.

Xu, Gang Gary: *Flowers of Shanghai*: Visualising Ellipses and (Colonial) Absence. In: Chris Berry (ed.): *Chinese Films in Focus: 25 New Takes*. London: British Film Institute 2003, pp. 104–110.

Yeh, Emilie Yueh-Yu: Poetics and Politics of Hou Hsiao-hsien's Films. In: Sheldon H. Lu / Emilie Yueh-Yu Yeh (eds): *Chinese-language Film: Historiography, Poetics, Politics*. Honolulu: University of Hawai'i Press 2005, pp. 163–185.

Yeh, Emilie Yueh-Yu / Darrell William Davis: *Taiwan Film Directors: A Treasure Island*. New York: Columbia UP 2005.

Yeh, Emilie Yueh-Yu / Xiaoyin Shen / Zhenya Li / Wenqi Lin: Goodbye South, Goodbye: Roundtable. In: *Chung Wai Literary Quarterly* 26,10 (1998), pp. 65–73.

Zhang, Yingjin: *Chinese National Cinema*. London: Routledge 2004.

Interviews

Egoyan, Atom: The Accented Style of the Independent Transnational Cinema: A Conversation with Atom Egoyan. In: George E. Marcus (ed.): *Cultural Producers in Perilous States: Editing Events, Documenting Change*. Chicago: University of Chicago Press 1997, pp. 179–231.

Pevere, Geoff: Difficult to Say: Atom Egoyan Interviewed by Geoff Pevere. In: *Exotica*, co-written with Atom Egoyan. Toronto: Coach House 1995, pp. 43–67.

Porton, Richard: Family Romances: An Interview with Atom Egoyan. In: *Cineast* 23,2 (December 1997), pp. 8–15.

Literary Works

Faulkner, William: *The Sound and the Fury*. London: Cape & Smith 1929.

—: *Light in August*. New York: Smith & Haas 1932.

—: *Absalom, Absalom!* New York: Random House 1936.

Filmography

21 Grams (USA 2003, D: Alejandro González Iñárritu)

24 City (*Er Shi Si Cheng Ji*, CN 2008, D: Jia Zhangke)

35 Shots of Rhums (*35 Rhums*, FR 2008, D: Claire Denis)

36th Precinct (*36 Quai des Orfèvres*, FR 2004, D: Olivier Marchal)

71 Fragments of a Chronology of Chance (*71 Fragmente einer Chronologie des Zufalls*, AT / DE 1994, D: Michael Haneke)

The Adjuster (CA 1991, D: Atom Egoyan)

Amores Perros (MX 2000, D: Alejandro González Iñárritu)

Amour (FR / DE / AT 2012, D: Michael Haneke)

And Your Mother Too (*Y tu mamá también*, ES 2001, D: Alfonso Cuarón)

Ararat (CA / FR 2002, D: Atom Egoyan)

The Assassin (*Nie Ying Niang*, TW / CN / HK / FR 2015, D: Hou hsiao-hsien)

Au Hasard Balthazar (FR 1966, D: Robert Bresson)

Babel (USA / FR / MX 2005, D: Alejandro González Iñárritu)

Bad Education (*La mala educación*, ES 2004, D: Pedro Almodóvar)

Bamako (ML 2006, D: Abderrahmane Sissako)

Beau Travail (FR 1999, D: Claire Denis)

Benny's Video (AT / CH 1992, D: Michael Haneke)

Birdman or (The Unexpected Virtue of Ignorance) (USA 2014, D: Alejandro González Iñárritu)

Biutiful (MX / ES 2010, D: Alejandro González Iñárritu)

Blind Chance (*Przypadek*, PL 1981, D: Krzysztof Kieślowski)

The Boys from Fengkuei (TW 1983, D: Hou Hsiao-hsien)

A Brighter Summer Day (*Gu Ling Jie Shao Nian Sha Ren Shi Jian*, TW 1991, D: Edward Yang)

The Burning Plain (USA 2008, D: Guillermo Arriaga)

Caché (FR / AT / DE / IT 2005, D: Michael Haneke)

Café Lumière (JP / TW 2003, D: Hou Hsiao-hsien)

Calendar (CA / AM / DE 1993, D: Atom Egoyan)

Carandiru (BR 2003, D: Hector Babenco)

Chants of Lotus (*Perempuan Punya Cerita*, ID 2007, D: Fatimah Tobing Rony et al.)

Cheerful Wind (*Feng Er Ti Ta Cai*, TW 1981, D: Hou Hsiao-hsien)

Chloe (US / CA / FR 2009, D: Atom Egoyan)

Chocolat (FR 1988, D: Claire Denis)

Chocolat (UK 2000, D: Lasse Hallström)

The Chorus (*Les choristes*, FR 2004, D: Christophe Barratier)

Chung-king Express (*Chung Hing Sam Lam*, HK 1994, D: Wong Kar-Wai)
City of God (*Cidade de deus*, BR 2002, D: Fernando Meirelles / Kátia Lund)
City of Men (*Cidade dos homens*, BR 2007, D: Paulo Morelli)
A City of Sadness (*Bei Qing Cheng Shi*, TW / HK 1989, D: Hou Hsiao-hsien)
Code Unknown (*Code inconnu*, FR / DE / RO 2000, D: Michael Haneke)
Contempt (*Le Mépris*, FR 1963, D: Jean-Luc Godard)
Crash (USA 2004, D: Paul Haggis)
Cute Girl (*Jiu Shi Liu Liu De Ta*, TW 1980, D: Hou Hsiao-hsien)
Darna Mana Hai (IN 2003, D: Prawaal Raman)
Daughter of the Nile (*Ni Luo He Nu Er*, TW 1987, D: Hou Hsiao-hsien)
Déficit (MX 2007, D: Gael García Bernal)
Diaspora (CA 2001, D: Atom Egoyan)
Do Over (*Yi Nian Zhi Chu*, TW 2006, D: Yu-Chieh Cheng)
Do the Right Thing (USA 1989, D: Spike Lee)
Double Happiness (CA 1994, D: Mina Shum)
The Double Life of Veronique (*La double vie de Véronique*, FR 1991, D: Krzysztof Kieślowski)
Dust in the Wind (TW 1987, D: Hou Hsiao-hsien)
The Edge of Heaven (*Auf der anderen Seite*, DE 2005, D: Fatih Akin)
El jardin del Eden (MX 1994, D: Maria Notaro)
Exotica (CA 1994, D: Atom Egoyan)
Fallen Angels (*Do Lok Tin Si*, HK 1995, D: Wong Kar-Wai)
Family Viewing (CA 1987, D: Atom Egoyan)
Fat Girl (*A ma soeur*, FR 2001, D: Catherine Breillat)
Felicia's Journey (CA / UK 1999, D: Atom Egoyan)
Festival (UK 2005, D: Annie Griffin)
"The Final Twist" in *Alfred Hitchcock Presents* (USA 1987–1988, D: Atom Egoyan)
Flight of the Red Balloon (*Le voyage du ballon rouge*, FR / TW 2007, D: Hou Hsiao-hsien)
Flowers of Shanghai (TW / JP 1998, D: Hou Hsiao-hsien)
Fragments (also called *Winged Creatures*, USA 2008, D: Rowan Woods)
Friday Night (*Vendredi soir*, FR 2002, D: Claire Denis)
Funny Games (AU 1997, D: Michael Haneke)
Funny Games U. S. (USA / FR / UK / AT / DE / IT 2007, D: Michael Haneke)
Game of Thrones (USA 2011–2018, HBO, Creators: D. B. Weiss / David Benioff)
Goodbye South, Goodbye (*Nan Guo Zai Jian, Nao Guo*, TW / JP 1996, D: Hou Hsiao-hsien)
Good Men, Good Women (*Hao Nan Hao Nu*, TW / JP 1995, D: Hou Hsiao-hsien)
Green Green Grass of Home (*Zai Na He Pan Qing Cao Qing*, TW 1982, D: Hou Hsiao-hsien)
Head-on (*Gegen die Wand*, DE 2004, D: Fatih Akin)
Highway 61 (CA 1991, D: Bruce MacDonald)

Historias minimas (AR 2002, D: Carlos Sorin)
I Can't Sleep (*J'ai pas sommeil*, ES 1994, D: Claire Denis)
In the Hands of a Puppetmaster (*Xi Meng Ren Sheng*, TW 1993, D: Hou Hsiao-hsien)
Intolerance (USA 1916, D: D. W. Griffith)
The Intruder (*L'intrus*, FR 2004, D: Claire Denis)
Jean de Florette (FR 1986, D: Claude Berri)
Jesus of Montreal (*Jésus de Montréal*, CA 1989, D: Denys Arcand)
Kaili Blues (*Lu Bian Ye Can*, CN 2015, D: Gan Bi)
Kicks (NL 2007, D: Albert Ter Heerdt)
La soledad (ES 2007, D: Jamie Rosales)
Last Night (CA 1998, D: Don McKeller)
Last Year at Marienbad (*L'année dernière à Marienbad*, FR 1961, D: Alain Resnais)
Late Spring (*Banshun*, JP 1949, D: Yasujiro Ozu)
Lemminge (AT 1979, D: Michael Haneke)
Life in a Metro (IN 2007, D: Anurag Basu)
Linha de passe (MX 2008, D: Walter Salles / Daniela Thomas)
Love and Human Remains (CA 1993, D: Denys Arcand)
The Lovers on the Bridge (*Les amants du Pont-Neuf*, FR 1991, D: Leos Carax)
Lumière and Company (*Lumière et compagnie*, FR / DK / ES / SE 1995, D: Hou Hsiao-hsien et al.)
Magnolia (USA 1999, D: Paul Thomas Anderson)
Memento (USA 2000, D: Christopher Nolan)
Midaq Alley (MX 1994, D: Jorge Fons)
Midnight (USA 1998, D: Woody Allen)
Millennium Mambo (*Qian Xi Man Po*, TW / FR 2001, D: Hou Hsiao-hsien)
Mooladé (SN 2004, D: Ousmane Sembene)
Mother and Child (USA 2009, D: Rodrigo García)
Mulholland Drive (USA 2001, D: David Lynch)
Nashville (USA 1975, D: Robert Altman)
Nenette and Boni (*Nénette et Boni*, FR 1996, D: Claire Denis)
Next of Kin (CA 1984, D: Atom Egoyan)
Nine Lives (USA 2005, D: Rodrigo García)
Open House (CA 1982, D: Atom Egoyan)
The Piano Teacher (*La pianiste*, AT / FR / DE 2001, D: Michael Haneke)
Pierrot le Fou (FR 1965, D: Jean-Luc Godard)
Platform (*Zhantai*, CN 2000, D: Jia Zhangke)
Possible Worlds (CA 2000, D: Robert Lepage)
Pulp Fiction (USA 1994, D: Quentin Tarantino)
Red Balloon (*Le ballon rouge*, FR 1956, D: Albert Lamourisse)
The Revenant (USA 2015, D: Alejandro González Iñárritu)

Roadkill (CA 1989, D: Bruce MacDonald)
Rudo and Cursi (*Rudo y Cursi*, MX 2008, D: Carlos Cuarón)
Run Lola Run (*Lola rennt*, DE 1998, D: Tom Tykwer)
Seediqbate (TW 2011, D: Wei Te-sheng)
The Seventh Continent (*Der siebente Kontinent*, AT 1989, D: Michael Haneke)
Sex, Lies and Videotapes (USA 1989, D: Steven Soderbergh)
Short Cuts (USA 1993, D: Robert Altman)
Short Sharp Shock (*Kurz und schmerzlos*, DE 1998, D: Fatih Akin)
Sin nombre (MX 2009, D: Cary Joji Fukunaga)
Slacker (USA 1991, D: Richard Linklater)
Sliding Doors (UK 1998, D: Peter Howitt)
Soul Kitchen (DE 2009, D: Fatih Akin)
Speaking Parts (CA 1989, D: Atom Egoyan)
A Summer at Grandpa's (TW 1984, D: Hou Hsiao-hsien)
The Sweet Hereafter (CA 1997, D: Atom Egoyan)
Tale of Tales (*Il racconto dei racconti*, IT 2015, D: Matteo Garrone)
Three Colours: Blue, White, Red (*Trois couleurs: Bleu, Blanc, Rouge*, FR 1993/94, D: Krzysztof Kieślowski)
Three Paths to the Lake (*Drei Wege zum See*, AU 1976, D: Michael Haneke)
Three Times (*Zui Hao De Shi Guang*, TW / FR 2005, D: Hou Hsiao-hsien)
Time of the Wolf (*Le temps du loup*, FR / AT / DE 2003, D: Michael Haneke)
"There Was A Little Girl ..." in *Alfred Hitchcock Presents* (USA 1987–1988, D: Atom Egoyan)
The Time to Live, The Time to Die (TW 1985, D: Hou Hsiao-hsien)
To Each His Own Cinema (*Chacun son cinéma*, FR 2007, D: Hou Hsiao-hsien et al.)
Too Many Ways to Be No.1 (*Jat Go Zi Tau Di Daan Sang*, HK 1997, D: Ka-Fai Wai)
The Top of His Head (CA 1989, D: Peter Mettler)
Toro Negro (USA 2005, D: Carlos Armella / Pedro González-Rubio)
A Touch of Sin (*Tian Zhu Din*, CN 2013, D: Zhangke Jia)
Traffic (USA 2010, D: Steven Soderbergh)
Videodrome (USA 1983, D: David Cronenberg)
"The Wall" in *The Twilight Zone* (USA 1989, D: Atom Egoyan)
Wer war Edgar Allan? (AT 1985, D: Michael Haneke)
White Material (FR 2009, D: Claire Denis)
The White Ribbon (*Das weiße Band*, DE / AT / FR / IT 2009, D: Michael Haneke)
The Widow of Saint-Pierre (*La veuve de Saint-Pierre,* FR 2000, D: Patrice Leconte)
Wings of Desire (*Der Himmel über Berlin*, DE 1987, D: Wim Wenders)
WWW: What a Wonderful World (FR 2006, D: Faouzi Bensaidi)
The Zone (*La zona*, MX 2007, D: Rodrigo Piá)

List of Figures

Hou

Fig. 15: A mountain's silhouette with the accompanying song's lyrics typed on the right margins of the screen space in *Good Men, Good Women*. Screenshot from DVD, Raro Video, 2007.

Fig. 16: The wandering gaze of the camera briefly stays with a television set on the floor projecting Yasujiro Ozu's *Late Spring* in *Good Men, Good Women*. Screenshot from DVD, Raro Video, 2007.

Fig. 17: During Liang's photo shooting for the film-within-the-film, a photographer's back blocks one third of the screen from the left margins in *Good Men, Good Women*. Screenshot from DVD, Raro Video, 2007.

Fig. 18: Chiang as the seer in the postwar and postcolonial any-space-whatever in Taiwan within the multilayered mise-en-scène in *Good Men, Good Women*. Screenshot from DVD, Raro Video, 2007.

Fig. 19: The brief moment of togetherness on screen between the couple during the pool game in *Three Times*. Screenshot from DVD, Artificial Eye, 2006.

Fig. 20: The inner silent space multilayered with engravings and ornaments in *Three Times*. Screenshot from DVD, Artificial Eye, 2006.

Fig. 21: Jing looks at Zhen's photographic portraits with fluorescent lighting from a lamp in *Three Times*. Screenshot from DVD, Artificial Eye, 2006.

Haneke

Fig. 22: Close-up of Anne's frightened face on an unframed stage in *Code Unknown*. Screenshot from DVD, Artificial Eye, 2001.

Fig. 23: Georges' portrait of a passenger in the Parisian metro, in *Code Unknown*. Screenshot from DVD, Artificial Eye, 2001.

Fig. 24: A sound operator with a boom, a steadicam operator, and a script supervisor are visible on screen in the film-within-the film in *Code Unknown*. Screenshot from DVD, Artificial Eye, 2001.

Fig. 25: The vague figure of Anne is illuminated in the background whereas two stage staff in the foreground are indiscernible shadows immersed in complete darkness, in *Code Unknown*. Screenshot from DVD, Artificial Eye, 2001.

Fig. 26: Anne and Georges rewinding and fast-forwarding the video footage of their house façade in *Caché*. Screenshot from DVD, Artificial Eye, 2006.

Fig. 27: Georges in Majid's flat which is piled with objects and full of colours in *Caché*. Screenshot from DVD, Artificial Eye, 2006.

Fig. 28: Georges' family house shot from inside a shaded barn, with the car in the background waiting to take Majid away in *Caché*. Screenshot from DVD, Artificial Eye, 2006.

Fig. 29: Anne's greyish blue baggy dress makes her blend into the background with wallpaper of the same colour in *Caché*. Screenshot from DVD, Artificial Eye, 2006.